ON WITHDRAWAL

ON WITHDRAWAL

SCENES OF REFUSAL, DISAPPEARANCE, AND RESILIENCE IN ART AND CULTURAL PRACTICES

EDITED BY
SEBASTIÁN EDUARDO DÁVILA, REBECCA HANNA JOHN,
ULRIKE JORDAN, THORSTEN SCHNEIDER,
JUDITH SIEBER, NELE WULFF

DIAPHANES

GEFÖRDERT DURCH DIE DEUTSCHE FORSCHUNGSGEMEINSCHAFT (DFG)
—PROJEKTNUMMER 2114
FUNDED BY THE DEUTSCHE FORSCHUNGSGEMEINSCHAFT (DFG, GERMAN RESEARCH FOUNDATION)
—PROJECTNUMBER 2114

DFG Deutsche Forschungsgemeinschaft

KULTUREN DER KRITIK

LEUPHANA UNIVERSITÄT LÜNEBURG

K d K

ISBN 978-3-0358-0506-2

LAYOUT AND PREPRESS: 2EDIT, ZURICH
PRINTED IN GERMANY

WWW.DIAPHANES.COM

Contents

Sebastián Eduardo Dávila, Rebecca Hanna John, Ulrike Jordan, Thorsten Schneider, Judith Sieber, and Nele Wulff

Introduction

How can withdrawal—meaning either that which withdraws itself, or which is being withdrawn—be represented, thus made visible and negotiable? This publication takes this paradox as its starting point, which remains present as a tension throughout. The book aims to draw constellations of different instances of withdrawal, ranging from passivity, failure, and refusal to disappearance and remembrance and to resilience and resistance. Understanding withdrawal as a concept that encompasses both cutting ties and reaffirming relations, the contributions collected here trace the ambivalences and ambiguities set loose by this term. In doing so, the volume inscribes itself in recent discussions on withdrawal and its relationship to society and politics.[1] Our understanding of withdrawal is informed by different discourses and is based on specific examples or problems delineated by the authors throughout the book. Something or someone withdraws or is withdrawn, but only in specific contexts do agents of this movement become tangible. On the one hand, withdrawal can take on various forms of not-doing, like pausing, failing or refusing; thus undermining expectations and constraints within oppressive power mechanisms. On the other hand, there are contexts in which withdrawal is violently enacted

1 See Pepita Hesselberth and Joost De Bloois, eds., *Politics of Withdrawal: Media, Arts, Theory* (Lanham, Maryland: Rowman & Littlefield Publishers, 2020). Instead of reading withdrawal as a depoliticized form of retreat, the book aims to position it as a political concept and strategy for action. In their Introduction the editors define withdrawal as being "primarily about *re*affirming relations rather than about cutting ties." Hesselberth and De Bloois, *Politics of Withdrawal*, p. 4.

by those in power, leading to the erasure and invisibilization of life. Furthermore, withdrawal can be understood as a double movement in which, like in the logic of resilience, the relationship between subjective agency and imposition from the outside remains tense.

The authors explore these aspects of withdrawal from different perspectives: as a political and aesthetic strategy of refusal, but also as a violent form of silencing critical voices; as an instrument of control and power, but also as something uncontrolled or uncontrollable. The publication navigates a variety of writing practices, ranging from interviews, to artistic or literary texts and visual contributions, to more academic texts. Across these heterogeneous contributions, located between art and theory, withdrawal emerges in all its complexity, whereby its material, physical, and bodily aspects are questioned.

Approaching withdrawal through "scenes," we chose a term that pertains to the field of theater. In ancient stage architecture the "skene" not only referred to the location of the stage, but also to the dressing rooms behind it.[2] Scenes are frames where the visible is structured and ordered, honing focus and attention on specific connections and contexts. Scenes reveal themselves as produced and are therefore self-reflexive, making it possible to question the production of meaning. In the logic of theater, a scene is a spatial and temporal structure in which some constellations are shown and others are hidden from the visual field of an audience. Scenes have long transcended the space of theater and the body as their points of reference and have also been proposed for theories of language and literature, within which

2 See Josef Früchtl and Jörg Zimmermann, "Ästhetik der Inszenierung. Dimensionen eines gesellschaftlichen, individuellen und kulturellen Phänomens," in *Ästhetik der Inszenierung. Dimensionen eines künstlerischen, kulturellen und gesellschaftlichen Phänomens*, ed. Josef Früchtl and Jörg Zimmermann (Frankfurt am Main: Suhrkamp, 2001), pp. 9–47.

the text becomes the stage of linguistic performance.[3] The concept of the scene makes it possible to analyze moments in which the—seemingly—withdrawn comes into view, its dynamic becoming observable. Moreover, the term has potential as a means for engaging with the past. Diana Taylor uses the related notion of the "scenario" as an analytical category that highlights the interaction between bodies and space in historical contexts.[4] The term allows for the constellation of different contexts in order to find connections between them, without comparing or subsuming them under one narrative.

In *The Origin of German Tragic Drama* Walter Benjamin describes his concept of constellations in an astronomical metaphor: By grasping the elements as points in such constellations, the phenomena are divided and saved at the same time.[5] The historical materialist searches for constellations where the sign of a messianic standstill of the events, in other words, of a revolutionary chance in struggle for the suppressed past[6] becomes tangible. According to Benjamin, thinking in constellations has the capacity "to make the continuum of history explode."[7] Informed by Benjamin and Taylor, this publication presents scenes of withdrawal, pointing out potentials for resistance against a seemingly predetermined history.

Bringing together the concepts of scene and constellation, the book is divided into three sections, each char-

3 See Gerhard Neumann, "Einleitung," in *Szenographien. Theatralität als Kategorie der Literaturwissenschaft*, ed. Gerhard Neumann, Caroline Pross and Gerald Wildgruber (Freiburg im Breisgau: Rombach Verlag, 2000), pp. 11–34, here p. 15.

4 See Diana Taylor, *The Archive and the Repertoire: Performing Cultural Memory in the Americas* (Durham, N.C. and London: Duke University Press, 2003), pp. 53–78. Also see the interview with Diana Taylor in this book, pp. 159–177.

5 See Walter Benjamin, *The Origin of German Tragic Drama* (London and Brooklyn N.Y.: Verso, 2009).

6 Ibid.

7 Walter Benjamin, "Theses on the Philosophy of History," in Benjamin, *Illuminations*, ed. Hannah Arendt (New York: Schocken Books, 1968), pp. 253–263, here p. 261.

acterized by a constellation of terms—passivity, failure, and refusal; disappearance and remembrance; resilience and resistance—that brings multiple movements, directions, and understandings of withdrawal into relation. In this way, connecting lines appear within and also between the sections.

Many contributions stem from the field of art or seize upon ideas present in artworks, the latter having specifically immanent structures of display. Art makes contexts accessible and visible—stages them—in a variety of ways. At the same time, art practices and artists are themselves permeated by ambivalences which mirror the tension within various forms of withdrawal. These practices have the potential to counter hegemonic forms of knowledge and build new infrastructures for living and imagining.

Passivity, Failure, and Refusal

This section explores the potentiality in non-heroic acts of not-doing that are experienced as passivity, failure, or refusal. These terms appear as forms of withdrawal in French Theory of the twentieth century, as well as in contemporary positions within Queer and Black Studies. Refusing to follow the norms of society as a form of withdrawal from the world can, for example, be traced back to the tradition of Cynicism in Ancient Greece that Michel Foucault described in *The Courage of the Truth* as a risky form of the art of living.[8] In this line of thinking, Kathrin Busch described a whole aesthetics of inability and self-loss that she calls "radical passivity."[9] Passive

8 See Michel Foucault, *The Courage of Truth (The Government of Self and Others II): Lectures at the Collège de France 1983–1984*, ed. Frédéric Gros, trans. Graham Burchell (Basingstoke: Palgrave Macmillan, 2011).

9 See Kathrin Busch, *P–Passivität* (Hamburg: Textem, 2012); Kathrin Busch and Ilse Lafer, *Radical Passivity: Politics of the Flesh*, exhib. cat. (Berlin: neue Gesellschaft für bildende Kunst, 2020).

strategies of withdrawal can also be found in Georges Bataille's interest in meditation practices, which he explored in the middle of World War II as ways of negating or deconstructing the mind.[10] Jack Halberstam's search for a "shadow archive of resistance"[11] that does not speak the language of action but instead articulates itself in terms of refusal, passivity, unbecoming, and unbeing is situated differently: it is part of a contemporary reflection on failure as a critique of heteronormative and capitalist understandings of success. With a focus on forms of resistance to slavery, Fred Moten and Saidiya Hartman have discussed a refusal of that which has been refused by withholding consent to be a subject, by living wayward lives, and by refusing to work. This field of references is not brought into one linear narration here. Instead, the different contributions of this section are arranged as a set of constellations that shed light on such forms of withdrawal from specific perspectives, so that a reading in relation can help in discerning the continuities as well as the disparities between the different understandings of passivity, failure, and refusal. While such forms of not-doing that abjure power do not necessarily generate immediate instances of assembly, as Bonnie Honig mentioned in *A Feminist Theory of Refusal,*[12] the authors of this section explore their potential for later repercussions. The contributions do this with a focus on personal points of view, ranging from theoretical and auto-theoretical to poetic, collaborative, and essayistic forms of writing.

The negation of the subject and recurring focus on the body—with its lived experiences of powerlessness and

10 See Georges Bataille, "Method of Meditation," in *The Unfinished System of Nonknowledge* (Minneapolis: University of Minnesota Press, 2001).

11 Jack Halberstam, "Shadow Feminisms: Queer Negativity and Radical Passivity," in *The Queer Art of Failure* (Durham, N.C.: Duke University Press, 2011), pp. 123–145, here pp. 126–128.

12 Bonnie Honig, *A Feminist Theory of Refusal* (Cambridge, Mass. and London: Harvard University Press, 2021).

suffering, but also as the location of a possible detoxing and re-assembling—is what connects the texts despite their diverse forms of writing as well as different geopolitical and temporal contexts. The questions of how to undo the ever-repeating history of violence, exploitation, and racism, how to withdraw from the oppressive power mechanisms of White[13] supremacy—in short: how to learn from failures and refuse to be governed by systems of exploitation and oppression—create echoes throughout the texts, as open tasks that find articulations in artistic and textual practices.

In "Self-Loss as a Form of Knowledge,"[14] Kathrin Busch excavates a thinking of self-loss in twentieth century philosophy and art. In opposition to the mastery of the self, a technique which has been the governing ideal of modern theories of subjectivity, the deliberate *undoing* of the self is explored as an "other" knowledge.[15] In the writings of Antonin Artaud, Maurice Blanchot, Emmanuel Lévinas and Paul B. Preciado, Busch shows traces of a thinking of self-loss and impotentiality that reveal this "other" knowledge as a new kind of self and world relation. In experiences of alienation, insomnia and artistic inspiration, one encounters a form of passivity that is not merely the opposite of activity, but an "archi-passivity": a form of passivity that shows the self as always already decentered, vulnerable and "open" to the world. Busch shows that art is one of the primary modes for disclosing these "generative" forms of self-loss, undoing and un-becoming.

13 When referring to their socio-cultural construction, we capitalize White as well as Black.

14 First published in German: Kathrin Busch, "Selbstverlust als Wissensform," in *Selbstverlust und Welterfahrung. Erkundungen einer pathischen Moderne*, ed. Björn Bertrams and Antonio Roselli (Vienna: Turia + Kant, 2021), pp. 212–225.

15 See Kathrin Busch, ed., *Anderes Wissen. Kunstformen der Theorie* (Paderborn: Wilhelm Fink, 2016). Furthermore see https://www.andereswissen.de/de (accessed December 6, 2022).

The starting point for Helen Cammock's artistic contribution "They Call It Idlewild Extended II" was a residency in which the artist was invited to create a work responding to the institution's archive.[16] The inspirational moment for the work, though, was an act of not-doing, of looking out of the archive's windows instead of into the content of its boxes, which can be understood as a subtle form of refusal. For this publication, Cammock combines text fragments and film stills, to which she adds her own poetic writings on moments of silence, mourning, waiting, and impotentiality. The topic of insomnia reappears when a new set of references casts a different, critical light on sleeplessness: from sleep deprivation as a torture technique, to the racist image of the sleeping, "lazy" enslaved man obliged not to rest but work, and to sleepless migratory birds as a model for today's image of the sleepless soldier—or of the worker in general.

The conversation with Mutlu Ergün-Hamaz takes his poem "Germany Detox"[17] (2012) as a starting point for discussing acts of refusing and being refused within the context of racism in Germany. Expanding the notion of detox—drug withdrawal—to the dismantling of White supremacy, Ergün-Hamaz and Rebecca Hanna John discuss not only the need to analyze White supremacy as a structure that racializes both BIPOC and White subjects, but also that the academic framework in which this analysis is taking place must be decolonized. Through the metaphor of the drug in Ergün-Hamaz' poem, the body can be understood both as the center of various dehumanizing forces and as the very location at which a potential detoxing, re-assembling, and empowerment can begin.

16 Helen Cammock's film *They Call It Idlewild* was shown as part of an exhibition of the same name at Wysing Arts Center in 2020, which is where the residency was taking place.

17 In the German original: Mutlu Ergün-Hamaz, "Entgiften," *freitext* 20 (October 2012), pp. 38–41.

Starting with the open question of how to read texts on withdrawal that were written from a White, male, Orientalist viewpoint, Knut Ebeling's auto-theoretical text "War in the Head: Meditating with Bataille" explores the theme of meditation in Georges Bataille's work as a form of withdrawal from war, as well as a methodological refusal directed towards conventional forms of writing. As Ebeling demonstrates in a close reading of *Method of Meditation* (1947), the central idea that underwrites all of Bataille's writing is that meditation is primarily a practice, an experience, and not a form of contemplation. Or: meditation is something that the writing subject actively brings about, as a form of writing against language and thinking against thought—an attempt to ultimately desubjectify the self. The form of negativity that is released in this practice, however, must be carefully distinguished from the idealist understanding of negativity as both reflection and struggle. For Bataille, Ebeling argues, meditation results in a form of negativity that counteracts the negativity of the war that surrounded Bataille.

The question of how to read and possibly even think-with—as Donna Haraway would say—Orientalist scholars appears again in Arnika Ahldag and Rebecca Hanna John's text on the journeys made by Hermann Goetz and Robert Lachmann from Germany to, respectively, India and Palestine in the 1930s. Their biographies serve as a starting point for thinking about the figure of the Orientalist as an outsider whose projects more often fail than succeed. Instead of essentializing and boycotting the figure of the Orientalist as the source of all evil—with a direct link to either French and British colonialism, as argued by Edward Said, or German nationalism, as argued by Sheldon Pollock—the authors explore the conditions under which German Orientalists like Goetz and Lachmann worked, in what was then defined as "the Orient." Foregrounding their failures helps in undoing the fixed opposition between silenced object of study and dominant researcher, to potentially find allies in a field that is often thought of as the enemy.

The interview with Akram Zaatari, conducted by Rebecca Hanna John, opens with a discussion on the artist's work *Letter to a Refusing Pilot* (2013). Looking back at the gesture of refusal in the main video of this multi-part installation, which refers to the Israeli pilot Hagai Tamir, who refused to bomb a school during the invasion of Lebanon in 1982, leads to questions still relevant in today's world of ongoing wars and other disasters: How to refuse to see the other side as an enemy to be eliminated? How not to drop a bomb if in the position of the soldier during a mission to attack? How to undo the course of history even if seemingly being caught in repetitions? While reflecting on the work ten years after its making, Zaatari makes a clear differentiation between refusal and boycott, the latter being an attitude which hinders all communication with the supposed enemy and any possible mutual process of change. The artist explains how refusing an order means to disengage from a collective act that one sees as criminal; an act of not-doing which may not change history in an immediate way but can have surprising repercussions years later.

Disappearance and Remembrance

While the first section deals with withdrawal as an act of refusal that might bear an unforeseen and possibly emancipatory potential against dominant power structures, this section discusses the violence inherent to the act of being forcefully withdrawn. We thus start by outlining a concept of withdrawal that inverts the notion of actively withdrawing to one of being withdrawn by violent means from one's very life and social context. Being denied the right to live among family and friends—the right to inhabit the world—leaves a void that raises crucial questions for those left behind: How can one mourn a body that has been forcefully disappeared? Can there be ways of grieving that create other forms of presence? What role can witnessing play in these processes? And how might it be possible to mark sites of violence that are subject to denial or forgetting in hegemonic narratives?

Throughout the section, the authors explore the tension residing between, on the one hand, the absence of bodies that have been disappeared by the state or other perpetrators and, on the other, personal and political attempts to restore the presence of those who have been forced into a state of absence. Looking at concrete historical and regional scenes as well as forms of disappearance and practices of remembrance, the authors ask whether it is possible to transform grieving, otherwise marked by intimacy, into a political resource in the search for justice. Practices of mourning and remembrance are of particular importance here, since they often mean resisting forces that seek to erase the memory of those who have disappeared, or rather, *have been* disappeared.[18] As Judith Butler points out, mourning *all* the lives lost means to acknowledge our fundamental vulnerability and inalienable humanness.[19]

The painful absence of the disappeared correlates with an absence of traces of violence in physical spaces. Unlike the lives lost, these places continue to exist. Acts of violence are inscribed in space and sometimes even overlap; yet at the same time, their traces are often erased or made illegible. How can the past be made visible, not only by means of spatial markers but also as a way to reconnect to the histories of those lost? In the

18 This grammatical shift responds to the tactic of enforced disappearance, specific but not exclusive to Latin American dictatorships throughout the twentieth century.

19 See Judith Butler, "Violence, Mourning, Politics," in Butler, *Precarious Life: The Powers of Mourning and Violence* (London and New York: Verso, 2004), pp. 19–49.

shadow of the history and traces of transatlantic slavery, Saidiya Hartman has discussed the desire to recuperate the dead's experiences and their voices—and the impossibility of doing so—both in space and the archive.[20] There is no one right way to do this, but there are many ways to try. The identification of various forms of writing may prove a useful tool in countering the disappearance of the dead from official narratives.

Together, the texts in this section map forms of disappearance and their aftermaths, focusing on artistic and cultural practices as the terrain where these can reverberate and on the many protagonists who grieve, witness, and commemorate. The contributions alternate between, on the one hand, a retelling of the crimes of disappearance and murder where the state is oftentimes co-responsible and, on the other, an engagement in processes of mourning and the search for justice and reparation through varying artistic media and political strategies. The authors highlight the role of the bereaved as agents, sometimes accompanying family members, friends, and witnesses in their processes of grief and protest.

The section opens with Ulrike Jordan and Sebastián Eduardo Dávila's interview with Diana Taylor, author of several books dealing with disappearance and presence throughout the Americas. Starting with the ethical question of how to speak about the forcefully disappeared, they discuss the ways in which violence is inscribed in unmarked everyday places, as well as in official memory sites like Villa Grimaldi, a former detention and torture center during the Augusto Pinochet dictatorship in Chile. Taylor emphasizes the role of the body as a recipient and transmitter of violence, experienced or witnessed, relating corporeality to various forms and practices of remembrance like archives, writing, art, and

20 See Saidiya Hartman, *Lose Your Mother: A Journey Along the Atlantic Slave Route* (New York: Farrar, Straus and Giroux, 2007), pp. 110–135.

narration. Proposing concepts like the repertoire and the scenario, she argues for the body's capacity to communicate and perform traumas, to remember and transform itself, other bodies, and the places where (state) violence has taken place. The interview concludes by discussing the varying strategies of mourning and protest that put the body at the center and that contest the disappearance and silencing implied in official ways of remembering and narrating.

Marivi Véliz' close reading of Regina José Galindo's performance series *Presence* from 2017 further complicates the binary of absence and presence, focusing on spirituality, silence, and the body as sites of resistance and healing. In each iteration of *Presence*, Galindo stood silently wearing an assassinated woman's clothes, given to her by family members of the victims. Tracing Galindo's personal exchanges and her rituals of preparation for the performances—which included Mayan spiritual elements and knowledge—the author argues that it is through silence that the women are called into presence. Putting herself in the victim's place, the artist's body functions as a medium, creating a grieving community around pain made perceptible. Drawing on theorists such as Peter Pál Pelbar and Peggy Phelan, Véliz' analysis of the performance and its mechanisms of presence-making includes "incorporeal yet real" and unknown, invisible forces and presences. She situates Galindo's practice in multiple contexts, stretching from necropolitics and violence against women—including feminicides in contemporary Guatemala—to the healing practices from women-led Mayan organizations.

Pınar Öğrenci's contribution *Purple Panic: 43* also looks at the Latin American context of (para-)statal violence and enforced disappearance, but by adopting a spatial approach.[21] Her text interweaves two instances

21 This text has previously been published in Andrea Caroline Keppler, Katharina Koch and Dorothea Nold, eds., *Revolt She Said. Dekoloniale*

of state violence in Mexico—the massacre by police forces during a peaceful rally in Tlatelolco, Mexico City, just before the Olympic games in 1968, and the enforced disappearance in 2014 of 43 students from a college in Ayotzinapa who were on their way to a commemoration of the former massacre—with an analysis of forms of spatial governance exerted by the modern authoritarian state. Based on her 2015 performance in public space in Mexico, she maps the connection of state violence to the sites on which it occurs. Tlatelolco is not merely the site of the 1968 massacre: it has also been defined by "conquest and destruction" throughout its passage from an Aztec center in pre-Hispanic Tenochtitlan to a colonial monastery and, more recently, to a working-class neighborhood cleared for middle-class housing in the 1960s. Öğrenci argues that violence is inscribed in architecture—embodying social, economic, and political structures—and raises the question of how justice might be obtained for the victims of such violence.

Delving further into questions of space and violence, Sebastián Eduardo Dávila and Ulrike Jordan explore the readability of places where violence took place, discussing inscriptions or sedimentations of violence in space, the disappearance of bodies, and the (im-)possibility of remembering them through artistic and spatial practices. They do so by analyzing four contemporary artworks, located in different historical, political, and spatial contexts and characterized by the artists' desire to remember the victims of murder and disappearance in the face of dismissal and denial by the state and society. Faced with the predominant absence of official acknowledgements of violence, the artists seek to map, reflect upon, and reinscribe the traces of the disappeared in space. They translate processes of grief

und feministische Perspektiven auf 68 (Berlin: District Berlin/alpha nova & galerie futura, 2019), pp. 34–45. It has been slightly revised for publication in this book.

and remembrance into films, performances, and installations, expanding the circle of witnesses to violence. Narrating and marking the disappearance in space, it becomes clear that this is an ongoing process, one that generates modes of remembrance and mourning that transform the vulnerability of our bodies and existences into a political resource.

Deniz Utlu takes on these questions of mourning and grief in relation to racist pogroms and murders in Germany.[22] Building on Judith Butler's discussions on "grievable lives," he analyzes how those bereaved by such forms of violence have been claiming a space for commemoration and justice while their losses are being disregarded and official commemoration is motivated more by anxieties about the public image of the state than by emotional necessity. Utlu locates the reasons for this dispossession of grief in the structure of a "bureaucratic-racist state apparatus," both shaped by and shaping the actions of its agents. He calls for commemoration from the perspective of the victims, valuing them as individuals, and turning against the dehumanizing effects of an "economy of remembrance." The text dates from 2013, but sadly remains relevant today. As right-wing terrorist attacks in Munich in 2016, Halle in 2019, and Hanau in 2020 and the often deficient public reactions have painfully shown, the question of whose lives are considered grievable is still marked by racialized perceptions of the victims in present-day Germany.

22 This essay was first published in November 2013 as part of the Rosa Luxemburg Foundation's publication series *Standpunkte* (13/2013) and has been slightly revised for its publication in Azar Mortazavi, Tunay Önder and Christine Umpfenbach, eds., *Urteile. Ein dokumentarisches Theaterstück über die Opfer des NSU mit Texten über alltäglichen und strukturellen Rassismus* (Münster: Unrast Verlag, 2016) as well as for its English translation in this book.

Resilience and Resistance

The third section discusses withdrawal in terms of resilience as a neoliberal mode of subjectivation, which first of all promotes both passivization and isolation of subjects and thus counteracts the formation of active refusal and collective resistance. Across individual scenes emerges the question of possibilities for (collective) resistance in a time marked by multiple crises. There is an increasing and complex feeling of exhaustion, not only as an individual experience but also as a diagnosis on a global level.

The imperative of resilience permeates more and more areas of life and, with the help of neoliberal approaches of positive psychology, ultimately suppresses possibilities for collectivity and criticality. It individualizes responsibility and discourages critique; all the while subjects are passivized and encouraged to simply adapt to systemic catastrophes. The diagnosis brought forth by the critique of resilience once again underscores the phrase prominently reintroduced in 2009 by Mark Fisher: "It's easier to imagine the end of the world than the end of capitalism."[23] Following Mark Neocleous and Sarah Bracke, Stefanie Graefe speaks of a "colonization of the imagination." Neoliberalism promotes constant demands for resilience, which atrophies any ability to "imagine otherwise."[24] This is a dynamic we regard as highly problematic. To resist, to (go on) strike against the various crises produced by capitalism—as Sofia Bempeza suggests—or to rebel and evade its demands requires a vision of something else: namely that another world is possible. In this section, the authors are brought into an exchange that inaugurates a search for collective possibilities of resistance, including in places where

23 Mark Fisher, *Capitalist Realism: Is There No Alternative?* (Winchester: zer0 books, 2009), p. 7.

24 Stefanie Graefe, *Resilienz im Krisenkapitalismus. Wider das Lob der Anpassungsfähigkeit* (Bielefeld: transcript, 2019), p. 191.

resilience all too often leads to passive acquiescence, resignation, or even fatalism, or is (mis)used to silence resistance. Despite the central critique of the concept of resilience it is not so easy to fix an opposition between resilience and resistance. It is clear that resilience can be an important coping mechanism in harmful situations, for instance in the very act of not giving up or not dying. In this sense, criticizing the concept is also connected to one's own position or resources. The opposing tendencies of withdrawal arise time and again, oscillating between activation and passivation, thus re-emphasizing the ambivalence of the concept.

As Lauren Berlant makes clear, artistic works and other forms of knowledge production and mediation can be demonstrations of resistance: an unlearning, but likewise a shared worldbuilding and the forging of new affective infrastructures in which ambivalences are foregrounded. A form of withdrawal that gives room for being different (in the world). In this sense art—and the issue of representation—are key points of reference. Moreover, while art can reveal forms of domination and offer possibilities for worldbuilding, artists are at the same time uniquely exposed to neoliberal individualization.

This section opens with Stefanie Graefe's sociological critique of the concept of resilience in work and life under neoliberalism. The author argues against taking vulnerability as a basis for political empowerment and shows how the two concepts have been incorporated into global governmental programs with a wide range of different agendas and consequences. Resilience has become a new socio-political imperative, a fix for problems experienced both by individuals and by communities. In a discursive movement "from an ontological excess to the naturalization of violence," Graefe points out the "transformative power of catastrophe" as a contemporary mode of biopolitics. She questions the usefulness of the concepts of resilience and vulnerability as tools for better dealing with the manifold challenges of the present and near future or for questioning the organizational and structural policies of a neoliberal withdrawal that are still—and might always be—in play.

Thorsten Schneider sketches out a number of corollaries that emerge when transposing recent critiques of resilience into discourse on art and culture. Over recent decades, artists have become role models for *the resilient subject* par excellence, while a critique of creativity and contemporary entrepreneurship has been discussed extensively. While art is criticized as a playground for a highly speculative system of capitalist investment, the organization of artistic work has not been discussed in the same way. Artistic self-organization is not only a matter of artistic autonomy, it is also a huge challenge in the everyday practice of artists themselves. The idealized image of artists living only for and from their art is remote from the realities of a great number of practitioners. Schneider problematizes the gap between art as symbolic form for social and political critique—especially neoliberal working conditions—and the conditions of the versatile withdrawals under which this artistic critique is produced.

Building on her own experiences as a writer, artist and cultural producer Sofia Bempeza reflects on the significance of working in art and culture in the era of Covid-19 in the neoliberal societies of the Global North. From a queer feminist perspective, she focuses on structural maladjustments that pervade and sustain the artistic-cultural field. Precarious, often project-based modes of working and living often lead to exhaustion and depression if the producer does not have a social background enabling them to deal with difficult financial conditions, for example. Bempeza argues for dealing with negative affects in a way that resists increased demands for resilience and adaptation as imposed by the capitalist creative economy. In contrast, and considering past and contemporary examples of (art) strike, the author demonstrates the importance of temporary withdrawal, processes of "thinking-feeling," and practices of commoning for developing forms of resistance to the pressures of the temporal economies of meritocracy.

In her contribution, Nele Wulff takes up the idea of collective organization against the norms and values of mainstream society and combines it with a reflection on failure as a critique of heteronormative and capitalist notions of success, as addressed in the first section. The author asks how an understanding of failure might help in efforts to develop resistance. Wulff examines the functions of various dimensions of failure for the construction of what she calls, following Lauren Berlant, a queer "transformational infrastructure." Social exclusion and marginalization are experiences shared by the Colombian performance collective House of Tupamaras as members of the local LGBTIQ+ community. With artistic-activist performances and the creation of spaces for queer subculture, they counter cis-heteronormative notions of value and life with refusal and appropriation rather than with adaptation and retreat. If, as Stefanie Graefe writes, resilience as a new technology of the self suppresses people's imaginative capacities, the collective practice of House of Tupamaras can be read as a shared "imagining otherwise" that opens up new spaces of possibility for existence.

Judith Sieber's text points to the critical potential of the infographics that W.E.B. Du Bois and his team at Atlanta University developed for the Paris World's Fair in 1900. These unconventionally designed charts depict the lives of the Black population of the nineteenth-century United States in an ambivalent way, showing the improvement of living conditions after the official end of slavery in 1865 alongside a persisting undercurrent of racism. This combination could lead to the assumption of a growing resilience of the Black community. But the charts do not merely subvert the conventionalized form of infographics, they also refuse the notion of a monocausal and reductionist narrative of Black life. Referring back to section one, Sieber's text elaborates on a subtle refusal, which is a not-doing in terms of not following the norms of representation. With this, she also shows a refusal's potential for later repercussion: in this case, the potential for the deconstruction of a hegemonic perspective on history. In reflecting on historical constellations, it becomes clear that discussions on resilience and resistance are linked to questions of media and, in particular, to everyday visual forms that generate evidence.

The importance of ambivalence is elaborated in the text "Unlearning the Common" by Lauren Berlant, which is an excerpt from their posthumous book *On the Inconvenience of Other People*.[25] In the chapter from which the excerpt is taken, Berlant explores the potential of the "common," a concept they distinguish in a previous passage from a normative Enlightenment ideal, in particular that of Kant's "Sensus communis." Discussing the latter concept, Berlant makes a strong case for the role of ambivalences "as the tactics of commoning." They describe a process of unlearning as a blocking of normative imaginaries and emphasize the role of imagination for worldbuilding. The examples in the text explore political scenes of crisis; however, beyond merely illustrating the potentiating crises of the present—such as unemployment, opioid epidemics, police violence, racism, and the Covid-19 pandemic—they also present new potential forms of the common that oscillate between fiction and protest. At stake are poetics and, at the same time, concrete modes of relation in order to create new infrastructures. Beyond probing the intersection of resilience and resistance—a key concern of the last section—this excerpt also opens up a view of the future or, as Berlant writes: "Individuals may be exhausted, but as a whole they've not yet given up on the world."

25 See Lauren Berlant, *On the Inconvenience of Other People* (Durham, N.C. and London: Duke University Press, 2022).

Acknowledgements

The sections of the book are based on workshops and public conversations held between 2021 and 2022 in the framework of the DFG Research Training Group "Cultures of Critique" at Leuphana University Lüneburg. The first section began with a reading workshop in December 2021 hosted by Rebecca Hanna John and Malte Fabian Rauch, on the critical potentials of refusal, fugitivity, failure, and waywardness. Together with Kathrin Busch and Knut Ebeling, the participants discussed the film *They Call It Idlewild* (2020) by Helen Cammock and texts by Saidiya Hartman, Jack Halberstam, Georges Bataille, Giorgio Agamben, and Fred Moten, alongside two texts by Busch and Ebeling that have been revised and expanded for the present anthology. Based on the writings of Diana Taylor and a variety of artistic practices, discussions on disappearance and presence were key for the development of the second section. Organized by Ulrike Jordan and Sebastián Eduardo Dávila in March 2022, Marivi Véliz's event *Absentees: Some Effects of Violence in Latin American Performance Art in the 21st Century* comprised a lecture and workshop in cooperation with neue Gesellschaft für bildende Kunst (nGbK) that nurtured and enriched this process. The third section evolved from a workshop hosted in January 2022 by Nele Wulff, Judith Sieber, and Thorsten Schneider. The participants discussed the relationship between resilience, vulnerability, and resistance, based on texts by Stefanie Graefe, Sofia Bempeza, Sarah Bracke and Lauren Berlant, combined with videos from TJ Cuthand, Liza Johnson, and Mouaad el Salem.

We would like to thank all authors and participants of the workshops for their contributions and for the engaged discussions. A special thanks goes to Malte Fabian Rauch with whom we started this book and who played a central role in its conceptualization, as well as in the search for authors and contributions. For their manifold support of the whole process of the workshops' organization and the publication we wish to thank Beate Söntgen, Catharina Berents-Kemp, Liza Mattutat, and Susanne Leeb. We furthermore thank Stephanie Braune and David Mielecke for their help. For working patiently with both authors and editors on multiple revisions, we thank the translators Angela Anderson, Valentine A. Pakis, Matthew James Scown and Katherine Vanovitch. Catherine Lupton copy-edited this volume with care and diligence. Our sincere gratitude goes to Michael Heitz and Hendrik Rohlf from Diaphanes for their confidence in the series and all their efforts to ensure its timely release. Finally, we also want to thank the German Research Foundation DFG for the generous funding that facilitated the entire venture. And last but not least, we thank all our colleagues, mentors, interlocutors and partners at the Leuphana University Lüneburg.

Passivity, Failure, and Refusal

Kathrin Busch

Self-Loss as a Form of Knowledge[1]

In the arts, one encounters yet again, and with remarkable frequency, references to an "I."[2] Especially in literature, the use of the first-person singular appears commonly in the so-called genre of autofiction. A counterpart to this can be found in the visual arts in the forms of essayism characterized by personal points of view.[3] What is apparently taking place is a return to the self, which is quite surprising after theoretical positions on the "death of the author," the dissolution of the self-determined subject, or in light of current post-humanist approaches. Upon closer inspection, it becomes clear that this new self-referentiality, with its modes of subjectivation, is concerned to a significant extent with self-loss. Particularly in literary autofiction, the self-evasive "I" becomes the source of a different sort of knowledge. It arises from forms of experience that require self-loss: knowledge that derives not only from undesired and unintended adversities but also from a fundamentally different relationship to the world—from an oddly a-subjective experience. Self-loss is a precondition for a form of knowledge that transcends any objectification, structured by consciousness and language, of the object of this knowledge itself. What is interesting about these autofictional depictions of self-loss is their unheroic

1 First published in German: Kathrin Busch, "Selbstverlust als Wissensform," in *Selbstverlust und Welterfahrung. Erkundungen einer pathischen Moderne*, ed. Björn Bertrams and Antonio Roselli (Vienna: Turia + Kant, 2021), pp. 212–225.

2 See Alex Kitnik, "I, etcetera," *October* 166 (2018), pp. 45–62.

3 For a discussion of literary autofiction within the context of the visual arts, see volume 115 of the journal *Texte zur Kunst* (2019), which is devoted to the topic of literature.

nature. They are not sacrifices or negations of the self that serve higher ends. Instead, these diminutions of the self are indicative of fundamental passivity. In these self-losses, what is underscored is not the over-expenditure of a stable subject but rather the condition of his or her formation. Obsession, deprivation, and exposure determine the constitution of the self. Unlike the heroic self-loss associated with sacrificial or transgressive characters, the sort of self-loss in question is associated with falling short, with inability and involuntary dispossession instead of any grand gesture of self-sacrifice or annihilation.[4] Especially in times when all sorts of self-techniques tacitly take for granted the controllability of the self, these involuntary losses, failed appropriations, and shameful deviations represent crucial aspects of a different form of subjectivation. They are a radicalized form of loss because they are suffered, unchosen, clumsy, and in fact unaffirmable. It is a potentiated self-loss that has interestingly led to a new and self-lost way of saying "I." These testimonies of unsuccessful self-determination and involuntary self-loss are part of a painful history of undermining the ideal of free self-determination.

1. Self-Loss and the Concern for the Truth

Unheroic self-loss belongs to a tradition that Michel Foucault referred to in his final lecture at the Collège de France in 1984. The lecture recalls self-techniques of self-deprecation or self-disclosure in classical philosophy, the aim of which was to expose the unchosen aspects of existence: that which, in other words, eludes self-determination and pushes the self to the edge of its dispossessions. The lecture bears the title "The Courage of the Truth,"

4 Georges Bataille and Jacques Derrida in particular have discussed the aporias created by expenditure, as when even a loss can be counted as a gain.

and it is devoted to the topic of parrhesia—speaking candidly—in classical philosophy. Of special interest are the sections on Cynicism, a deviant form of philosophy that, via a scandalously permissive way of life, makes visible to the public all that is generally hidden. One aspect of this philosophy is that it is essential to speak truths about oneself and others, and these truths might be unpleasant: forms of embarrassing and self-revealing speech, and also forms of self-disparagement or self-deprecation. These are ways of speaking that bring to light the baseness of existence, thereby ushering into the space of philosophical truths that which is typically not open to discussion. In classical Cynicism, this is less about the shame of speaking the truth than it is about revealing what is shameful; it is a matter of pointing out that the lowly and the scorned are a condition of the truth. The truth is not limited to the pure and the sublime; it also includes the dejected, and courage is needed to express this and embody it openly. Not only must this truth be expressed; it also needs to be tested and lived—in the original sense of askesis: as an exercise in a way of living that corresponds to the truth. Whereas the aim of ascetic practices is normally to conform oneself to certain philosophical ideas or ideals, the Cynic performs this in reverse: it is not what is known to be true that should be lived; rather, living should reveal the true life. This practice involved being truthful and speaking openly about what really defines existence: namely, the inevitable and inescapable factors that constitute the conditions of life, which included the bodily needs that Cynics satisfied on the side of the road like dogs (kynicos), hence their name. What the Cynics brought to the discourse of truth was thus the raw and existential. They slept, ate, masturbated, and urinated in public space. In this way, they exposed indispensable aspects of life such as sleeping, eating, desiring, and digesting by performing such things in the public sphere. This requires courage. It requires courage to reveal what is normally rejected because it lies outside of our own control: the passive conditions of existence, vulnerability, and arousal, which lie outside our powers and precede our own activity. As such, they are not at our disposal and they occur at the point of our own existence that evades the self and is beyond the control of our subjective capabilities. The genuine concern of Cynicism was to expose these elementary aspects of life: to lend expression to what is unchosen in our own existence, to speak of what is elementary and beyond our realm of possibility. We have no choice but to accept such things as the body's base materiality. In contrast to the more commonly preferred idea of self-empowerment, it is interesting that Foucault devoted attention to the rejected and the base—as well as to powerlessness and self-loss—in his late research program devoted to the "aesthetics of existence."[5] Unreserved self-exposure and the "scandalous manifestations of [this] other [baser] life" are techniques of the self.[6] Or inverted techniques of the self, if one thinks of the common philosophical programs of self-governance, the intention of which since antiquity has been to stylize self-control and self-refinement as mankind's loftiest achievement. It seems self-evident that the arts of life serve self-determination, and that ascetic trials and exercises serve self-empowerment. In Foucault's work, however, the opposite becomes conceivable: one must train oneself to develop the courage to face that which evades the self—the inevitable and the shameful. This is an asceticism of disavowal that confronts what is unpleasant. It is directed toward those truths of the subject which express her or his inability and baseness, the disclosure of which inevitably brings

5 Michel Foucault, "An Aesthetics of Existence," in *Politics, Philosophy, Culture: Interviews and Other Writings, 1977–1984*, ed. Lawrence D. Kritzman (New York: Routledge, 1988), pp. 47–53.

6 Michel Foucault, *The Courage of Truth (The Government of Self and Others II): Lectures at the Collège de France 1983–1984*, ed. Frédéric Gros, trans. Graham Burchell (Basingstoke: Palgrave Macmillan, 2011), p. 269.

to light a truth that, though unpleasant and painful, must be expressed.

According to Foucault, this risky form of the art of living, which exposes self-loss, has survived into modernity. There is a "trans-historical Cynicism,"[7] but it persists today not in philosophy but rather in art. The habitualization of a deviant mode of existence, which reveals an elementary truth, and the courageous examinations of concealed, rejected, or discarded incapacities can be found in modernity's artistic conceptions of existence.

The thesis that a truer form of subjectivation was preserved in the lives of modern artists has been refuted—or so it might seem—in the studies by Luc Boltanski and Ève Chiapello.[8] They have demonstrated how the artists' critique of bourgeois society and its conventions, in the name of freedom and deviant self-determination, in fact encouraged the economization of creativity and neoliberal project work. Paradoxically, it is precisely the insistence of artists to maintain independence and freedom that led to the precarious nature of creative work. Throughout their book, Boltanski and Chiapello often interpret Foucault's techniques of self-governance as precursors to neoliberal subjectivation, and they criticize these techniques in their analysis of self-optimization. Despite this critique and these arguments, Foucault's thesis in favor of a different "aesthetics of existence" has not been invalidated. Its critical potential simply no longer lies in the promise of self-actualization, which is often associated with the lives of artists. If one understands Foucault's theses on the art of living in terms of his reconstruction of Cynicism, a different image emerges. For, what tends to be overlooked in cursory interpretations of Foucault's "aesthetics of existence" is

7 Ibid., p. 174.

8 Luc Boltanski and Ève Chiapello, *The New Spirit of Capitalism*, trans. Gregory Elliott (London: Verso, 2005).

that it concerns the history of artistic self-deprecation and the exposure of self-loss. The artistic way of life thus seems exemplary not in the way that it explores freedom but in the way that it investigates a lack of freedom. The artistic life is not one of self-empowerment but one that seeks to represent disempowerment; it is not a matter of showcasing self-chosen ability but of exposing inability. There is in fact a whole tradition of an aesthetics of inability, of artistic confessions of self-loss and self-rejection, presented as way of surrendering to a different sort of truth. This aesthetics of inability, self-loss, or passivity is directed toward the forces that are at work in artistic production processes, which dispossess their creators and turn their self-lapses into instances of a different form of knowledge.

2. Aesthetics of In-Ability

In the twentieth century, Antonin Artaud's courageous articulation of inability should be mentioned above all, because it has been especially important to French thought—from André Breton to Jacques Derrida—and because, here, self-loss also affects the ability to think. In the early 1920s, the still unknown Artaud had submitted poems to the renowned literary journal *Nouvelle Revue Française* and received a rejection. The poems, according to the journal's editor, were not good enough. Artaud did not accept this rejection and, in a now famous exchange of letters, he attempted to persuade the editor that the poems—though indeed not very good (as he openly admitted)—nevertheless deserve to be published because they testify (entirely in the spirit of courageous truth-telling) to an intellectual inability that is fundamental to thought itself. Artaud argued that his failure does not derive from a poor command of language; rather, his work reveals that there is something insistent in thinking that resists all his abilities: "My thought abandons me at every level."[9] His poems are intended to demonstrate this loss or abandonment and illustrate the fact that there is an inherent dynamic in thinking that evades conscious and volitional thought and therefore dispossesses the thinker. In the inability to control his thinking, Artaud reveals the uncontrollable nature of the thought process itself, which gains its dynamics from non-knowledge and inability and is permeated by involuntary lapses. Maurice Blanchot, who wrote about Artaud's famous correspondence, emphasized this relation between suffering and thinking. Artaud, he remarked, "is in contact with something so grave that he cannot suffer its reduction."[10] He makes it clear, according to Blanchot, that art cultivates an experience of impossibility, and that thinking takes place along the edges where it is extinguished. Artaud's aim is to walk along and test out these borders on the fine seam of inability. For his part, Blanchot uses the term "archi-passivity" to underscore the constitutive significance of this self-lost or dispossessed state of suffering. What is meant by this is not the opposite of activity, but rather the opposite of potency. The notion goes hand in hand with the far-reaching insight that "the limit of the human" does not lie "in possibility itself."[11] This rejection of the vita activa is central to Blanchot's aesthetics. The realm of the day—with its activity, with domination, history, and power—is opposed by the passive space of the night. This image of radical passivity, however, is not one of the inactivity of sleep but rather the unease of insomnia, in which the night is experienced while the ability

9 Antonin Artaud, "Correspondence with Jacques Rivière," in *Collected Works: Volume One*, trans. Victor Corti (London: John Calder, 1968), pp. 25–42, here p. 31

10 Maurice Blanchot, "Artaud," in *The Book to Come*, trans. Charlotte Mandell (Stanford: Stanford University Press, 2003), pp. 34–40, here p. 35.

11 Emmanuel Lévinas, "The Vision of the Poet," in *Proper Names*, trans. Michael B. Smith (Stanford: Stanford University Press, 1996), pp. 127–139, here p. 127.

to sink into sleep is extinguished: a potentiated passion or involuntary powerlessness. It is insufficient to distinguish art from what is useful, interesting, or sensually knowable and to associate it merely with sensual experience and aimless contemplation. What is decisive is not the limitation of action but the transcendence of ability. Art creates access to passivity in the sense of inability or self-loss. It disables ability and leads to the "desolate field of impossibilities incapable of constituting themselves as worlds."[12] It is a lament for power, a farewell to ability, an element of powerlessness. To write is to sever the ties between language and the ability to act. Only in self-loss—if this is understood as the suspension or transcendence of ability—can something be encountered "before which the I loses its ipseity."[13] Writing is this motion of becoming unable, and it is precisely in this transition toward inability where a new mode of knowledge lies.

Another relevant example is F. Scott Fitzgerald's autobiographical essay "The Crack-Up" (1936), which Gilles Deleuze analyzed in "Porcelain and Volcano" (a chapter included in *The Logic of Sense*).[14] Fitzgerald's text concerns an author who, like a plate, becomes cracked. That is, the author in question suffers a sort of damage that is irreducible. A defect that henceforth renders the person extremely fragile—ever in danger of breaking apart from the event that has inscribed itself in his body in the form of a crack. The knowledge of being broken comes, according to the essay, not as a heavy blow but as a crack that inscribes self-loss into one's awareness almost imperceptibly at first and yet inevitably leads to "the disintegration of one's own personality."[15] One does not

12 Ibid., p. 131.
13 Ibid., p. 132.
14 See F. Scott Fitzgerald, *The Crack-Up*, ed. Edmund Wilson (New York: New Directions, 1993), and Gilles Deleuze, "Porcelain and Volcano," in *The Logic of Sense*, trans. Mark Lester and Charles Stivale (London: The Athlone Press, 1990), pp. 154–161.
15 Fitzgerald, *The Crack-Up*, p. 76.

recover from the crack that results from an overestimation of one's own possibilities.[16] There is an open confession of alcoholism and financial hardship in the essay, as well as an implicit theory on the connection between depression and addiction. At the same time, addiction seems to be intimately related to the literary as a form of dependency that dispossesses the self. In his analysis of this essay, Deleuze makes it clear why the fragility of a subject at risk of self-loss belongs to the tradition of Cynical aesthetics. He detects in the text and in the literary representation of the crack a form of counter-actualization. Instead of simply realizing the crack, the artistic confession of self-loss rehearses it to some extent in the events and encounters that are beyond our control: "But each time we must double this painful actualization by a counter-actualization which limits, moves, and transfigures it."[17] Art exists in this act of doubling. One must, that is, reembody and showcase what really happened, the event, however self-alienating this might be. Instead of confining what has happened, the crack-up, in its actualization, one must test it through this reenactment. At the end of his commentary, Deleuze remarks that this should be a matter of transforming the techniques of social alienation into revolutionary means of exploration.[18] Alienation in today's society, which is oriented toward self-improvement, is alienation from inability. To reembody it would be a form of resisting the self-improvement that society demands. As a continuation of the Cynical aesthetics of existence discussed by Foucault, art should be a test of the infeasible, of de-potentialization; it should be an act of speaking the truth with respect to that which is left unregistered in life's margins of possibility: experiences that, as impingements and traumas, cannot be intentionally created but

16 Ibid.
17 Deleuze, *The Logic of Sense*, p. 161.
18 Ibid.

only repeated. In this sense, Cynical art would be an act of exercising the inability of representing one's own losses and wounds. It is through such exposure that we can "become worthy of what happens to us."[19] In this sense, Cynical art is affirmational. Rather than seeking self-improvement, we should seek to incorporate what is unpleasant: "Become the man of your misfortunes; learn to embody their perfection and brilliance."[20]

To some extent, Chris Kraus does exactly this in her autofictional novel *I Love Dick*, which was first published in 1997. This novel was rediscovered in the German-speaking world thanks to a 2017 translation and thanks to the eponymous television series filmed by the American director Joey Soloway. *I Love Dick* follows an aesthetics of weak self-loss. The text depicts the experience of self-loss as one of self-deprecation and a shameful lack of sovereignty. The book, which is a cross between an epistolary novel and a piece of confessional literature, mixes different genres and connects them with an essayistic tone, all the while exposing a self-dispossessing experience of falling in love. It thus brings into play the question of self-loss and our relationships with others. In a casual style, Kraus paints a picture of a failing artist who regards herself as "wantonly unhappy,"[21] unattractive, and unsuccessful—not only in matters of love but also in her work. She describes how she falls apart in her efforts to connect and transfer her love to a man with whom she is obsessed. The writing here is also an example of counter-actualization that repeats self-loss, which is formally expressed in the asymmetry of the protagonist's correspondence with her love interest, who does not respond to her letters.[22] From this

19 Ibid., p. 149.
20 Ibid.
21 Chris Kraus, *I Love Dick* (Los Angeles: Semiotext(e), 1998), p. 228.
22 The casual or amateurish nature of the writing is intensified all the more by the fact that the two male characters in the novel—her husband Sylvère Lotringer and Dick Hebdige, the object of her desire—are identifiable.

manner of writing, which is unreturned, the self empties itself out in a sort of draining relationality. Thus we read toward the end of the book: "For years I tried to write but the compromises of my life made it impossible to inhabit a position. And 'who' am 'I'? Embracing you & failure's changed all that 'cause now I know I'm no one. And there's a lot to say …"[23] This connection between being "no one" and having "a lot to say" carries the book: a text that confesses to a lack of sovereignty while simultaneously allowing Chris Kraus to become a writer. The self-exposing and humiliating writing sets in motion a transformation that cannot simply be derived from the disgraceful situation and is not executed for the purpose of self-empowerment; what it does instead is restage self-loss, which is reflected in the text by way of Félix Guattari's schizo-analysis: "I was becoming you."[24]

3. The Flesh of Knowledge

A radicalized form of becoming other (and of knowledge gained through self-loss) can be found in Paul B. Preciado's *Testo Junkie*.[25] The book can be understood in terms of the Cynical practice of displaying the elementary aspects of life in a blunt manner. First published in 2008 under the name Beatriz Preciado, the book documents a self-experiment with what is precariously called one's "own" gender, while providing an account of testosterone addiction and an erotic love affair. At the same time, it is an effort to expose and test a certain discursive truth through this experience. Preciado examines the present biopolitical regime and comes to the conclusion that today's biopower operates according to

23 Kraus, *I Love Dick*, p. 221.
24 Ibid., p. 254.
25 Paul B. Preciado, *Testo Junkie: Sex, Drugs, and Biopolitics in the Pharmacopornographic Era*, trans. Bruce Benderson (New York: The Feminist Press, 2013).

the pharmacological and pornographic regulations of desire. The analysis presented in the book leans on Foucault's thesis that gender and sexuality have been a central object of political power since the beginning of the nineteenth century, and it traces their current pharmacological and pornographic conditions. Preciado analyzes the biopolitical significance of the pill and Viagra as paradigmatic examples, and then examines the porn industry as the dominant visual technology for controlling and producing desire. At the same time, Preciado's book formulates a new connection between theoretical insights and autofiction (in the sense of its courage to reveal the truth). In addition to its theoretical analyses, *Testo Junkie* also documents the author's self-experiment with intoxication: "This book is not a memoir. This book is a testosterone-based, voluntary intoxication protocol, which concerns the body and affects of BP [i.e., Beatriz Preciado]. A body-essay. Fiction, actually. If things must be pushed to the extreme, this is a somato-political fiction, a theory of the self, a self-theory."[26] *Testo Junkie* operates in multiple registers; it contains Foucauldian discourse analysis, a genealogical reconstruction of pharmacopornographic biopower, a description of an intoxicating and gender-disidentifying self-experiment, and autofictional pornographic writing. In this montage, which juxtaposes theory, confessional literature, historical reconstruction, and instructions for sexual practices, Preciado's book revives the Cynical practice of combining bodily exposure with unsettling truth. This truth takes the form of theoretical fiction, a published self-experiment undertaken on Preciado's own flesh. This self-experiment is reflected in the essayistic style of the work. Knowledge, pharmacology, and pornography are treated as the constitutive elements of subjectivation and Preciado, via the example of his own intoxicated and stimulated body, melds them with the episteme by

26 Ibid., p. 11.

allowing post-pornographic sex and the illegitimate use of testosterone to inform the theoretical side of the book. This sort of knowledge must be lived and exposed to the "force of testosterone."[27] This is an extremely risky aesthetics of existence, not only because the testosterone gel is addictive but also because Preciado is undergoing an uncontrolled process of becoming another gender.[28] In this engagement with contemporary forms of power the elementary aspects of existence are exposed. Preciado reembodies the power to which he is subjected and affects readers with the techniques of arousal that *Testo Junkie* reveals. At the same time, the empowering gesture of having hormonal and erotic control repeatedly turns into extreme passion or suffering. In this process of becoming, which involves the administration of hormones, the author runs the risk of self-loss and exposes the ambivalence, uncontrollability, and toxicity of self-empowerment:[29] "In order to transform conventional frameworks of the 'cultural intelligibility' of human bodies, it is necessary to evolve toward practices of voluntary autointoxication," which disidentify.[30] Preciado adds: "I don't recognize myself."[31] To lose oneself, according to this line of thinking, is the condition of every subjectivation. Subjects are formed when they become unrecognizable to themselves.

The book concludes with a reflection about thinking. Philosophy, according to Preciado, is a praxis of "decapitation": "I wanted to decapitate myself, cut off my head that had been molded by a program of gender, dissect

27 Ibid., p. 21.

28 The open-ended form of this process leads to an uncertain existence devoted to a "becoming" that defies traditional masculine-feminine categories.

29 See Giorgio Ferreti, "Grenzen von Gewicht: Körper und Freiheit in den Werken von Marina Abramović und Ulay im Vergleich mit Paul B. Preciados *Testo Junkie*," *Kritische Ausgabe* 33 (2017), http://www.kritische-ausgabe.de/artikel/grenzen-von-gewicht (accessed on January 10, 2019).

30 Preciado, *Testo Junkie*, p. 351.

31 Ibid., p. 397.

part of the molecular model that resides in me."[32] Whenever Preciado applies this to himself and reembodies, in the Deleuzian sense, what he analyzes as the technology of power, his act of counter-actualization—the act of taking testosterone—repeatedly tumbles into self-loss and powerlessness, despite the grandiloquent, inflated, and self-aggrandizing language with which he describes this experience.

4. Arts of Knowledge

What significance does Foucault's thesis—again, that the Cynical tradition has survived in the arts—have for aesthetic theory? Whereas theories of aesthetic experience predominate in the German-speaking world, Foucault's approach in "The Courage of the Truth" paves the way for a different theory of art and a different artistic form of knowledge. Theories of aesthetic experience have as their starting point the concept of aesthetic reflexivity. By aesthetic means, art has the ability to reflect the present in a critical manner. In aesthetic experience, processes of reflection are set in motion that resist any definitive content and thereby sharpen the critical view of the present. This is different from art with genealogical roots in Cynicism. Here, truth is reembodied, deviant practices of truth-telling are practiced, and forms of radicalized sensibility are incorporated in exposures of traumatic events or are revealed as deviant counter-actualizations in the wounds of inability. If, according to Foucault's reconstruction, parrhesia encompasses not only the courage to speak the truth but also concern for the self, then this is a type of concern that is open, exposed, and devoted to that which is uncontrollable. As a form of knowledge, self-loss articulates a weak, non-dominant knowledge, a knowl-

32 Ibid., p. 424.

edge created from debilitated positions that have not strengthened into consensus. A minority knowledge, to the extent that the majority is the norm of consolidated knowledge. This norm includes normative ideas about the progress of scientific knowledge in which insights are consolidated until everything fragile is replaced by secure knowledge.[33] The history of science—as a history of discoveries, correcting false assumptions, and solving problems—is a history of the ways in which knowledge and power are intertwined. On the one hand, there are the powerful effects of knowledge; on the other hand, there are the powers within knowledge itself to reject, deny, and regulate.[34] Foucault analyzed this interrelation of knowledge and power in his essay "The Order of Discourse." Here, with reference to a number of specific historical practices of knowledge, he traces how an empowering form of scientific knowledge emerged from precarious insights and from the threatening unrest of the discourse. This scientific will to knowledge has ultimately come to dominate all other forms of knowledge.[35] In his analysis of the relationship between knowledge and power, Foucault's distress about the impossibility of weak knowledge is almost palpable. So much is clear when he traces the trajectories of excluded and different forms of knowledge articulated in the unheard or unheeded voices of insane, abnormal, or infamous people. For Foucault, it seems evident that minor and ostracized forms of knowledge can only come to expression when they intersect with power.[36] Not until his final lectures did he redirect his attention from the will to

33 See Moritz Epple et al., eds., *Weak Knowledge: Forms, Functions, and Dynamics* (Frankfurt am Main: Campus, 2019).

34 See Michel Foucault, "The Order of Discourse," trans. Ian McLeod, in *Untying the Text: A Post-Structuralist Reader*, ed. Robert Young (Boston: Routledge & Keagan Paul, 1981), pp. 48–78, esp. pp. 52–53.

35 See ibid., pp. 55–56.

36 See Michel Foucault, "The Life of Infamous Men," in *Power, Truth, Strategy*, ed. Meaghan Morris and Paul Patton (Sydney: Feral Publications, 1979), pp. 76–91.

knowledge to the concern for truth. To the concern for the self and the concern for others, he adds the concern for an endangered truth. Today, one finds this concern for weak and vulnerable truth in art.

Translation: Valentine A. Pakis

Helen Cammock

They Call It Idlewild Extended II

Brighton / 2022

Very recently I wrote a song lyric in collaboration with a group of women who all had an uncommon yet shared loss —the song looped around different reflections on the permutations of silence; its vibrations and hums, its vacuum-ous nature and the bravery required to endure it through moments of deeply penetrating trauma.

I'm listening in your silence
I'm listening in your silence

Sometimes the reflective tomb squeezes, requiring us to endure the labour involved in walking through walls of solitude
this tomb can also offer the kind of breathless sanctuary needed for metamorphosis
to
another shape
another colour
something bright winged and weary can emerge exhausted yet beautiful

My therapist talked of pennies at the bottom of the well
static underground swell dark and voluminous
eyes cold and aching
diving so deep
'til you can hear yourself

a pumping refrain spinning on the skin of the coin
and something begins
shape taking
awaiting the moment you decide
to break the edge of surface
and
although there is concerted effort
pockets edges and emotional edifice
exist
in all of us

The well
The cave
The studio
The pillow
The belly of another
The cleaning cupboard
The empty street
Can house what lies
dormant

sometimes   in

all of us

New Orleans / 2022

Fan overhead, that chops and glides through air heavy with water and sun. A rivulet runs down and into the stitches cinched and strained on a hot waist.

My desk a little high

My skin too hot

My eyes look through and beyond glass

I shuffle and understand that again I have finally found a slightly folded wet lipped cave to push away the thoughts of what I should do—to do something else

The brick dust falls in sprinkles

The mustard door is wide

I feel a splinter rip sock and a cockroach feigns death

Birds are cackling

A possum swings a stomach full of promise

A gecko stretches and a caterpillar spiked and resplendent climbs, rope free and without a belayer hair upon hair bristling through muscle every rock face brown painted rendered stair

Cumbersome auto gearbox
Slurred notations and crawling crescendo
I will collect cars one day
Staccato and sleek
gearbox notched serenade

Rubber and engine
Hot bodywork
Colour to suck on
Boiled sweets move forward and back

I run from my finger nails
Peeled and discarded
I look to the squirrel who runs up the bark
I feel invisible and yet everyone sees me
I understand the nod
Respond to it the left side of expected
I bounce on my trainers green mint choc chip soles
Pavements are cracked yet smoother than roads outside my new cave
Full of heat and friction and life
I am on top then inside then alone and no one really cares when they look
I don't feel alone
Generosity and gold teeth
Eyelashes and air con
White wine and wheezing laughter
Where privilege and death clash if you look
Clash if you listen
Clash if you feel
I choke then I laugh
I'm touched and I sigh
I sleep then I don't
I sit still here and breathe

Laredo / 2022

Waiting to move
As a deer who hears a hunter
Limbo liminal ice
Numbing tingling legs
Fighting the need to move
To be angry
I sit alongside 200 or maybe 300 or maybe more Trapped in a hangar waiting for a plane
I am impotent
I do nothing I wait I am impotent I do nothing all I can do is do nothing and bear the wait

Wysing / 2019 / 2020
They Call It Idlewild - Script

Condensating window
Thread pile
Meccano bolted loft
Full to itself
wound
With tightly
Folded stories
Spines and edges of stuttering stacked casings of text
Managers manual to fast thinking
Subtitle
Of what?
35mm slides
Of frames and shapes and shadows
Daylight fading
Tracing through grey leaf blown sky
Fly suspended as
Box file contents
On a spider's string
Singular web line
Swings to the rhythm
Of draft streams

Two boxes say "A Mock Up" another says "fragments" So, I sit with the mock up and the fragments and my head and still waiting for the chasm that needs to fall sharply into somewhere dark or somewhere cold or somewhere palpably wet or is it dusted and dry—some-where plants can't grow but ideas can

A germination as stomach tightens, chest relaxes, shifting synapses or is it something different for you? I must stand and walk or sit and stare…is it the same for you?

o

Plastic and chrome
Swing and sway
Camera operator says
If you sway like that
You appear at best unsure
At worst as if you're lying (PAUSE)
But I always sway when I write
Green box file
Textured
Hessian-imitating
A colour I want to touch
Cd's
Black hand written
Drawings
Randomness is like idleness Route
to possibility—keychain Never the
sepulchre
For word
Or line
Or frame

And this morning the heat is strong
Thin heat
With a strong shafting
A fly lies in light
On desk
A beautiful corpse
Leg flicks
And I realise it's the "not-dead"
fly I tried to let out last night
But it couldn't find the door
And I couldn't find the patience For
the endless
Window
Door
Collisions
And so this not quite dead corpse
With one leg flicking
I carry outside to live
Or to die
In that shafting
Damp

Bright
    Fresh
light
Of

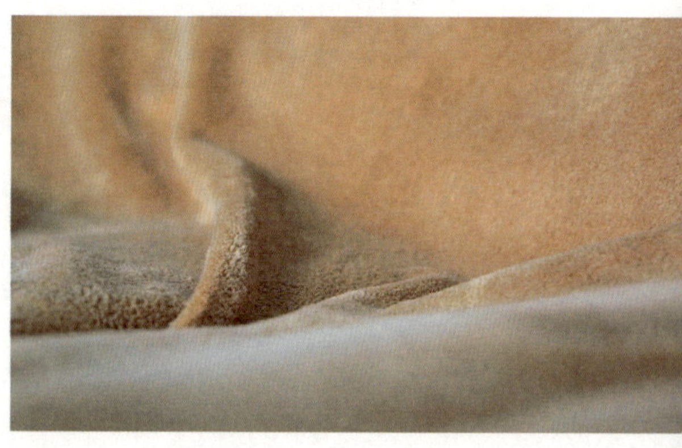

November

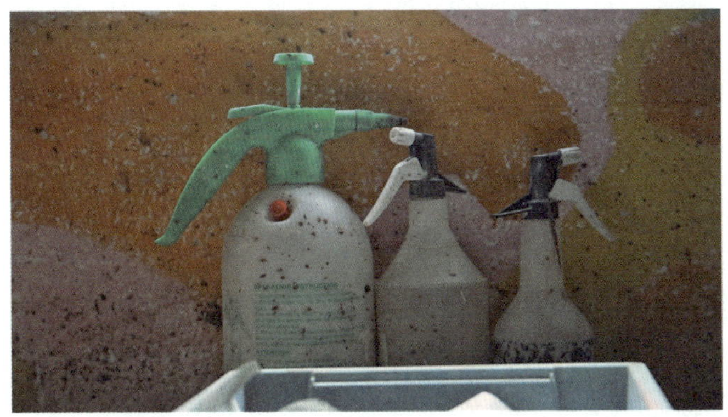

°

Futile acts in futile times
Grasping for something that the light on my skin brings I think again
Of stillness
Idleness
I am caught by a text lying clipped in a box
ENTER_ARCHIVE
Titled *Killing me softly* by Krzysztof Fijalkowski
A wandering across historical moments and dislocated genres
And I consider what it means to engage with sound And what is at stake in embracing silence
To be forced into silence is one proposition
But to be forced into a world devoid of silence is quite another

°

Wet grass and the possibility of poisonous
Funghi
Stops me
I look around
And my skin feels everything the air has to offer
My toes feel damp and the cold pops the epidermis of green suede

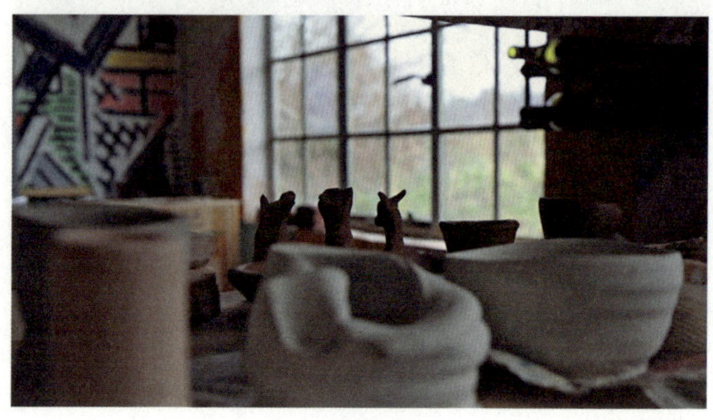

And I remember the words of Chris Davis:

All living creatures have to work to stay alive
Some have to work harder than others
Those creatures that need to do little work to stay
alive Are more likely to survive periods of difficulty

than those that must work harder and longer......

One shouldn't confuse inactivity with idleness. The fisher-man may look like he's idle as he sits, intent on his line, but at that moment he is constrained, not free.

When he isn't fishing, he may go for a walk and look more active, but he is actually free to do anything in that moment and so is idle in evolutionary terms;

His stationary fishing is active, his walking a form of idle-ness which he engages in for pleasure.

The artists model, sitting still, is theoretically active, the amateur sculptor chiselling away at the block is theoreti-cally "idle."

Joyce in his 1903 notebooks wrote:

All art, again, is static for the feelings of terror and pity on the one hand, and the feeling of joy on the other hand are all feelings which arrest us.

Afterwards it will appear how this rest is necessary for the apprehension of the beautiful—the end of all art, tragic or comic,—for this rest is the only condition under which the images, which are to excite in us terror or pity or joy, can be properly presented to us and properly seen by us. [1]

°

Mary Oliver says:

No one yet has made a list of places where the extraordi-nary may happen and where it may not. Still, there are indications. Among crowds, in drawing rooms, among easements and comforts and pleasures, it is seldom seen. It likes the out-of-doors. It likes the concentrating mind. It likes solitude. It is more likely to stick to the risk-taker than the ticket-taker. It isn't that it would disparage com-forts, or the set routines of the world, but that its con-cern is directed to another place. Its concern is the edge, and the making of the form out of the formlessness that is beyond the edge. [2]

°

And Audre Lorde says:

As they become known to and accepted by you, our feelings and the honest exploration of them become sanctuaries and spawning grounds for the most radical and daring of ideas.

They become a safe-house for that difference so necessary to change and the conceptualisation of any meaningful action.

Right now, I could name at least ten ideas I would have found intolerable or incomprehensible and frightening, except as they came after dreams and poems. This is not idle fantasy, but a disciplined attention to the meaning of "it feels right to me."

So, the daydream can create idle space—and that space is host for both ideas and feeling to co-exist and multiply or intersect. There is nothing inactive about that.[3]

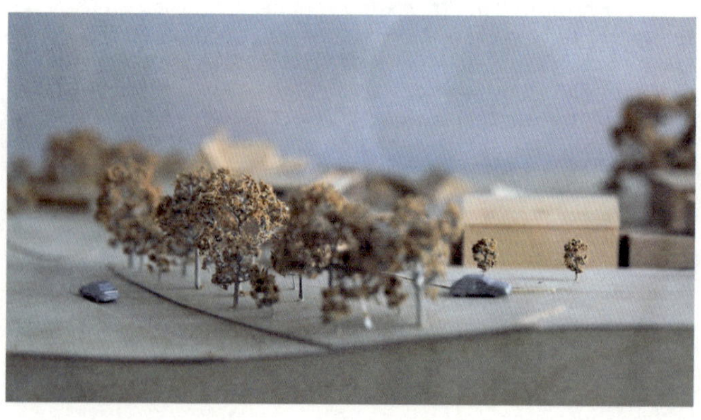

°

A tree rises from wet earth
Yellow through russet
And it settles on the
Tone of my skin
When it's warm
It punctures cloud
And the leaves gently
Caress the bones
Of a smaller perhaps more urgent
But commanding tree behind

The wind aids the connection
And I catch sight of the leaves on the architects'
model It is a world of ambition
Perspex
Encasement
Plywood
Base
Screws hold the foundation
Like the lugs in the meccano of this loft

Modern dry
Older frieze blocked
Concrete path
Gravel
Dirt road mud bath
Trees and wood so much wood
If I listen hard I can
Hear the noise of scraping chair
Feel the breath on my neck of a frustrated sigh Traces
Yet something will come it always does

°

Chip on my windscreen
Large car fast too fast
Red, yellow
Russets springs then
Sound of rustle blast rain
Memories of country living
Shiver and shake me
I feel the wet slide
Down my wrist bones
And prickle my elbow
I stroke my hands
On my lips
Soft skin

Ridges
And remember how it
Feels to kiss
Gravel under foot
Satisfying sounds
Of chipped stone crackle
I'm waiting for a flow that is already
here

°

Lazy bones sleeping in the sun
When you gonna get your day's work done?You can't
get your day's work done
Sleeping in the noon day sun.

Lazy bones layin' in the shade
How you gonna get your cornmeal made?
You can't get no cornmeal made
Sleeping in that evening shade.

When taters need sprayin', I bet you keep prayin'
The bugs fall off the vine
And when you go fishin', I bet you keep wishing
Them fish don't grab your line.

Lazy bones loafing all the day
How you spect to make a dime that way?
You won't make no dime that way
Loafin' in the shade all day.[4]

°

And maybe Johnny Mercer didn't know the extent of what he'd ingested—what he admired so much was so undermined by what those words perpetuated.
Lazy black man who lay under a tree, well fed, clean clothes and straw hat… sleeping the day away… fingers grass sliced, burnt soil, heatstroke, snake bite, whip, no sleep, gnawing hunger… plantation to farm hand to dustbowl disaster; project to projects… the space for the irresponsible lazy black person never fades.

°

But the plantation owner… the landowner—the per-son owner… the knighted landed peer—the Tory MP with business interests that belong to him but are never worked by him… which came to him at birth, who believes in nothing but the furtherment of this entitled existence is of course the faithful lazybones who needs the slave, the indentured labourer, the child in the Congo, the disabled parent, the projects, the coun-cil estate, immigrants all to hide their own laziness… to ensure they can live off the labour of others, the impov-erishment of others, while all the time hiding their own parasitic embodiment through the projection of the lazy in all those who keep him or her there… head of the straw chewing, toe bouncing, shade grabbing tree of bet-terment.

(PAUSE)

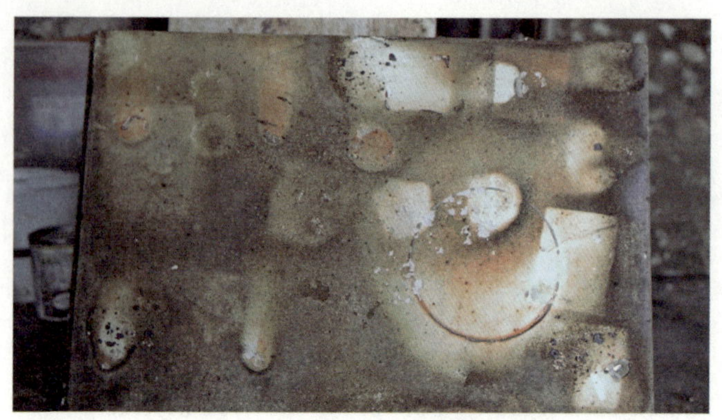

So is it in the activeness in doing nothing,

not the passiveness in working without question

that we should cite our song

lilting jazz melodies in a world of

frozen step bodies

and

dawn breaking cleaning jobs

o

And surely sleep is the ultimate act of idleness… cer-tainly not purposeless but definitely idle… Is sleep then also contested ground…? I hear conversations of people claiming how little they need as often as I hear conver-sations of how much they need.

But Jonathan Crary says:

Anyone who has lived along the West Coast of North America may well know that, each year, hundreds of species of birds migrate seasonally up and down for various distances along the continental shelf. One of these species is the white-crowned sparrow.[5]

Unlike most other birds, this type of sparrow has a highly unusual capacity for staying awake, for as long as seven days during migrations.[6]

Over the past five years, the US Defence Department has spent large amounts of money to study these creatures. Researchers with government funding at various universi-ties, notably Madison, Wisconsin, have been investigating the brain activity of the birds during these long sleepless periods, with the hope of acquiring knowledge applicable to human beings. The aim is to discover ways to enable people to go without sleep and *to function productively and efficiently. The initial objective, quite simply, is the creation of the sleepless soldier.*[7]

The scientific quest here is not to find ways of stimulating ways of wakefulness but rather to reduce the body's need *for sleep.*[8]

24/7 markets and global infrastructure for continuous work and consumption have been in place for some time, but now a human subject is in the making to coincide with these far more intensively.[9]

o

Fingers tingle from cold
School voice serenade downstairs in action
Action and
sound
Envelope marked

Unknown slides

Drawing colour face of mind
They click through my own
Sequence
Unsequential
Unknown slide is unremembered moment Day
Movement
Drawer
Painting
We are all forgotten one day

°

Lazy Bones sleeping in the sun when you gonna get your day's work done?
You won't get your day's work done
Sleeping in the midday sun

°

Sleep deprivation as torture can be traced back many cen-turies, but its systematic use coincides historically with the availability of electric lighting and the means for sus-tained sound amplification. [10]

In experiments, rats will die after two to three weeks of sleeplessness. It leads to an extreme state of helplessness and compliance [11]

These are techniques and procedures for producing this abject state of compliance, and one of the levels on which this occurs is through the fabrication of a world that radi-cally excludes the possibility of care, protection, or solace. [12]

Confucius said: Thinking leads to bewilderment; think-ing without learning results in idleness.

Somehow this underestimates the way the human mind has potential to work
and when this mind belongs to one body surely it doesn't have to stand against or in the way of the collective
bewilderment can be essential and structured learning a covert trap
yet still we move tripping and stalling with ever grind-ing movement either forward, backwards, or sideways

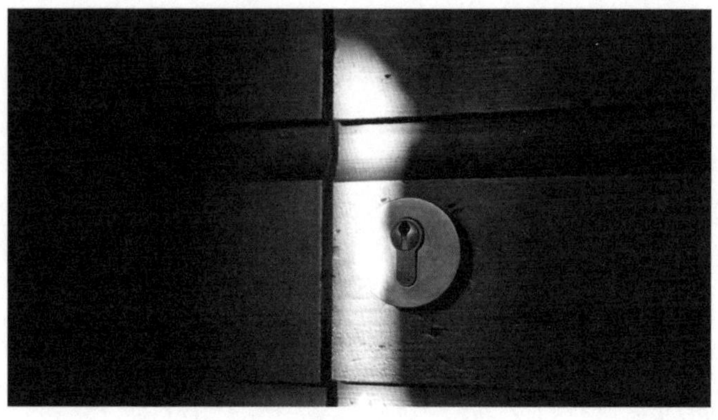

But the colour remains
The shape
The form
Is alive now in the cold loft
A different way to yesterday
And in a different form to tomorrow
Tomorrow when I slip
Them willingly into
Slide projector
Arm
To take another turn
Blazing on an empty

Hungry

Wall

They will

shine

and

speak and

fade

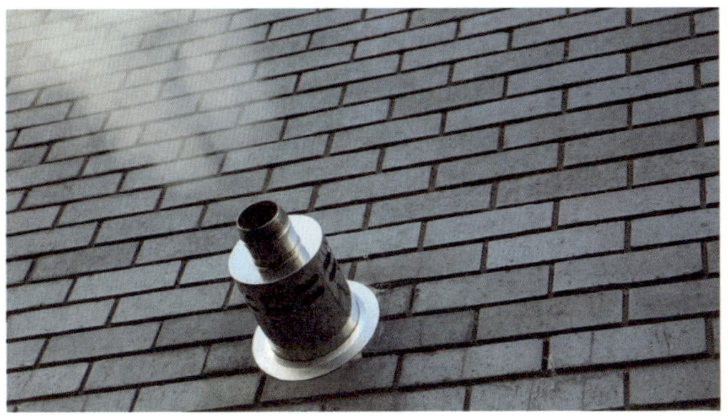

o

So, the struggle to justify actively doing nothing—and the problematics and bind of the labour cascade are murmurs then echoes then shouted assaults and yet still we must hunt like the tracker in search of the glade, for that light shaft of nothing-ness in order for some-thing-ness to scratch the back of the mind and tingle the senses and then whoever we are and whatever the hunger

something something will come

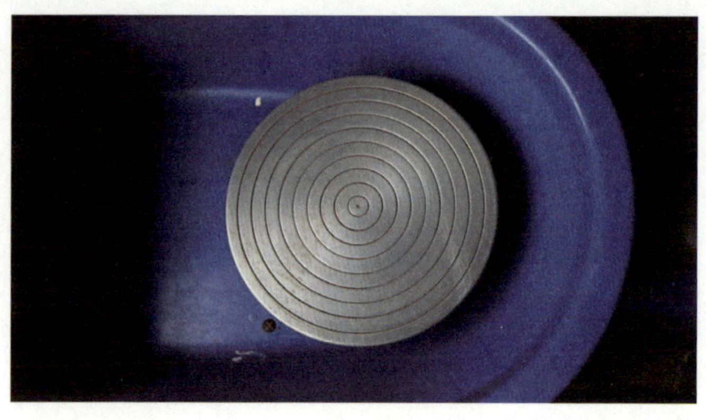

I need to know that we are seen   not forgotten
attended to   without erasure
witnessed   with open eye

I don't need much

just the sky

locked in

and still

holding the eye of my storm

Notes

1 Gregory Dobbins, *Lazy Idle Schemers: Irish Modernism and the Cultural Politics of Idleness* (Dublin: Field Day Publications, 2010), p. 92; original quote in James Joyce, "Aesthetics," in *Occasional, Critical and Political Writing* (Oxford: Oxford University Press, 2000), pp. 102–107, here p. 103.

2 Mary Oliver, "Of Power and Time," in *Upstream: Selected Essays* (New York: Penguin Press, 2016), pp. 23–30, here p. 28.

3 Audre Lorde, "Poetry Is Not a Luxury," in *Your Silence Will Not Protect You* (London: Silver Press, 2017), pp. 7–11, here p. 9.

4 Johnny Mercer and Hoagy Carmichael, *Lazy Bones*, 1933.

5 Johnathan Crary, *24/7: Late Capitalism and the Ends of Sleep* (London and New York: Verso, 2013), p. 1.

6 Ibid.

7 Ibid., pp. 1–2.

8 Ibid., p. 2.

9 Ibid., pp. 3–4.

10 Ibid., p. 6.

11 Ibid., pp. 6–7.

12 Ibid., p. 8.

"Germany must detox, Germany has to go on withdrawal"

Email Conversation between Mutlu Ergün-Hamaz and Rebecca Hanna John

Rebecca Hanna John: In your text "Entgiften," published in the magazine *freitext* in 2012[1] and later translated into English as "Germany Detox," you wrote about the need for Germany to "go on withdrawal" with which you meant detoxing or getting clean after having been high on drugs for a very long time. You did not refer to any chemical drug, but to what you call a "racial drug" that can be called White supremacy. The text was written from a very specific place and time and, at least in the way I read it, with a lot of anger. Could you say a bit more about the contexts in which and for which you wrote this text which you define as "lyrical guerrilla"?

Furthermore, I would be very interested in getting to know how you look at it now, ten years later and at a moment which seems to be marked by a new "welcome culture" in Europe that is directed towards refugees arriving from Ukraine, which is seen by many people as a very good sign that gives hope but that also leaves a bitter aftertaste if we consider who was and still is not welcomed in the same way.[2]

1 Mutlu Ergün-Hamaz, "Entgiften," *freitext* 20 (October 2012), pp. 38–41.

2 The Russian invasion of Ukraine started on February 24, 2022. When we began this e-mail conversation on March 24, 2022, it got clearer that one result from this ongoing war would be the largest refugee crisis that Europe had experienced since the Second World War. In the months that followed, discussions increased around the racial bias behind the "welcome culture" shown by many European countries that had not been equally welcoming in 2015, when over one million people arrived on the continent to request asylum, coming mostly from Syria, but also other countries like Afghanistan, Nigeria, Pakistan, Iraq, and Eritrea.

Mutlu Ergün-Hamaz: I wrote the text in late 2011, I think. I had just returned from London, where I had been living and studying for five years. I thought it was the right time to return to Berlin and focus on my PhD research project, which was about racialization and empowerment in Germany. And then, this huge emotional bomb exploded into almost every Turkish or Kurdish German face, but also other people's faces: the self-exposure or self-uncovering of the National Socialist Underground (NSU), a German White supremacist, right-wing terror organization which had been murdering owners of small businesses, most of them men who had migrated from Turkey to Germany within the past ten years. The NSU was only able to continue their murderous terror acts since the police assumed that the men of color were murdered because they were involved in criminal activities. Even though the family members and other people in the surrounding communities of color were pointing at right-wing terrorism, the police victimized the families and friends of the murder victims for a second time, investigating what they thought were mafia-like structures and a parallel society which they had no access to. The notion that these people had been murdered by Nazis was ruled out very quickly, since the *Verfassungschutz* (Federal Office for the Protection of the Constitution) withheld—and is still withholding—crucial information from the investigators. The NSU was only discovered by their own doing, and it highlighted that Nazi terror was covered from within government institutions. It was in this context that the protest slogan "State and Nazis – Hand in Hand" came up.

I wrote "Germany Detox" at the time in a state of bewilderment. Here was another concerning confirmation that there are people in the government who simply lack basic humanity or human decency, who ascribe no value to human life, in particular a human life of color. I actually do not even think that I wrote the text with a lot of anger, I just went into the core of the issue. In the first verse of the first part of the text, which I wrote in November 2011, I focused on White supremacy and how highly dependent it is on the construction of the racial other. In addition, similar to an addict who is in denial of their addiction, being in denial of White supremacy means being in denial of something that is harmful to society *as a whole*. Whilst there might be some people who are aware of toxic masculinity and how harmful it can be to men, despite them being privileged by patriarchy, there seems to be very little discourse about toxic Whiteness and how it can be harmful to White people despite them being privileged by White supremacy. The second verse, which I added a few months later, was much more thoughtful and intersectional, I would say. It also reflected my own entanglement in power structures that I benefit from.

I do not think that ten years later, the text has lost much of its currency. Resmaa Menakem, a Black trauma therapist, conceptualizes White supremacy also as White body supremacy.[3] So, there is little surprise that the migration caused by war and displacement of White (Slavic) bodies does not evoke the same White hysteria and rejection as the presence and migration of Black and Brown bodies in the European borderland. Whiteness may generate empathy to some extent for other White bodies, but it surely does not generate compassion for all—to a certain extent not even for itself. This even means that if White people become victims of White supremacy, such as Michèle Kiesewetter, Walter Lübcke, or Gabriele R., the mother of the White supremacist terrorist from Hanau, it does not necessarily lead to a thorough investigation of how racialized terrorism is supported by government institutions such as the *Verfassungsschutz* or the police.

3 See Resmaa Menakem, *My Grandmother's Hands: Racialized Trauma and the Pathway to Mending Our Hearts and Bodies* (Las Vegas: Central Recovery Press, 2017).

RHJ: While reading your reflections on the state's refusal of thorough investigations in cases of racialized violence, e.g. the NSU, and its structural conditions, I was wondering if literature, visual arts, music, theater, or dance might possibly allow for other forms of investigation, as well as empowerment and resistance. I am thinking of theater plays like "Fahrräder könnten eine Rolle spielen" (Bicycles Could Play a Role), written by Deniz Utlu and Sasha Marianna Salzmann, which had its premiere at Berlin's Ballhaus Naunystraße in November 2012, the same year as you published "Germany Detox" in *freitext* magazine.[4] Could you share your thoughts around that collective spirit that brought you all together and explain the term lyrical guerrilla, maybe also in its relationship to hip hop culture?

MEH: Well, hip hop is a great example of empowerment and resistance, of other forms of investigation and reporting on social issues, which the dominant culture would rather like to forget or silence. I am thinking about the early days of hip hop in particular, such as "The Message" by Grandmaster Flash or Public Enemy, but also much later DeadPrez and whoever is around now who creates conscious critical rap music. The cultural critique is usually reflected in the lyrics.

Guerrilla warfare is a very special type of warfare. It is about fighting an enemy who is more powerful and has more resources. In contrast to this enemy, the guerrilla blends in with the land and the people, it's as if they hide in plain sight. They cause so much damage until

4 Nine years after the premiere of the piece, the story was retold in the form of a reading and discussion with Deniz Utlu at Gorki Theater in the context of the exhibition "Offener Prozess" (October 1, 2021–March 13, 2022), curated by Ayşe Güleç & Fritz Laszlo Weber, which disentangled the complicated backdrop that paved the way to the serial murders committed by the NSU between 2000 and 2006. See the chapter "Disappearance and Remembrance" of this book for a text that Deniz Utlu wrote in 2013, shortly after the theater play, pp. 239–257.

the other side, for example the colonial oppressor, opts for leaving since it is not worth the costs and the trouble. Being a lyrical guerrilla to me meant being a writer who attacks the dominant culture through their writing in a smart and strategic way.

I was very much socialized by hip hop music. I also used to perform rap music until I decided to leave it to those who were actually good and more serious about it than I was. Nevertheless, hip hop has influenced my writing significantly and even when I joined Phoenix[5] and learned to become an empowerment trainer, it always came back, for example in the form of the question: What do you center around, what is your focus? This question is central to both, empowerment movements and hip hop culture. I am thinking of a house track called "Energy" by the British duo Disclosure which says: "Where your focus goes, your energy flows." If you center around Whiteness, all your energy will go towards Whiteness. But since Whiteness is already at the center of almost everything, I wondered why I should put my focus there. I began to see my writing as a form of resistance, I thought about putting the empowerment of BIPOC into the center of my work—which does not mean that I ignore White people, but their role in the empowerment of BIPOC can be seen as a secondary one.

When I met Deniz and Sasha, they had already founded *freitext*. We immediately got on and recognized something in each other. In Berlin of 2002, it was rare to talk about racism, White supremacist patriarchy, but also about POC empowerment at a cultural event like a reading, for example. It was even radical. And without

5 The Phoenix anti-racism and empowerment trainings were developed in the 1990s by the Afro-German Austen Peter Brandt. He had previously been trained in London by the Black British woman Sybil Phoenix in the pedagogy of racial awareness training. The Phoenix group was founded in January 1993 on the initiative of some training participants. Over three decades, the Phoenix trainings evolved also to include biographical work as well as body work. See www.phoenix-ev.org (accessed December 6, 2022).

discussing it much, the three of us knew that this was what we had to do. Deniz said: "Let's use *freitext* as our platform." The "tausend worte tief" (thousand words deep) readings at the Café :vor Wien became another one of those spaces where we gave writers and musicians of color a platform to show and perform their art.[6] This was our form of resistance, where we simply said: "We don't need your White platforms, we can just create our own spaces." And we had a lot of fun doing that.

RHJ: And this collective energy that you created together comes across even when reading your texts ten years later. What you just said about creating your own platforms apart from the predominantly White mainstream spaces also reminds me of a conversation that our PhD group had with Julia Grosse and Yvette Mutumba in January 2021, moderated by our colleague Nelly Yaa Pinkrah. Julia and Yvette told us how they founded *Contemporary And (C&)* and later also *Contemporary And America Latina (C& AL)* as an art magazine and platform for issues around contemporary art from African, Latin American, and Caribbean perspectives. The idea was to create a space where they could create a collective energy with likeminded people who shared similar experiences of not wanting to fight the mainstream anymore, where one constantly needs to explain why the works and perspectives of BIPOC are important. Interestingly, *C&'s* founding moment (2013) was very close to your publication of "Germany Detox." When I think back to this year myself, I realize that "Race" did not appear as a central category of analysis in the BA program in literature, art, and media studies that I

6 The reading series "tausend worte tief" was started in 2003 by Mutlu Ergün-Hamaz and Deniz Utlu, with the support of Kerim Atasever who ran the Café :vorWien at the time. It consisted of monthly readings for the time span of two years, at Café :vorWien in Berlin Kreuzberg, https://tausendwortetief.wordpress.com/about/ (access December 8, 2022).

then graduated in. If racialized othering was mentioned at all, it was in optional courses that we could choose, whereas the theoretical canon that we were introduced to in the foundation courses rehearsed a White European or North American perspective. This meant that the main work of anti-racist sensitization was done by students who organized events, for example in the format of the *festival contre le racisme*.[7] I also remember that the AStA (general students' committee)[8] invited you for a talk about racism after the publication of your book *Kara Günlük: Die Geheimen Tagebücher des Sesperado*,[9] which was a true eye opener for me since it was the first time I heard anyone address the topic in a lecture hall.

Now, ten years later, the issue is not solved at all. What has changed, though, is that especially in academia, but also in cultural institutions, seemingly everyone wants to be aware of structural racism and is therefore busy with decolonizing themselves, their research, and the discipline they are working in. Unlearning and undoing are high in trend.[10] I am wondering what you as someone who has been engaged in anti-racism for so long

7 See https://www.contre-le-racisme.de/ (accessed December 6, 2022).

8 Louise Haitz was one of those in the organization team, and an active member of AStA Gleichstellungsreferat Universität Konstanz since 2013. I am thankful not only for her and all their collective engagement back then, which was the starting point of an ongoing row of "aha moments" for me and surely for others as well, but also for her remarks on this text.

9 Mutlu Ergün-Hamaz, *Kara Günlük: Die Geheimen Tagebücher des Sesperado* (Berlin: Unrast Verlag, 2012).

10 This conversation happened before the accusations made in the context of documenta fifteen against postcolonial studies and decolonial movements as being structurally antisemitic. At the panel discussion "Anti-Semitismus in der Kunst" (Anti-Semitism in the Arts) in Kassel on June 29, 2022, Nikita Dhawan explained that contrary to those accusations, post-colonial studies and the fight against antisemitism are necessarily to be thought and taught together. This reflects the position in the so-called Historikerstreit 2.0 taken by scholars like Michael Rothberg who plead for studying a global history of collective violence, namely antisemitism and racism, in relation to each other in what he calls multidirectional memory. See Michael Rothberg, *Multidirectional Memory: Remembering the Holocaust in the Age of Decolonization* (Stanford: Stanford University Press, 2009).

thinks about this current moment in which the mainstream seems to want to fight for those minority issues that it has ignored for such a long time.

MEH: I welcome this development. Twenty years ago, when I called a person "White," it was not unlikely that this person would shout at me and call me a racist. I appreciate that I can talk about White and BIPOC and even if people might frown a little or feel insecure, at least these do not seem like total alien concepts. At the same time, I believe that it is important to be mindful of this development. Within the dominant culture, there has always been an ebb and flow when it comes to ethics. So, on one side it is great that racism and decoloniality seem to have arrived as ethical issues in mainstream academia, but if it is just a fashion, then it will simply pass. We should not forget that academia played a role in justifying colonization and genocide, the enslavement and murder of African people, the Shoah and on and on. It might just take another serious economic downturn or a war in Europe or in the US and the dominant culture might deem anti-racism and decoloniality as unfashionable, maybe even look to academia for ways to explain why genocide is actually okay in certain situations. I truly believe that this can be avoided, but it is going to take a lot of work. And what is this work that we need to do? Especially in academia, we assume that through a cognitive reflection of colonization and how it has affected the production of knowledge etc., we will automatically evolve and arrive at a decolonized university. I believe that we must go deeper, that it is just as important to decolonize our emotional lifeworld. Particularly in academia, this might raise a couple of question marks. Western epistemology is all about being "objective" and neutral, about putting your feelings aside. Some social researchers criticize the notion of a "*realist objectivity*," another baby from late Enlightenment thought, namely Kant, in which knowledge production is almost equated with representing, reflecting or reproducing the truth.[11] Objectivity necessitates neutrality, it can be considered a standard which marks something as scientific or if it lacks as unscientific, it could also be understood as the removal of subjectivity.[12] However, examining human behavior is not about a universal verification of the truth and Karl Marx criticized objectivity as a tool to disguise power structures, since it is those in power who define what is objective or not.[13] If a researcher got too emotionally immersed and involved into their fieldwork, it was said about them—and this highlights again the colonial character of Western sciences—that they had "gone native." Obviously "going native," becoming emotionally involved with their research subjects was not considered and is still not considered a good thing in academia. With more "natives going researcher," standpoint theory was developed:[14] also White, Western, male subjects perceive reality in a certain type of way, and they cannot abstract that perception of the world from their research subjects. There is more and more research that indicates that before White Europeans went out into the world, they had to colonize themselves in order to colonize others.[15] And what does that mean to the White, Western subject of today, being subjected to colonization and

11 See Martyn Hammersley, *Methodology: Who Needs It?* (London: SAGE Publications, 2011), p. 95; Mukesh Kumar Khatwani and Farida Panhwar, "Objectivity in Social Research: A Critical Analysis," *Asia Pacific* 37 (2019), pp. 126–142, here p. 129.

12 See Khatwani and Panhwar, "Objectivity in Social Research," pp. 129–130.

13 See Otto Friedrich Bollnow, "The Objectivity of the Humanities and the Essence of Truth," *Philosophy Today* 18 (1974), no. 1, pp. 3–18; Karl Marx and Friedrich Engels, *Die deutsche Ideologie* (reprinted as *The German Ideology, Part I*), ed. C. J. Arthur, trans. W. Lough (New York: International Publishers, 1970 [1846]), pp. 65–66.

14 See Sandra G. Harding, *The Feminist Standpoint Theory Reader: Intellectual and Political Controversies* (New York: Routledge, 2004).

15 See Theodore W. Allen, *The Invention of the White Race, Vol. 1: Racial Oppression and Social Control* (London and New York: Verso, 2012); Edward W. Said, *Culture and Imperialism* (London and Sydney: Vintage, 1993).

racialization? This is not a cognitive process, so how can it be deconstructed cognitively? Being racialized also as a White person is a physical, visceral, and emotional experience and it is only through trauma therapy and body work that we are finding new tools to address this. So, in order to decolonize, to "detox" so to speak, deeply and sustainably, it needs a lifelong process of emotional and body work. Societal change, structural, cultural and institutional change does not happen in a short time, it does not happen in a few days, weeks or months, it does not even happen in a few years or in a lifetime, it is a process that will take many decades, maybe even a few centuries. However, as individuals we can set the seeds for this change—and thereby, there are more and more collectives and communities forming—but it does take that personal work for this change to happen and to stay. Luckily.

RHJ: Now I can grasp even better why you used the image of "detoxing" in your text: because it addresses the problem of racism in such a drastically bodily way. And if I understand you correctly, what you are saying is that it needs to be addressed in this way because the body is the very place where racism resides, and where it can therefore be tackled.

Interestingly, the body was also the first point of reference for us to think about this publication, as a point that connects our different research interests, even though we all approach it from various angles, disciplinary backgrounds, and in different contexts. But throughout our time at the university, we have also felt that the moments in which the body is actually addressed in a *bodily* and not in a theorized way are extremely rare in academia, if not non-existent. We had been playing with the idea of introducing workshops that include body work, possibly performance and dance, and I think it is very telling that none of these ideas got through.

Instead, we are working on a book, seemingly *the* academic format per se.

What do you think, what are the strategies that we can all work on to introduce the body into writing in particular, but also into academic work in general, in a way that the change that you are speaking about can actually happen within these "non-bodily" spaces? I would guess you are also thinking of anti-racist trainings, a work you have been engaged in for many years now.

MEH: Yes, that is exactly what I mean. As academics in particular, we might fall into the trap of believing that racism is something that happens solely in the head. But our strategies will be flawed or incomplete if we assume that racism is just a matter of what we think. In my workshops or trainings, I sometimes ask the participants if they remember how they learned how to eat, how to have table manners. Are we aware that these body techniques have developed over the centuries? When we eat now, is it a conscious process or is there a lot of bodily automatism involved? Norbert Elias did some fundamental research on that.[16] Racialization has deeply inscribed itself into our bodies and very often, we feel and act in racialized ways that have very little to do with our thinking. How would theory be going to change that? I am not saying "let us forget about theory." Of course, the scholarly work of people such as Judith Butler, Frantz Fanon, Edward Said, bell hooks etc. is invaluable. But I also think of Lauren Berlant[17] who in *Cruel Optimism* writes that academics can very easily fall into the trap of inflating the power of

16 See Norbert Elias and Edmund Jephcott, *The Civilizing Process: Sociogenetic and Psychogenetic Investigations,* (Oxford: Blackwell Publishing, 2000 [1994]); Dmitri N. Shalin, "Norbert Elias, George Herbert Mead, and the Promise of Embodied Sociology," *The American Sociologist* 51, no. 1 (2020), pp. 526–544.

17 See also Lauren Berlant's text "Unlearning the Common" in this book, pp. 361–378.

reparative reading.[18] Berlant writes that especially those who think for a living might overestimate the power of writing and ideas, in particular when those ideas are very much detached from everyday life.

If I would express it very provocatively, and I do this being a scholar and a writer myself, I would ask: how is writing or reading a book going to repair or heal the wounds and trauma that racialization has left on our minds, bodies and souls, on our whole society, on our planet? When I am at a central train station and I get stopped and searched, it does not happen because of my brains, the way I think, or my beautiful spirit. It happens because of the way a usually White police officer reads my body. Their racialized reading of my body leads to my body being policed. Luckily—and here I laugh at my own provocation—there are a few scholars and writers who address the issue of racialization and the body: I think of Resmaa Menakem's *My Grandmother's Hands*, Ruth King's *Mindful of Race* or George Yancy and Emily McRae's *Buddhism & Whiteness.*[19] So, it *is* important that we write about these things. At the same time, I am not only a scholar or a writer, but also an anti-racism and empowerment practitioner as you have mentioned, which is why I say that it is not only about writing and reading, but also about *doing* the work. About applying this knowledge about "Race," trauma, and the body in our lives. And here, it becomes clear that the dominant style of Western academia is very limited, regulated, and sometimes removed from the world—and again, I say this as a scholar holding a PhD from a Western elite university. This critique of Western epistemology is as old as colonization itself. Very early on, the colonized

18 See Lauren Berlant, *Cruel Optimism* (Durham, N.C.: Duke University Press, 2011).

19 Menakem, *My Grandmother's Hands*; Ruth King, *Mindful of Race: Transforming Racism From the Inside Out* (Boulder: Sounds True, 2018); George Yancy and Emily McRae, *Buddhism and Whiteness: Critical Reflections* (Lanham: Lexington Books, 2019).

looked at the dominant Western knowledge production and asked: what kind of weird science is this, which is solely about cognitive abilities and where body work, emotional or spiritual learning is devalued? This goes back to early Enlightenment thinkers and their ideas of being rational in the sense of the principle "I think therefore I am," widely attributed to Descartes, even though he was not the only one to mention it. A basic task of this philosophical enterprise was to conceptualize an ontological divide between a purely mental and a purely physical domain, which Silvia Federici analyzes in *Caliban and the Witch* as the foundation of capitalism with its equal commitment to racism and sexism.[20] Neutrality, objectivity, and scientificity were claimed as masculine and White traits, while the body and emotions were thrust into the realm of the feminine or the racial "Other." Federici writes how from the beginning of the Women's Movement, feminists have seen the concept of the body as key to an understanding of the origins of male dominance and the construction of female social identity.[21] Similarly, this focus on the body has characterized the literature produced by the anti-colonial revolt and by the descendants of the enslaved.

I do hope that maybe after you have finished this anthology, you might return to the idea of doing body work as well, because I truly believe it is one of the keys in addressing and understanding intersectionally what it means to navigate these bodies that we have through the societies we live in and how they shape the way we experience, perceive, feel, and *relate* to the world and the people that live in it.

20 See Silvia Federici, *Caliban and the Witch: Women, the Body and Primitive Accumulation* (New York: Autonomedia, 2004).

21 Ibid., p. 15. She adds that it is not surprising that a valorization of the body has been present in nearly all the literature of "second wave" twentieth-century feminism.

RHJ: I hope so too. I think that the anti-racism training[22] that we were luckily able to invite you for was a very good first step in this direction, and I am hopeful for many more steps to come. Speaking of body work and of relating: I am reading your last lines while on a research trip to the UK and what you said seems to relate very much to the artist's talk by Palestinian dancer and choreographer Farah Saleh that I attended after her performance *Gesturing Refugees* at Fruitmarket in Edinburgh.[23] She spoke about how in her understanding of living archives, body and mind have to be thought together, also in order to make any process of decolonization effective, and in order to arrive at something that we could call allyship. She pointed at the fact that we have to start with the body and the gestures that we have incorporated into our bodily archive, most often without actively noticing it. She lays her focus on affective experience which, in her performances, translates into a sharing of very personal gestures and narratives of refugeehood. To break the imaginary fourth wall between performers and spectators, she invites the audience to join in and share gestures of their own body archive. This approach aims at deconstructing victimizations and instead wants to create an empathic link between people who come from different contexts and carry very different sets of experiences. It even feels a bit strange to write about it because one actually needs to experience her performances in order to really feel what this approach does. I am not sure if I am forcing this similarity between her dance and choreography practice and what you described as your anti-racism and empower-

22 In the context of the research training group "Cultures of Critique," we invited Mutlu Ergün-Hamaz and his colleague Mel Irmey from Phoenix e.V. to conduct an anti-racism training with us from January 18–20, 2022.

23 After the performance on April 29, 2022, Farah Saleh was in conversation with her collaborator Claricia Parinussa at Fruitmarket Edinburgh, see https://www.fruitmarket.co.uk/farah-saleh-past-inuous-and-gesturing-refugees/ (accessed December 6, 2022).

ment practice, or if you can also see links between the approaches?

MEH: Oh, I think this is perfectly fitting. Our bodies are archives, not only of our own stories, but also of our ancestral stories, as many cultures of color highlight, e.g. when practicing communication with their ancestors, and as epigenetics is figuring out more recently. I find it very fascinating that something seemingly small and simple such as sharing a gesture, which is very personal and vulnerable, and others repeating it and sharing theirs can be so (re-)humanizing. And we don't all need to read Giorgio Agamben's *Homo sacer* to understand how precariously dehumanizing it is to be a refugee in our current global societies.

In my early years as an activist, I often assumed that anti-racist or empowerment work has to be big and triumphant, but through my work and my research, I began to realize that it is not, and it does not need to be. Being subjected to racialization, and that is also why I mentioned Norbert Elias earlier, turns us in racialized contexts into an embodiment of "Race." This embodiment and upholding of "Race" sometimes is a conscious, intentional, and rational act, but mostly it is unconscious, unintentional, and motivated by emotions and affects—and it is physical. Even our psyche resides in our body, in our brain, in our nerve tracts, our limbic system etc., not somewhere in space. Sufism, but also other mystics have generally questioned that dichotomy of body and soul/psyche. In the Alevi tradition that my parents come from, there is the idea that a person is the perfect embodiment of the "human whole"—and the divine. This centuries old belief system assumes that humanness is a direction, a compass that guides us through our relationships. White supremacy, or White body supremacy as Resmaa Menakem calls it, patriarchy, the supremacy of the cis-male body, deform the relationships that we have to each other, but most importantly to ourselves. If racialization, being gendered etc. does not go past any person in society—White, Black, or of color—it dehumanizes us in different ways. Whilst the White cis-male, heterosexual body might be granted full humanness, it is a humanness that is based on the dehumanization of other human beings. How does that work? I am human because you are not? Therefore, it is okay if your bodies (of color etc.) are sacrificed for our wealth and living standard? In this dynamic, bodies of color either become hyper-physical, or invisible, expendable, and less worthy of mourning when they die on and on and on. The Black Lives Matter movement was essentially saying: recognize our humanness, our bodies are not worthless, they are worth being mourned for just as much as a White body is.

I am returning to that Western notion of the human subject, the "I think therefore I am." Buddhist tradition would say: if you think, you are not; you are actually just thinking, but not being.[24] Ubuntu, Alevi traditions, but also an Eliasian sociology says that a person becomes a person through other persons: our humanness is embodied in the relationships that we have to each other and to ourselves. If that relationship is dehumanizing, it dehumanizes us all, and if that relationship is humanizing, it humanizes us all. This is why I am totally in favor of any type or form of bodily practice which helps us to reconnect to that part that racialization or being gendered etc. has taken from us.

RHJ: Thank you very much, you touched upon topics that had been central starting points of this book project: the body and various "de-semantics" that every human body is confronted with, even if in different ways, depending on its positionality. On the one hand, you spoke of racial othering as *de-humanizing,* and you

24 See Thích Nhất Hạnh and Katherine Weare, *Happy Teachers Change the World* (Berkeley: Parallax Press, 2017).

also mentioned thinking as a mode of *not-being*. On the other hand, you brought in embodied practices that can help to work against these specific de-semantics, which I think beautifully shows that what you called detoxing and withdrawal ten years ago could also be understood as re-assembling, re-connecting, and re-practicing.

Germany Detox

By Mutlu Ergün-Hamaz

Refrain:
Germany must detox, Germany has to go on withdrawal,
Germany has to straighten the course, Germany is on a nosedive
Germany must detox, Germany has to get clean,
Otherwise, my crew and I will roam through your streets

Germany must detox,
Germany needs to go on withdrawal,
Germany is high on a drug,
A drug named "White supremacy."
White people in Germany have been high for so long on this drug,
That they no longer remember.
This drug makes them so high,
It gives them wings, it opens almost any door,
The door to power, knowledge and culture,
To employment, housing and only because the skin color and the name is right.
This drug makes you high because it is such an ego boost,
The "I'm-better-because-you-are-all-shit"-lie,
We indulge ourselves.
The "I-am-a-human-and-you-are-all-uncivilized savages-shit"
We persuade ourselves to believe in.
But this drug is not cheap,
This drug has a terrible price:
It can cost People of Color their lives,
It can cost People of Color their existence,
It can cost People of Color their mental and physical health,
And even more,
It costs White people their gaze,
Their view of the "Other"

**But above all, their views of themselves,
Because they are dependent,
They are hooked,
They are junkies,
They depend on the needle,
They are addicted to the idea that there's an "Other,"
That's standing below them, so that they can feel superior,
Which is less worth living,
So that they can feel like real humans,
This toxic White-supremacy-heroin poisons and eats away the hearts and souls of white people.
The needle with the racial poison is put so early in the veins of our children,
How can they fight back?
And with the dependence on the White-supremacy-heroin begins the descent of humanity,
The loss of what it really means to be human.
People become Döner,
The innocent criminals,
Criminals the extended arm of the state.
Loss of humanity, empathy,
Let us empathize:
"Blutwurst-killings"? Special Commission "Spreekanal" or "Hansel & Gretel"? Informant known as "Little Osama"?
But my comparison is inappropriate,
Neither the people in Turkey nor Osama are or were White supremacy junkies,
Which gave them the power
To be the greatest players on the planet.
Germany needs to go on withdrawal,
Germany needs to go cold turkey,
Germany must come off the White-supremacy-heroin.
But that will not be easy,
It will not work with candle lights or lip service,
This does not work with denial,
Not with the non-acknowledgement that we hang on the White-supremacy-heroin.**

This will only work with a long hard look in the mirror,
This only works with a warm look in the face of the White supremacy junky,
With the admission,
Of the fact that we are dependent on the racial drug,
But that we are ready to make a detox from now on,
And try to stay "clean."

Refrain:
Germany must detox, Germany has to go on withdrawal,
Germany has to straighten the course, Germany is on a nosedive
Germany must detox, Germany has to get clean,
Otherwise, my crew and I will roam through your streets

Germany must detox,
Hans-Joachim must detox,
Petra must detox,
Sakine must detox,
Mutlu must detox,
I have to detox, I have to detox, I have to detox.
I'm addicted,
I am dependent on a drug named "I-am-because-you-are-not."
I'm high on being (cis)-male because you're not (cis)-male
I'm high on being hetero, because you're not a hetero,
I'm high on being light-skinned, because you are not light-skinned,
I'm high on education, because you do not have what I understand as education,
I'm high on ... damn, the list is long.
I look in the mirror and I hate myself in you?
I do not want to be high, for being high makes me static,
Being high gives me an answer for every shit,
Who you are, who I am, where I belong, what I can, what you don't,
But the truth is,

There are no answers,
There is no static I that can be found somewhere on my skin between my legs, hiding behind my bum hair,
There is only a constant changing I,
That despite the lack of answers,
Has no fear to ask questions continuously,
For something that moves, can only be found if we are searching for it while we're moving.
I want to ask myself who, when and why told me the shit, about masculinity and sexuality?
I want to ask myself how much bullshit I've learned in school or college? And how much of misinformation or non-information this has left in me?
I want to ask myself how much dirty crap I've already consumed, that has poisoned another person's life? How much I could change in the world just by changing my consumption?
I want to ask myself why it's so easy to see the errors in the others and so difficult, to ask yourself critical questions?
I want to ask myself... damn, the list is long.
Asking questions helps me to know where I stand,
Helps me know where you can put your Integration Awards,
Helps me to know to whom I speak,
What I say and why.
It also helps me to know that I'm not free,
Of the toxin.

Refrain:
Germany must detox, Germany has to go on withdrawal,
Germany has to straighten the course, Germany is on a nosedive
Germany must detox, Germany has to get clean,
Otherwise, my crew and I will roam through your streets—with the antidote...

Knut Ebeling

War in the Head: Meditating with Bataille

For some in the critical sphere, the French writer and philosopher Georges Bataille is a model of the privileged white, male, and even pornographic gaze—one he subjects a wide range of women to in his texts, in the most scandalizing possible manner. But especially in his writings of the 1940s, the Somme athéologique, *Bataille works with strategies of withdrawal, negativity, and refusal—as is shown in the refusal and contestation of a conventional philosophical mode of writing. How can we discuss Bataille's texts today, following on from a range of feminist, queer, postcolonial, and black revisions to strategies of refusal, negativity, and withdrawal—strategies that reclaim and re-occupy those concepts in the light of very different political experiences? How do we handle and read Bataille's concepts today, in the light of these important markers? These are concepts that, while operating with withdrawal, refusal, and negativity similarly to many postcolonial, black, feminist, and queer authors, ultimately do not correspond with any immediate political experience of refusal (of rights, for example), withdrawal (of recognition, for example), or negation (of, for example, gender) and are entirety formulated from the privileged position of a white, Western, and male viewpoint. Is there any path that leads from Bataille's contestations to, for example, Saidiya Hartman's "waywardness," or from surrealist* desinvolture *to queer disobedience? And can Bataille's autotheoretical efforts, such as* Inner Experience *(1943) or* Method of Meditation *(1947), become part of an updated autotheoretical project—by, for instance, interspersing one's own meditative experiences in repetition of Bataille's withdrawal from philosophical writing?*

***

There is sound. A group session. For the lack of anything else to write on I am scrawling these words onto toilet paper, all other options having been confiscated from learners upon arrival at this meditation retreat. I came here shortly after a conference at the Grüner Salon in Berlin, where I spoke with Alex Goss about Georges Bataille's activism, his secret groups, and their projects and meditations.[1] During the first few days of meditation, my mind is still haunted by the discussions, especially by the contributions I failed to make. I neglected to say that Bataille's theory represents a theory of "other knowledge"; I neglected to say that his act of writing was less a depiction and more an embodiment of that theory. And I neglected to say that Bataille is concerned not with writing *about* this other knowledge, but rather with a "neutral" writing of the other, one in which the writing should preferably record itself, like a phonograph, like an electrocardiogram.

I thus write here in a state of total withdrawal from any kind of writing. I am thus not concerned with writing *about* meditation, with a "theory" of meditation, or even with a *Method of Meditation* as per the title of Bataille's book (which was quickly forgotten)—my interest lies rather in their withdrawal, in the "mechanical" recording of the embodied, materialized scene of withdrawal that is meditation. But how do I record a scene of the withdrawal of writing?

1 "Forschungsmaschinen: Verschränkte Verfahren in Kunst und Theorie" (Research machines: entangled processes in art and theory), Volksbühne Berlin, September 21, 2019.

It is after all impossible to meditate and write simultaneously. Ultimately, the meditation practiced here aims directly at the subversion of normal, everyday thinking; at avoidance of the habitual use of the mind. The mind is to be deprived of thought—of "its own" thought— with the intention that a perception-led, representational thought should give way to the creation of an alternative space of the mind, now no longer constantly distracted and arriving instead at its "own self" and materiality, like when seeking to discern the "touch of the breath." None of this is without reason: I do meditate badly after or while writing. Thoughts rattle around my head, which continues to think thoughts rather than exorcising them to focus on meditation.

Since at least today, the third day of meditation, the effects of withdrawal have been making their presence felt: I can sense the disruptive operations that interfere with my day-to-day being in the world. My eyes suddenly begin soaking up every letter of every word on the premises, even the ones just explaining the rules for use of the pool. Learners are also asked to refrain from any form of representation, symbolization, or production of perception during the post-meditation breaks, when they head to the park to stretch their legs; previously, they have apparently often dug tracks into the soil or made carvings in the trees. Or piled small stones on top of one another.

Given these tortuous operations, fairly reliable in their ability to unhinge our working consciousness, these scenes of withdrawal—of negation of the mind—are anything but pleasurable for the conscious mind. They are a pure agony, experienceable as an ordeal or as torture: which at any rate explains Bataille's central but fairly puzzling use of the *supplice* concept in his theoretical works of the 1940s. Practices of withdrawal agonize the mind as they force it to endure other experiences: ones not of thinking but of the materiality of the body, the breath, the limbs, and then naturally of thought

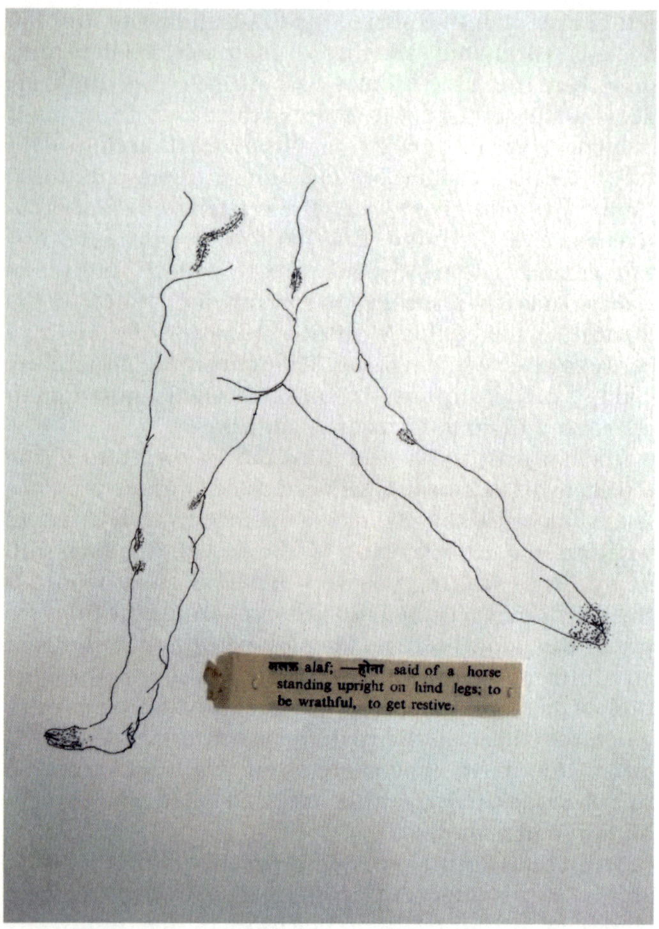

Fig. 1: Pallavi Paul, *Elsewhere 7*, ink, thread and collage on paper, 9 x 7.5 inches, 2018.

itself's materiality too. Sitting around unproductively for hours in meditation that produces no thought—working instead to exclude the production of thought—is torture for the mind. This imperative to not think, to disidentify with your own thoughts, lops off the mind's head; "decapitates" it, if you will.

This scene of the mind's decapitation was of course a central image for Bataille, who even set up a group and a journal for these practices: *Acéphale* was a kind of activist surrealist dissidence, whose machinations we chronicled at the Grüner Salon. In his search for practices that could put his anti-idealist program into action, Bataille began mediating in 1938 shortly after *Acéphale* was founded. It was a practice he initially dubbed as "Hindu concentration exercises."[2] In narrowing down these two pieces of biographical information—a practice of headless thinking, and one of meditation—the latter can be understood in Bataille as an acephalic practice with a "severed head" or, even better, as a practice of disintegrating, disseminating, and deconstructing a mind. For Bataille too, meditation consists precisely in the systematic undermining and undercutting of thought: "Prolonged calm, deep breathing, as in sleep, like an enchanting dance, slow concentration, irony, thoughts toward the void, a skillful juggling of the spirit on meditational themes, the sky, the earth, and the subject successively collapse."[3]

These words appear in a slim book entitled *Méthode de méditation*, published by Bataille in 1947 shortly after World War II, which has, in all subsequent (French and German, but not all English—translator's note) editions, been incorporated into a central theoretical work—*Expérience intérieure*. Both books are in turn part of the larger *Somme athéologique* project, an atheological cor-

2 Georges Bataille, "Method of Meditation," in *The Unfinished System of Nonknowledge* (Minneapolis: University of Minnesota Press, 2001), p. 78.

3 Ibid.

pus that begins with the thought diary *Le Coupable* in 1939 and ends with *Sur Nietzsche* in 1944: *Méthode de méditation* was then not a guide to practice-oriented thinking and writing, but rather an esoteric appendix to *Inner Experience*. The meditation that appears in the book's title was thus never understood directly *as* meditation, and the volume was read neither as a report on meditation nor as a meditative book; a misunderstanding for which Bataille does not entirely escape blame. His book contains barely any information on meditation, even his own—evidently, he did not understand his title as an imperative to provide information on the methods of meditation that he himself used.

In keeping with the entire *Expérience intérieure*, *Méthode de méditation* turns its back on meditation as a subject matter, shifting its position from object to subject. The book on meditation becomes a meditative book: because it disseminates no knowledge on meditation and commits itself instead to *writing meditation*, the impression could easily arise that Bataille knew hardly anything about the subject itself. Everything about Bataille's meditation can, however, be found elsewhere.[4] Only with *The Tears of Eros* in 1961 did he publicly state that "in 1938, a friend initiated me into the practice of yoga."[5]

This friend of Bataille's was Jean Bruno, his Bibliothèque Nationale colleague from whom he had gotten

4 He puts it thus in a *Notice autobiographique* twenty years later: "Bataille en effet s'est dès 1938 adonné à des exercises de yoga, à la vérité sans suivre de près les préceptes de la discipline traditionelle, en grand désordre, et dans un tumulte d'esprit poussé à l'extrême." Georges Bataille, *Œuvres complètes VII* (Paris: Gallimard, 1974), p. 462. ("Indeed, Bataille devoted himself to the practice of yoga from 1938 onward, in truth without following the discipline's traditional precepts, in great disorder, and in a tumult of spirit pushed to the extreme.")

5 Georges Bataille, *The Tears of Eros* (San Francisco: City Lights Books, 1989), p. 206.

"decisive pointers on mysticism and yoga."[6] While Bataille is still speaking of "Hindu concentration exercises,"[7] Bruno is more properly engaged not with yoga but with *meditation*.[8] Bruno reads Bataille less as a theorist and the *Expérience intérieure* not as a theoretical text, but rather as evidence of practices—more specifically of meditation practices. Correspondingly, Bataille speaks in one of his earliest meditations of writing being able only to "leave behind traces of the path followed."[9] Bataille had been on this path for quite some time, having been exposed to mystical Christian practices and Jesuit meditation during his youth and adolescence.[10] They are later discarded in just the same manner as Western philosophy's concept of meditation; for Descartes or Husserl, for example, this had meant the mind's interior monologue or objectless reflections on method.

Bataille turns his focus instead to practice—to Buddhist meditation practices that distinguish themselves from a comparatively theoretical Christianity. He claims that "Christian practices" lack "an initial movement, without which we remain subordinated to discourse."[11] Bruno too sees the significance of Bataille's meditations in them having "rediscovered the phantasmagoria of our sensory universe":[12] he claims however that the authenticity of Bataille's texts on meditation had not

6 Bernd Mattheus, *Georges Bataille. Eine Thanatographie I* (Munich: Matthes & Seitz, 1984), p. 433.

7 Bataille, "Method of Meditation," p. 78.

8 Jean Bruno, "Les techniques d'illumination chez Georges Bataille," *Critique 195–196*, August–September 1963, pp. 706–720.

9 "Un écrit ne peut que laisser des traces du parcours suivi"; Georges Bataille, "L'amitié," in *Œuvres complètes VI* (Paris: Gallimard, 1973), p. 296.

10 See Bruno, "Les techniques," p. 714; Mattheus, *Thanatographie I*, p. 433.

11 "les pratiques chrétiennes," "un premier mouvement sans lequel nous restons subordonnés au discours"; Bataille, "L'amitié," p. 274.

12 "Avait ... redecouvert ... la fantasmagorie de notre univers sensorial"; Bruno, "Les techniques," p. 717.

yet been recognized. This is a judgement that, sixty years later, remains largely unchanged.

What is the history of Bataille's meditations? What was it that he knew about these practices? What discourse did he participate in? In 1938, Bataille—who Bruno regards as "exceptionellement doué" and confirms as making "rapid progress"[13] in the style of the teacher—begins meditating, a full ten years before the publication of *Méthode de méditation*. The teacher laments the student not having presented a more systematic manual,[14] feeling the book to have been rather about the "modalities and implications of experience."[15] Regardless, Bataille had availed himself of the "traditional precepts" to which he had privileged access as a librarian at the Bibliothèque Nationale. Bataille is initially enamored with this Orientalist tradition: "For the first movement, the traditional precepts are indispensable, they are marvelous. I took them from a friend of mine, who took them from an Eastern source."[16] In 1938 alone, Bataille ingested an astonishing amount of contemporary literature on yoga, both from translated South Asian sources and French vulgarizations.[17]

Bataille even claims in *Le Coupable* to have known a Hindu monk: "Read two 'causeries' by a Hindu monk that I knew, I saw him for an hour."[18] But this same *Méditation selon le Vedanta* by Swami Siddheswarananda triggers an increasing frustration in Bataille: "Depressed by this literature compliant with occidental

13 "rapides progès"; ibid. p. 707.

14 Ibid., p. 719.

15 "modalités et implications de l'expérience"; ibid. p. 719.

16 "Dans le premier mouvement, les préceptes traditionnels sont indiscutables, ils sont merveilleux. Je les tiens d'un de mes amis, qui les tenait de source orientale." Bataille, "L'amitié," p. 274.

17 Bataille read, for example, Constant Kerneïz, *Le yoga de l'occident* (1938), Swami Vivekananda, *Raja Yoga ou conquête de la nature intérieure* (1930), and W.Y. Evans-Wentz and Lama Kazi Dawa-Samdup, *Le yoga tibétain et les doctrines secrètes* (1938).

18 "Lu deux 'causeries' d'un moine hindou que j'ai connu, je l'avais vu une heure"; Bataille, "L'amitié," p. 281.

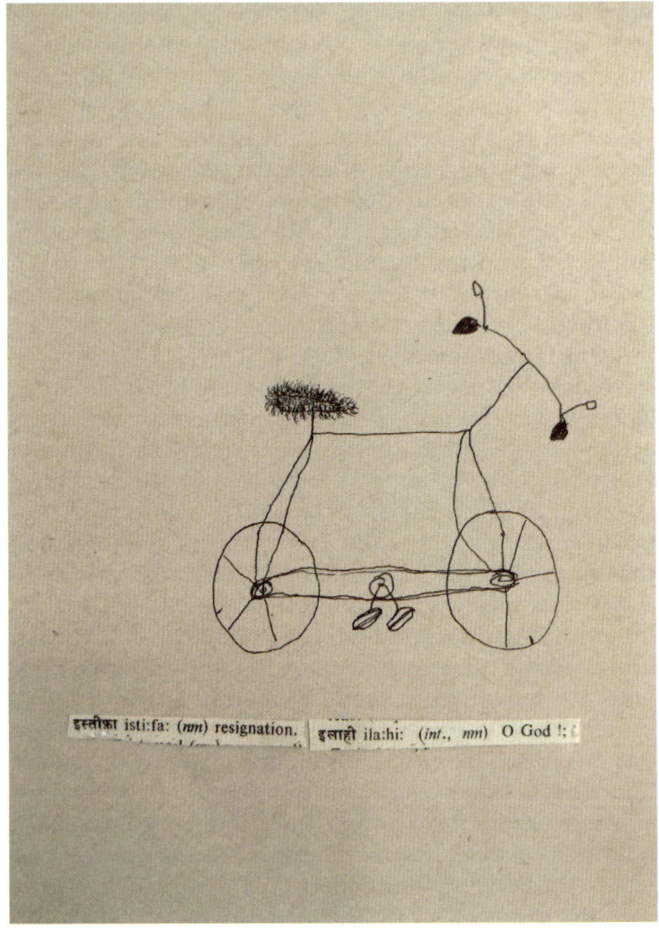

Fig. 2: Pallavi Paul, *Elsewhere 8*, ink, thread and collage on paper, 9 x 7.5 inches, 2018.

morality."[19] When Bataille was writing these notes in 1938, there were almost 300,000 persons still resident in French India, prior to the end of British colonial rule in 1947:[20] correspondingly, the sources Bataille read were shot through with the era's Orientalism. Constant Kerneïz (aka Félix Guyot), who Bataille read, regarded things such as Indian meditation techniques as a means for Western readers to get back to their roots. Upon finishing his reading, Bataille concedes that "I know little, at bottom about India ... The few judgments which I abide by—more in antipathy than in receptivity—are linked to my ignorance."[21]

Bataille's engagement with "Orientalist sources" is coupled with an anti-idealist attack on any and every activity of the mind, as is evident in the early literary and philosophical texts he produced in the sphere of the journal *Documents* (1929–1931). Meditation thus became an anti-idealistic practice for Bataille, one that systematically undermined any mental activity or reflexivity, idealistically understood as negativity: quotidian thought is restrained, the wandering of the mind inhibited, the flow of associated thought is stopped.

At my retreat, it is made clear to learners that we should not be thinking about some object or another, but rather following the sensations of our own bodies: "Start again, start again, start at the top of your head and move from head to feet and from feet to head"— I follow the teacher's instructions and focus my attention on physical feelings and sensations, seeking to drop any

19 "Déprimé par cette littérature conforme à la morale des Occidentaux"; Bataille, "L'amitié," p. 282; see also the corresponding endnote in Geroges Bataille, *Œuvres complètes V* (Paris: Gallimard, 1973), p. 520, and Bernd Mattheus, *Georges Bataille. Eine Thanatographie II* (Munich: Matthes & Seitz, 1984), p. 17.

20 See Arghya Bose, *A Wrinkle in Empire: Reflections on Colonial and Nationalist Imaginations of Territoriality in French Chandernagor* (Kolkata: Avenel Press, 2019).

21 Georges Bataille, *Inner Experience* (Albany: State University of New York Press, 1988), p. 17.

thought of anything else. I concentrate on the very top of my head, causing me to automatically stretch my back. It is a point that remains vaguely defined—is the highest point at the rear of the head or at the vertex, the *œil pinéal*, the sun-eye that Bataille had studied with such intensity prior to his meditation? Bataille's anti-idealistic interpretation of meditation corresponds to my experience. In undermining representation, it becomes possible to understand meditation as an attack on the central activity of perception; the meditating mind represents the world no longer as notional objects, nor as objects of the mind. Each thought of each object is abandoned, as is the object of each thought. In dissolving every thought, the meditator avoids the representation of the objective world; the meditator knows something, without simultaneously possessing any *knowledge about* something capitalizable into an object of the mind.

But how do you write a book without the capital of your thought? How do you overextend your thoughts while writing? This radical withdrawal defines all Bataille's *Inner Experience* which, like *Method of Meditation*, aims at a dissolution of the distinction between interior and exterior objects of the mind. Both titles are equally misleading; for all its descriptions of mystical states, *Inner Experience* ultimately contains no praise for interiority, just as *Method of Meditation* is not a book about meditating. But it is because meditation had always been a practical enactment of what Bataille pursued as a theoretical project that this practice assumed such a decisive role: for Bataille, meditation is the central method for implementing his *Inner Experience* project and for disintegrating all reflexive boundaries between interior and exterior, feeling and thinking, practice and theory. In this autoperformative turn against the activity of thought, it is impossible to continue reading *Method of Meditation* in relation to "Hindu concentration exercises"; it must instead—analogously to the concept of meditation in Western philosophy—be brought into relation with the repetition of central moments from Western metaphysics. No longer, however, to pursue their lines of thought but, as Bataille writes, to ruin them.[22]

***

What was it that led Bataille to such a radical project—one that he would adhere to for the entire duration of the Second World War? Key is that the ensemble of *Somme athélogique* starts with the first acts of war and ends in the ecstasy of *libération*.[23] The entire large-scale philosophical operation of *Somme athéologique* is suspended on the framework of the act of war, as if it had been launched as a means of withdrawing not only from a mode of thought but (apparently conterminously) also from a war, the two apparently linked for Bataille by the shared brace of negativity: in the post-idealist Hegel interpretation of Alexandre Kojève, which Bataille followed, both thought and war were regarded as negative with respect to creation, as if the diverse figures of withdrawal of thought and the desubjectification of his writing Bataille offers up here were a reaction to the violent negativity and desubjectification of war. At the end of *Somme athéologique*, war thus emerges as a struggle to transcend fascism—its *Führerprinzip* and its "illusion forcefully unleashed through the movement of transcendence"[24] against the very immanence Bataille's own writing advocates for. The negativity and transcendence of fascism were lies, he continues, exposed by the Second World War.[25].

A person begins meditating at the outbreak of war and meditates his way through the war. Bataille's retreat can

22 Bataille, "Method of Meditation," p. 78.
23 Georges Bataille, *Nietzsche und der Wille zur Chance. Atheologische Summe III* (Munich: Matthes & Seitz, 2005), p. 390.
24 Georges Bataille, *On Nietzsche*, trans. Stuart Kendall (Albany: State University of New York Press, 2015), p. 156.
25 Ibid., p. 161.

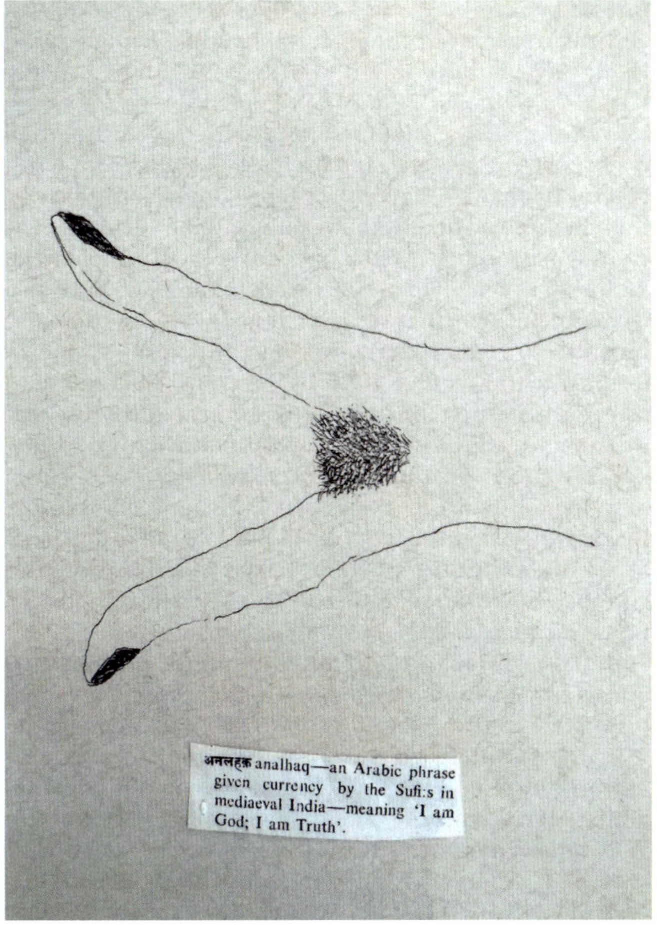

Fig. 3: Pallavi Paul, *Elsewhere 5*, ink, thread and collage on paper, 9 x 7.5 inches, 2018

indeed be interpreted as the same thing as his books: a gesture of retreat in the midst of chaotic, barbaric, and lacerating warfare. But it would be to underestimate Bataille's *Method of Meditation* to regard it as a "private exercise":[26] "Ecstasy [of meditation] itself is empty when envisaged as a private exercise, only mattering for a single individual."[27] Beyond the personal commitment, the theoretical, methodological, and political aspects cannot be forgotten, and beyond everything personal and private, these operations were at the same time also that which their titles suggested they were: method and medium to fight against the same war (understood in keeping with Kojève as the most severe, open, and brutal form of negativity of the mind) and to destroy the war in thought. Likewise (and contemporaneously), when his reflections on the concept of expenditure see him describe all its forms as parallel forms and alternatives to war, the latter also emerges in Bataille not in the form of a philosophical reflection, but as a cultural one. In contrast, however, to these culture-theoretical thoughts, his texts from *Somme athéologique* emerge as a radical and quasi–"final" form of a philosophical practice that aimed at dissolving within itself that which war had ultimately always been for Kojève and Bataille: negativity. War was here no longer to be fought—as Bataille felt an entire critical intelligentsia fought it—via that which kept it running, i.e., the machinery of negativity and reflexivity, but rather by arresting this machinery *in oneself*, simply pausing within oneself; by meditating.

While writing this, I am not meditating; I am keeping the machinery running. I am thinking about practices of non-violent resistance. Can Bataille's meditation be understood as a form of non-violent resistance? Would such an interpretation of Bataille not be too soft, given that his meditation practice was shot through with fan-

26 "Private Übung": Mattheus, *Thanatographie I*, p. 458.
27 Bataille, *Inner Experience*, p. 92.

tasies of violence? Thinking about all this, it becomes clear to me that Bataille's practice went much further than my own. I am not interested in unleashing a mental "war" within myself, as a means of fighting the wars in the world outside. At most, I fight my own depressions. In my meditation practice, reduced to individualism, I merely ask myself if I can detect feelings and where; in my left toe, my right elbow.

Bataille's meditations involved visions and scenes of violence, inner images and visions that largely give way to an incandescent self-consumption.[28] Keying into his affirmation of practicing meditation from 1938 onward, he goes into further detail: "It was on this occasion that I discerned, in the violence of this image, an infinite capacity for reversal. Through this violence ... I was so stunned that I reached the point of ecstasy."[29] Even while writing as indirectly about meditation as he does about war, traces of violent imagery emerge time and again in his language.

In Bataille's texts from the *Somme athéologique*, it is in fact the disruptive and at times violent language that stands out: it affirms, for example, that the divided individual must "be broken"[30] and "wish itself destroyed";[31] it speaks of "abuse committed against oneself";[32] of humanity being "war."[33] It is "rupture"[34] that will promote forces which exceed or destroy the individual, understood simultaneously as a "sacrifice."[35] We must "leave to the fire that which cannot be saved,"[36] as the

28 Ibid., pp. 126–127.
29 Bataille, *Tears of Eros*, p. 206.
30 Bataille, *Inner Experience*, p. 96.
31 Ibid.
32 "sévices exercés contre soi-même"; Bataille, "L'amitié," p. 257.
33 Bataille, *Inner Experience*, p. 37.
34 Ibid., p. 96.
35 Ibid.
36 "dem Feuer überlassen, was nicht zu retten ist"; Georges Bataille, *Die innere Erfahrung nebst Methode der Meditation und Postskriptum 1953. Atheologische Summe I* (Munich: Matthes & Seitz 1999), p. 137, and Bataille, *Inner Experience*, p. 96.

German-language translator of Bataille translates the French idiom (rendered very differently by the English edition's translator as "we are led to contain the fire within us"—translator's note) *faire la part du feu,* used likewise by Blanchot as a motto for his eponymously named book.[37] How can we avoid bringing this "sacrifice" into relation with the countless victims sacrificed to war while Bataille was writing? How can we possibly avoid automatically seeking correspondences between the negativity of war and Bataille's manifold negativities, highlighted at the latest with his famed formulation, in a letter to Kojève, of a "négativité sans emploi"—an unemployed negativity?

Le Coupable openly declares war and mystical experience to be interchangeable: "I will not speak of war, but of mystical experience. I am not indifferent to war. I would gladly give my blood..."[38] But Bataille does not give his blood. Rather, he writes with increasing frequency about his manic states, caused—among other things—by "moments of savagery, from which we proceed into the vicinity of death."[39] Death, both in Hegel's idealistic interpretation and in Bataille's absolute negativity, appears for the latter author not on the battlefield; rather, the battlefields transform that author's writing into a battlefield of desubjectification. In writing meditation, Bataille writes war. He kindles war in his head and meditates, fights, and writes against the war: writing meditation is to write the war, is to break the war.

Throughout *Somme athéologique,* Bataille time and again describes spending the war years living in complete retreat and meditation. It is rare that a direct correspondence between war and meditation is affirmed,

37 See Maurice Blanchot, *La part du feu* (Paris: Gallimard, 1949).

38 "Je ne parlerai pas de guerre, mais d'expérience mystique. Je ne suis pas indifférent à la guerre. Je donnerais volontiers mon sang"; Bataille, "L'amitié," p. 246.

39 "moments de sauvagerie auxquels nous accédons au voisinage de la mort"; ibid.

as when Bataille says of himself that "I write as I am just about to leave Paris, and Paris is at eight in the morning covered with a cloud of soot. I am in a hotel in the city center, it is dismal. I compel myself, on the fifth floor, to immerse myself in meditation."[40] How can this simultaneity of war and meditation be deciphered? How can these infernal data and texts still be read today? How can we situate a Bataille who wrote his main philosophical work in wartime, during a war in which he is never directly involved and which, as stated, he rarely directly commented on? And can his strategies of refusal, withdrawal, and negation be compared to current "scenes of withdrawal" as experimented with and invoked in postcolonial, feminist, and queer contexts?

***

It is indeed a very different—and perhaps incomparable—thing when experiments are conducted with strategies of aesthetic, literary, or artistic refusal in reaction to preceding political denials of civil rights, of political or social recognition, or even, on balance, of humanity *grosso modo*. Indeed, an aesthetic or literary operation like withdrawal assumes a different weight when it is in response to a preceding withdrawal of recognition: it is entirely natural that an account of a formerly enslaved woman's revolt—such as that of Esther Brown, who was denied her human rights—will always assume a very different status to Bataille's immanent operations of contestation that, as striking as they may be, are relatively risk-free, a storm in a teacup of a secure intellectual life and literary career, however existential and life-threatening

40 "J'écris au moment de quitter Paris, et Paris, à huit heures du matin, est couvert d'un nuage de suie. Je suis dans un hôtel du centre, et c'est lugubre ... Je m'efforce, au cinquième étage, de m'abîmer dans la méditation." Bataille, "Les Malheurs du temps présent," in *Œuvres complètes V*, p. 291.

the "change in historical conditions"[41] may seem from the perspective of the writer. The "ruin"[42] Bataille discusses—ultimately referring back to metaphysics—will always be read very differently to Brown's "willingness 'to be ruined by standing against what is instituted as right by law.'"[43]

It would be wrong to allow these very different operations—from such different and incomparable social and political contexts and whose modes of subjectification are situated so differently—to be played off against one another. Aesthetic strategies can rarely be reduced down to retrospective reactions to preceding political dispossessions; the operations of withdrawal and refusal described above can nonetheless be better deciphered by interrogating their political context. With the key data of the *Somme athéologique*, it ultimately becomes clear that the desubjectification of an author communicates with its immediate political context: moreover, it becomes clear that France's entry into and exit from the war represent the peak negativity to which the writing of *Somme athéologique*—"negative" and refusing of any positive philosophical position—reacts, without this writing thus being assigned a negating-negation position within a dialectical setting. It is evident that for Bataille, war represented the self-same preceding experience of desubjectification that the manifold desubjectifying procedures of the *Somme athéologique* are responding to, without being mirrored within them one-to-one; for Bataille, the great anonymizing nobody was war.

The imbrication of war and meditation is also a scene in which two figures of negativity (or the negative) encounter one another: an idealistic figure of negativity as reflection as deployed by Bataille following Kojève,

41 "changement des conditions historiques"; ibid., p. 298.
42 Bataille, "Method of Meditation," p. 78.
43 Saidiya Hartman, *Wayward Lives, Beautiful Experiments: Intimate Histories of Social Upheaval* (New York and London: Norton, 2019), p. 241.

and a deconstructive framing of negativity as (for example) decay and putrefaction, as developed by Bataille in his *Documents* texts. Likewise at my retreat, I define negativity both as reflection (refused to me by my environment) and as a meditative attack on the negativity of the mind. Are there transitions between these two framings? Why did Bataille replace and confront war with meditation? How exactly can their relationship be described? Bataille's entries into his thought diary become perceptibly bloodier as he depicts the abjectness of war:[44] this is a person meditating not *despite* but *because of* the war. This is not a person fleeing from the daily routine of war into the peace of meditation, but someone meditating *in light of* its cruel imagery and of fear; this is a person seeking to resist or counterbalance the war outside his door with a war in his head;[45] the external war spills over into the internal war, and vice versa. As if the two had become indistinctively merged, the external war becomes a war in the mind; the violence of war seems to be expressed in imagined scenes of violence.[46] Here, even peaceful meditation becomes something of a medium of cruelty, one that allows Bataille to recall or work through the gruesome images in his mind.[47]

***

This strategy—igniting a war within himself as a means of confronting the war without—distinguishes Bataille, per his own analysis, from a soldier: while the author embraces his fear and works with it, the "hommes de guerre" would flee from their own fear.[48] This diagnosis differs from the Bataille of the beginning of the

44 Bataille, "Le Coupable," Georges Bataille, *Œuvres complètes VI*, Paris 1973, p. 293.
45 Bataille, *Inner Experience*, p. 41.
46 Bataille, "Les Malheurs du temps présent," p. 293.
47 Ibid., pp. 294–295.
48 Ibid., p. 295.

war, who very much celebrated the soldier and war as figures of expenditure.[49] Correspondingly, he had read Ernst Jünger's 1922 book *War As an Inner Experience,* translated into French from the German in 1934. But as the war proceeded, his attitude evidently changed: "I hate the tastes of those who love [war] for its fighting. It attracts me, makes me afraid. Such feelings are foreign to 'men of war' ... they head to the front to avoid fear."[50] And from *Expérience intérieure*: "The horror of war is greater than that of inner experience."[51] Whereas Jünger particularly celebrated male invulnerability, Bataille's texts are distinguished by an extreme violability and vulnerability; the internal states he describes are, quite unlike those of the soldier, extremely fragile and prone to harm, both physically and psychologically. Above all, they can be infringed upon by others who confront you without warlike intent. Unlike with Jünger, these others are for Bataille not the soldier or the enemy but, we suspect, the equally controversial figure of the naked girl, another permanent resident in the *Somme athéologique.* The figure of the Other who, in for example Judith Butler's work, is the mourned-for person who tears me away from my own subjectivity,[52] is for Bataille the naked woman who dispossesses me of and desubjectifies my gaze. As some feminist authors have emphasized, however, this figure is, in its power to dispossess, distinct from the subject position of the dominating, power-affirming male gaze that appears in many pornographic works.[53]

49 Mattheus, *Thanatographie I*, p. 431f.

50 "Je hais les goûts de ceux qui l'aiment pour se battre. Elle m'attirait, me donnant de l'angoisse. Des 'hommes de guerre' sont étrangers à de tels sentiments ... Ils vont de l'avant pour éviter l'angoisse." Bataille, "Les Malheurs du temps présent," p. 295.

51 Bataille, *Inner Experience*, p. 45.

52 Judith Butler, "Violence, Mourning, Politics," in Butler, *Precarious Life: The Powers of Mourning and Violence* (London and New York: Verso, 2004), pp. 19–49.

53 Carolyn Dean, *The Self and its Pleasures: Bataille, Lacan and the History of the Decentered Subject* (Ithaca: Cornell University Press, 1992); Amy Hollywood, *Sensible Ecstasy: Mysticism, Sexual Difference and*

This dispossessed male gaze is not remotely subject to the political dispossession experienced by manifold black and feminist authors, for whom political discrimination is inscribed into the gaze's regime. Bataille's desubjectification is in turn distinct from Heidegger's fear—it may be equally white, male, and privileged, but it is every bit as radically related to the Other as in Levinas and Butler. My gaze and desire are withdrawn from me; the gaze is dispossessed, becomes vulnerable, while I look at the naked woman. This is, following the term coined by Levinas, exposition—both exhibition and representation, as remarked upon by Judith Butler in an interview:

> As you know, Levinas uses an interesting French expression, "exposition." This means being-exposed, but also an expository moment of explaining or demonstrating. What is demonstrated with exposure is the living being's fundamental dependence on life processes, on a set of life-sustaining conditions. When these life-sustaining conditions are destroyed or withdrawn, as in the case of precariousness—to return to that concept—then exposure increases: exposure to the elements, to all risks to which a body can be exposed.[54]

Likewise, meditation is exposition: It exposes me, places me in an exposed position. It exposes me not only to the Other that I become while meditating, but also to the painful withdrawal of a life-sustaining precondition of thought. Bearing life is hard when not thinking every moment. Likewise, the words I write here do not serve as a reparation of thought within writing, nor as a retrieval of something withdrawn, but rather as a risk of feeling myself exposed "to all risks to which a body can be exposed."

the Demands of History (Chicago: University of Chicago Press, 2002). Many thanks to Nadine Hartmann at the University of Siegen for these pointers.

54 Butler's words here have only been published in German: "Politik, Körper, Vulnerabilität. Ein Gespräch mit Judith Butler," in *Judith Butlers Philosophie des Politischen*, ed. Gerald Posselt, Tatjana Schönwälder-Kuntze, and Sergej Seitz (Bielefeld: transcript, 2018), p. 306.

Is robbing people of their own image a war crime?

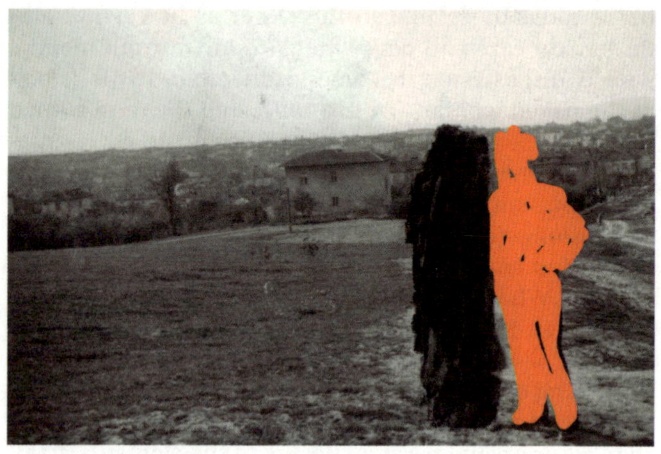

Fig. 4: Pallavi Paul, *Bluff check Omitted*, archival print, 11.7 x 16.5 inches, 2015.

Translation: Matthew James Scown

Arnika Ahldag and Rebecca Hanna John

"Very little resistance from the Orient's part"?

On Moments of Failure in Hermann Goetz's and Robert Lachmann's Orientalist Journeys

To study a subject where it resides, to understand its context, to work from within and not just "on" a field of study, especially in art history and ethnography, means to be physically present. This is what drew the main protagonists of this text, art historian Hermann Goetz (1898–1976) and music ethnologist Robert Lachmann (1892–1939), to leave Germany and enter their respective research fields in the British Raj and Mandatory Palestine.[1] As German Orientalists with an expertise in collections and archives, they were invited to settle and help build institutions for what were to become new nation states: the National Gallery of Modern Art in New Delhi and the Hebrew University of Jerusalem. Nevertheless, it was not only their urge to study, but also the increasingly charged political situation in Europe of the 1930s that pushed them to leave. We take their struggles as context for reflecting on the Orientalist researcher as an outsider figure. By laying the focus on specific moments of failure in their institution-building projects and

1 The reflections that led to this article came out of the multi-part program *The Whole Life*, facilitated by the Haus der Kulturen der Welt in Berlin (HKW) from 2019–2022. The specific workshop group in which the two authors exchanged thoughts on failure and luck and the position of the outsider sought to identify different types of "archive builders" and learn how their biographies are mirrored in archives.

archival work, we not only want to break away from glorified narratives of success, but also to reconsider the image of the Orientalist that resulted from readings of Edward Said's *Orientalism*.

In the nineteenth and twentieth centuries, the reasons for European scholars to academically situate themselves in and as "experts" of other parts of the world were plenty and have widely been discussed as being part of the colonial project. Edward W. Said prominently described how "the Orient"—which in the nineteenth century meant India and the "Holy Land"—is not a natural fact but "an idea that has a history and tradition of thought, imagery, and vocabulary that have given it reality and presence in and for the West."[2] He described how the construction of the Orient as Europe's Other imposed upon it a timelessness and incapability of self-representation and self-consciousness, and therefore a need to be represented by others.[3] The arguments made by detractors of Said's book *Orientalism*, like Bernard Lewis, Ibn Warraq, or Abdulla Al-Dabbagh, who claim that the Orientalist quest for knowledge about other societies was motivated by innocent curiosity and in fact "a labour of love,"[4] wanting to show Arabs in a positive light,[5] not only deny the affiliation of knowledge with power[6] but also risk erasing the disastrous consequences of colonization. Even if our sympathies lie with Said's goal of breaking up and reconceiving the field ruled by essentialist universalism, our interest in writing this essay is not to align with either side in this long existing polarized debate. Look-

2 Edward W. Said, *Orientalism: Western Concepts of the Orient* (London: Penguin Books, 2001 [1978]), p. 5.

3 See Edward Said, "Orientalism Reconsidered," *Cultural Critique*, no. 1 (Autumn 1985), pp. 89–107, here pp. 93–94, p. 97.

4 Abdullah Al-Dabbagh, *Literary Orientalism, Postcolonialism, and Universalism* (New York: Peter Lang Publishing, 2010), p. 29. Also, "The orientalist initially meant the person who loved the East and sympathised with it." Ibid., p. 15.

5 See Ibn Warraq, *Defending the West: A Critique of Edward Said's Orientalism* (New York: Prometheus Books, 2007).

6 See Said, *Orientalism*; Said, "Orientalism Reconsidered."

ing beyond generalizations about Western scholars,[7] we are focusing on the conditions under which they worked in Asia, the multilayered relationship they had to their research field, and the impact their personal biographies had on institution and archive building and vice versa. Moreover, we choose two figures who represent *German* Orientalism—a national stream of Orientalism that Said left unaccounted for in his analysis.[8] This gap was critiqued by authors like Sheldon Pollock, who not only drew connections between the German fascination with Indian languages and philosophy during Romanticism and the discourses of Aryanism in Nazi Germany, but also questioned the direct link between Orientalism and colonial rule.[9]

By bringing together our research interests, in this essay we analyze the trials and failures of two Orientalist[10] researchers whose biographies and scholarly work are partly known, but also leave questions open for spec-

7 *Orientalism* has been critiqued to single out the exaggerations, racism, and hostility of much Oriental writing, and thereby create a reverse essentialist image of Western culture, which reinforces the duality that the book wants to leave behind. See Robert Irwin, *Dangerous Knowledge: Orientalism and its Discontents* (Woodstock N.Y.: Overlook Press, 2006); Daniel Varisco, *Reading Orientalism: Said and the Unsaid* (Seattle: University of Washington Press, 2007).

8 In the introduction, Said describes "a quantitative as well as qualitative difference between the Franco British involvement in the Orient" and "the involvement of every other European and Atlantic power," following that "[f]rom the beginning of the nineteenth century until the end of World War II France and Britain dominated the Orient, and Orientalism." Said, *Orientalism*, pp. 3–4. To those critiques directed towards his exclusion of German Orientalism, which he calls "superficial or trivial," he sees no point in responding. See Said, "Orientalism Reconsidered," p. 90.

9 See Sheldon Pollock, "Deep Orientalism? Notes on Sanskrit and Power Beyond the Raj," in *Orientalism and the Postcolonial Predicament: Perspectives on South Asia*, ed. Carol A. Breckenridge and Peter van der Veer (Philadelphia: University of Pennsylvania Press, 1993), pp. 76–133. See also María do Mar Castro Varela and Nikita Dhawan, "Die Orientalismus-Kontroverse," in *Postkoloniale Theorie. Eine kritische Einführung* (Bielefeld: transcript Verlag, 2015), pp. 104–119.

10 We use the designation "Orientalist" here in the sense of the academic focus developed in the nineteenth and early twentieth centuries, spreading across the disciplines of European research institutions.

ulation. To reconstruct their biographies, one needs to read not only their research notes and publications, but also their letters and complaints. Furthermore, we pay attention to those who did that archival work before us, which in the case of Robert Lachmann leads us to the work of artist and filmmaker Jumana Manna.

Hermann Goetz's and Robert Lachmann's starting points and interests show many similarities, despite being situated in different disciplines: from the mid 1920s to the early 1930s, Hermann Goetz and Robert Lachmann both worked in Berlin and their decisions to leave Germany nearly coincided, even though their relation to the German state was as different as their reasons for departure. Goetz left Germany because of the economic decline of the Weimar Republic, first to the Netherlands in 1931 and then to India—at that time the British Raj—in 1936, with a stipend from the Kern Institut, whereas Lachmann left Germany later and witnessed the rise to power of Adolf Hitler's far-right National Socialist German Workers' Party (NSDAP). After the so-called *Berufsbeamtengesetz* of April 7, 1933, Jews and political opponents were dismissed from civil service, which made Lachmann as a Jewish German researcher lose his job at the Staatsbibliothek Berlin (State Library Berlin) and seek refuge in Mandatory Palestine in 1935, to work at the Hebrew University of Jerusalem.[11]

It is noticeable that both scholars chose to leave Nazi Germany to emigrate to what were then regions dominated by the British Empire, which only became independent nation states after World War II, namely the Republic of India and the State of Israel, with their respective histories of independence struggles, partition, and violence. As mentioned before, these were the regions at the heart of what had been defined by the

11 Lachmann was invited by Judah Leon Magnes, chancellor and later president (1935–1948) of the Hebrew University of Jerusalem.

West as "the Orient." In this essay, we trace the biographies of these two German scholars, reflecting on their role between invited guests and all-time outsiders, appreciated for their expertise but remaining minor figures of their fields. The background against which we observe these two scholars will be the histories of institution building and the colonial urge to document and study "other" cultures.

Hermann Goetz: Creating Counter-Narratives to Nationalist and Orientalist Art Histories

Prior to his travels to India and while still in Germany, Hermann Goetz had taken classes in Indology (Sanskrit and Pali) and received his doctorate in art history from the Ludwig Maximilian University of Munich. During World War I, he had conducted research on the Ottoman Turks, after which he widened his interests to Iran and subsequently India in the age of the Mogul Emperors. He worked extensively on a vast array of subjects in Indian art history, initially with a focus on Mughal miniature paintings, especially the *Jahângîr Album* to which he had access at the Staatsbibliothek Berlin.[12]

Goetz was an avid writer throughout his life and it is notable that he broke away from the ahistorical interpretations of non-Western art then prevalent in art history, and established a discourse on transnational cultural exchange between India and other Asian countries, by closely considering and incorporating social and political histories into art historical discourse.[13] In

12 See Karl Jettmar, "Hermann Goetz," *East and West* 26, no. 3/4 (1976), pp. 539–540.

13 See Hermann Goetz, *The Art and Architecture of Bikaner State* (Oxford: Bruno Cassirer, 1950), p. 11. This interest in transnational exchange—today rather called *entanglement*—is very different to the dichotomy European vs. non-European which dominated anthropology at that time and has organized art history for the longest time. See Susanne Leeb, *Die Kunst der Anderen. "Weltkunst" und die*

doing so, his work stands out in contrast to the Orientalist writing on Indian art of that time. His focus on transnational exchange and interest in modern art also offered a counter narrative to the emergence of so-called nationalist art historians in India who sought, in reaction to the colonial approach, to revalorize Indian art by insisting on the spiritual character of its ancient Hindu and Buddhist legacies.[14] In 1936 he and his wife, the granddaughter of the Jewish German mathematician Lazarus Fuchs, decided to move to India to conduct research. German speaking scholars of the time often stayed in India by the invitation of local rulers of princely states, because they did not benefit from the British logistical support. Their mobility was therefore limited and during World War II, German passport holders like Goetz were considered enemies of the state, hence often interned as "enemy aliens." Goetz himself was interned twice and spent a total of three years in prison camps in the present state of Maharashtra, during which time he undertook research on local monuments.[15] However, unlike many other European scholars, Goetz stayed in India after the end of World War II.

In 1943, the Maharaja of Baroda, Pratap Singh Rao Gaekwad, appointed Goetz as the Director of the Baroda Museum and the Picture Gallery, following the renowned Jewish German art historian Ernest Cohn-Wiener, who had overseen the Picture Gallery from 1934 until 1939. We can only speculate whether Cohn-Wiener had recommended Goetz for this position, or if Goetz had gained more popularity due to his lectures at the University of Bombay. In Baroda, Goetz expanded the Picture Gallery with a rich collection of European

anthropologische Konfiguration der Moderne (Berlin: b_books, 2015), p. 13.

14 For example, see Ananda K. Coomaraswamy, *Essays in National Idealism* (Colombo: Colombo Apothecaries, 1909).

15 See Hermann Kulke, "Life and work of Hermann Goetz," in *India and the West: Proceedings of a Seminar Dedicated to the Memory of Hermann Goetz*, ed. Joachim Deppert (Delhi: Manohar, 1983), p. 42.

paintings. He also added a collection of Indian art as well as Western artists working in India. In 1943, he founded the Bulletin of the Baroda Museum and joined the University of Baroda as Honorary Professor.

Goetz's remarkable contribution to Indian art history is that he not only offered a multilayered approach to ancient Indian art, but also defended Indian modern art against conservative, academic or revivalist currents of the Indian art establishment. His reading and contextualization of Indian contemporary art was informed by this knowledge of the past and the path breaking idea of that time, that contemporary art was as valuable as ancient culture. The first exhibition of the Progressive Artists' Group in Baroda in 1949 was organized by Goetz, long before the group became part of the canon of Indian Modernism. The acquisition of Francis Newton Souza's painting *The Blue Lady*, initiated at a time when the artist was still relatively unknown, is an example of Goetz recognizing and promoting artistic rigor.

After his directorship in Baroda, Goetz started working for The National Gallery of Modern Art (NGMA), an institution in New Delhi, established in 1954 at the behest of India's first Prime Minister Jawaharlal Nehru, with the intention to adequately store his personal collection of Indian Modernist paintings, including those of his friend, Amrita Sher-Gil. An outsider, but not entirely unknown in India's art world and growing institutional and academic landscape, Hermann Goetz became the museum's first director, and was given the task of building the gallery's collection. This is one of many examples of how such newly-initiated institutions, which were set up to narrate India's history, relied on outsider knowledge and expertise in collecting and building museum infrastructures.[16]

16 One of the most prominent examples is Grace Morley, the former director of the San Francisco Museum of Art, who served as director of the National Museum in Delhi from 1960 onwards.

Robert Lachmann: Studying Music Traditions Across Religious Divisions

Berlin-born Robert Lachmann's way to ethnomusicology was initiated by his experiences during World War I. Having studied English and French, as well as Arabic, he was sent back from the front to serve as an interpreter in a prisoner-of-war camp at Wünsdorf, Brandenburg, which became a place for a specific kind of knowledge exchange: here, he encountered North African music for the first time and developed an interest in the languages and music traditions of North Africa and India that he would later study.[17] He enrolled in ethnomusicology under Johannes Wolf and Carl Stumpf at Berlin University and obtained a doctorate with his dissertation on urban music in Tunisia in 1922, which was based on his own recordings and transcriptions. He undertook several further recording expeditions and was appointed librarian in the music department of the Staatsbibliothek Berlin in 1927. His comparative study *Musik des Orients* (Music of the Orient) was published in 1929, and one year later the research association *Gesellschaft zur Erforschung der Musik des Orients* (The Society for the Study of Oriental Music) was founded on his initiative.[18] From 1933 to 1935, he edited its quarterly journal *Zeitschrift für vergleichende Musikwissenschaft* (Journal of Comparative Musicology).

Among scholars of German comparative musicology, Lachmann is considered to be one of the founding figures of ethnomusicology and a world expert on Oriental Arab music. However, he remains a rather unknown

17 See Ruth Katz, *"The Lachmann Problem": An Unsung Chapter in Comparative Musicology* (Jerusalem: Hebrew University Magnes Press, 2003), p. 28. Lachmann wrote about "India" even before its independence, see Robert Lachmann, *Musik des Orients* (Breslau: Ferdinand Hirt, 1929).

18 He founded the society together with his former teachers Johannes Wolf, Curt Sachs, Georg Schünemann, and Erich Moritz von Hornbostel.

figure among historians and other scholars of Palestine during the British Mandate Period, as Gil Hochberg notes in her analysis of Jumana Manna's film *A Magical Substance Flows Into Me*—a film which can be regarded as an archive itself and to which we will come back later.[19] In the following section, we want to show that Lachmann's experience can be understood as that of a double outsider—a racialized outsider pre-emigration and an academic outsider post-emigration.

Lachmann's decision to seek refuge in Palestine was connected to his profession, not his religious beliefs, as Ruth Katz writes in her book *The Lachmann Problem*: "Palestine seemed like an ideal laboratory, offering unique research opportunities."[20] The Hebrew University in Jerusalem, to which Lachmann was invited by chancellor Judah Leon Magnes, was born in the Zionist movement and became one of the major institutions embodying the process of "the homeland on its way," which also led to conflicts about the definition of such a "university of the Jewish people."[21] Lachmann seems to have been at odds with those conflicts, since he was not interested in defining a purely Jewish musicology. His research interests and archival endeavors were driven by the conviction that local Arab musical traditions should be studied across divisions between the liturgical and the secular, as well as between the Arab and the Jewish. In his first report of June 14, 1935, he writes:

> It may be hoped that in the course of time it will be possible to study the ritual song not only of the different Jewish traditions, but also of the Christian Oriental communities of Palestine and, perhaps, recitations of the Koran, all

19 See Gil Z. Hochberg, "Revisiting the Orientalist Archive," in *Becoming Palestine: Toward an Archival Imagination of the Future* (Durham, N.C. and London: Duke University Press, 2021), pp. 37–52, here p. 37, p. 39.

20 Katz, *The Lachmann Problem*, p. 38.

21 Ibid., p. 47.

> of them in reliable renderings. Moreover, there still exists a wealth of secular song and instrumental music especially on the part of Arab peasants and Bedouins.[22]

Lachmann's view on musical connectivity across these divisions clashed with the agenda of the university, which might be one reason why he never succeeded in securing a permanent position at the Institute for Oriental Studies,[23] even though he was valuable for the university not only because of his expertise but also because he brought his own recording machine together with his technician, Walter Schnur.

Today, his archive is stored in the National Library of Israel, located on the campus of the Hebrew University of Jerusalem. The files include his correspondence, the manuscripts and recordings of the radio show that he hosted from 1936 to 1938, called "Oriental Music," as well as a large collection of sound recordings. Compared to Hermann Goetz, he is a less widely known figure and only a few people wrote about his work.[24] Thanks to Berlin-based Palestinian artist Jumana Manna's film *A Magical Substance Flows Into Me* (2015), Lachmann's work, which could be called a dead archive, recently resurfaced and was made accessible to a wider—mostly contemporary art—audience. But what also re-emerged with his work was the story around it: that of an ethnologist who was truly invested in recording, studying, and archiving Palestinian music, who tried to integrate him-

22 Robert Lachmann, "Section for the Study of Non-European Music. First Report," in Katz, *The Lachmann Problem*, pp. 111–112.

23 See Katz, *The Lachmann Problem*, p. 105.

24 Ruth Katz's *The Lachmann Problem* from 2003 is the only publication dedicated to Lachmann's work as a musicologist in both Germany and Palestine. A more recent publication includes the transcriptions of Lachmann's radio lectures and brings them in dialogue with more recent scholarship: see Ruth Davis, *Robert Lachmann: The Oriental Music Broadcasts, 1936–1937: A Musical Ethnography of Mandatory Palestine* (Middleton, Wisconsin: A-R Editions, 2013).

self within Jewish academia but failed in being accepted academically and in establishing a research department.

The Making of an Outsider: Hermann Goetz at the NGMA

Upon his arrival in Delhi and appointment at the NGMA, Hermann Goetz's immediate task at hand was to build up a collection. There was an urgency since the institution had been a storehouse for entire collections of artists' works which had been gifted, either to the gallery or to the first Prime Minister, Jawaharlal Nehru, himself. Through his exchanges with the Ministry of Education, we can trace the lack of appreciation and support that Goetz got from the newly formed ministries of the Indian state.

In a letter dated March 18, 1953 to the Ministry of Education, under whose direct mandate the NGMA fell at that time, Goetz asks for permission to change the procedure of appealing to the National Art Treasures Fund for permission to purchase a work of art. According to Goetz, the procedure was too slow, and he complains that he had missed out on opportunities to buy works that would have enriched the collection. His suggested solution is to have more autonomy, to be able to buy works on his own responsibility within a fixed budget.

In a second letter from November 1953, he explains further why he is unable to execute purchases. The committee of the National Art Treasures Fund was based on members from different parts of India who had to physically appear in Delhi to make decisions. Therefore, Goetz had to gather many proposals and offers from artists before the members even arranged a meeting. This led to the fact that only works that did not attract much attention from other buyers could be shown to the committee:

> When I select a picture or other work in exhibitions, the artists agree only under the condition that I may have it for offer to the Purchase Committee, in case nobody else buys it on the spot. But the really good and in this case also still comparatively cheap works are almost always sold to some embassy or private person before the exhibition is over.[25]

And secondly:

> When I request artists, even well-known ones, to make offers, I again obtain, in most cases, just those works which the artist could not sell, i.e. generally his less successful creations. And from private side only very few offers worth consideration have hitherto been received. How under these circumstances we shall be able soon to build up a National Art Gallery, I cannot see. [26]

Goetz's letters reflect the difficulties he faced in building up the collection. He requests the government to set up a small purchase committee in New Delhi consisting of local members that can react ad hoc and decide over more expensive works and in a similar manner he suggests committees for Calcutta, Bombay, Madras, Lucknow, Hyderabad, and Bangalore. Much to Goetz's disappointment, the deputy of the Secretary Vikram Singh responds to him only almost a year later, that he had never received any proposal to purchase a work. Yet he agrees that Goetz should have the autonomy to purchase works on the spot and that local committees should be initiated. Again, much to Goetz's frustration, having suggested scholars and art experts for the committees, he was merely being informed that such committees had been initiated but it remained unclear who selected the members. We speculate that meanwhile the

25 Letter from Hermann Goetz to the Ministry of Education, National Archives, File 8356/53-H.2.

26 Ibid.

local committees had gotten together and suggested a number of works that were not to Goetz's satisfaction, since he writes in a letter to Vikram Singh on June 4, 1954, that he is "not impressed at all by the selection" and doubts "whether most of the pictures are suitable for exhibition."[27] Goetz also reports that he neither is a member of the local committee nor knows the names of the members of the local committees. It seems that the Ministry of Education compromised their decision, and eventually set up committees but excluded Goetz from purchase decisions. Therefore, the autonomy Goetz had fought for was entirely taken from him and given to a committee he could not engage with. His question about the members of the committee gets answered only through the state of Hyderabad, sending a list with the names of all members of the local committee in Hyderabad. The remaining answers might be lost, or Hermann Goetz never received such answers.[28]

The issues the gallery is still facing today are revealed here for the first time: Being under a direct mandate of the government, the director of the gallery does not have the authority to make decisions, and even curatorial decisions are colored by state interventions. The institution was built upon cultural capital, personal relationships and likings, rather than an autonomous funding system and democratic decision-making processes, being completely dependent on donors who might have been attracted by seeing their works, or close relatives' works, in upcoming national institutions. From today's perspective, this set a precedent for collection building in India, despite Goetz's attempt to introduce a more systematic approach.

27 Letter from Hermann Goetz to Vikram Singh, National Archives, File FS-60/54-H.2.

28 This archival research was first published in Arnika Ahldag, "In transition: Collection building at the National Gallery of Modern Art in New Delhi," *The Chitrolekha Journal on Art and Design* 5, no. 1 (2021).

The collection of the NGMA has from its beginning in 1954 until today mainly been based on chance rather than systematically collecting artworks.[29] Goetz's struggle against and helplessness in dealing with the bureaucracy of the new state were connected to its systems of favoritism—promoting friends and relatives—and lack of transparency, systems that are still at the root of many institutions in India and actively being reinforced today.[30]

From Orientalist to Minor Figure: Robert Lachmann at the Palestinian Broadcasting Service

The fact that Robert Lachmann established a radio program for the Palestinian Broadcasting Station, in which he invited a different group of musicians each week to perform, shows that the inclination behind his large collection of audio recordings was to share it with a wider public, outside of academia. In Jumana Manna's film *A Magical Substance Flows Into Me*, which is based on her research in the National Library of Israel, we encounter Lachmann through the texts that he wrote for this radio program. When we hear his ideas of preserving what he calls "pure" Arab music traditions, read out by the artist, he comes across as a scholar with a rather patronizing tone, driven by an Orientalist thinking that imagines Palestine as a pure and unspoiled Bible land. The scene in which we hear his voice during a meeting of the advisory committee of the broadcasting service in December 1936, nevertheless, gives us some hints about him also being at the receiving end of critique:

29 At the time of writing, works are not purchased anymore due to fiscal limitations, and perhaps the anxiety of interfering with the market and being accused of favoritism of certain artists and galleries.

30 Many of these institutions are now crumbling, under the hyper nationalist drive of the current BJP-led Indian government.

> Gentlemen, I have invited you because of the shocking attacks and protests directed against our program and especially our musical program, both by the Arab and the Hebrew newspapers. You know that we have spared no trouble in securing the very best and noblest representants of music to be found in Palestine. Still our ardent efforts have been met with ill feeling and with insulting criticism. I would ask you now, to give me your most valuable advice as to possible changes in our programs and our method.

As the film develops, we also get to read his handwritten manuscripts which show some of his inconsistencies: "Although I am still a stranger to this country, I will say a few words about Arab music. If there is anything that entitles me to speak about this topic, it is my love of Arab song and knowledge of its history." In an even closer view on his handwriting, we can see that he crossed out the clause "and the fact that I have been studying it." Listening to these sentences, as well as seeing his multiple attempts to re-write these words, creates a multifaceted image of a Jewish German Orientalist who reflects upon and struggles with his own position, being a stranger in Palestine.[31] In the film, we also get a sense of the tragic failure of Lachmann's vision of music. While he imagined music being a path "towards a better understanding between Jews and Arabs," the state-owned radio station where he tried to promote this idea was of a different opinion. Their separatist principle assumed that "Arabs would listen to the Arabic sections, Jews would listen to the Hebrew

31 These thoughts on Jumana Manna's film were first developed in Rebecca Hanna John, "Giving a Voice to Gaps and Cracks. Archival Critique in Jumana Manna's 'A Magical Substance Flows Into Me'," *roots and routes* 33 (May–August 2020: Archivio è Potere), https://www.roots-routes.org/giving-a-voice-to-gaps-and-cracks-archival-critique-in-jumana-mannas-a-magical-substance-flows-into-me-by-rebecca-john/ (accessed August 30, 2022).

section."[32] In her film, which responds to Lachmann's struggles with a mix of critique and empathy, Manna foregrounds the gaps and cracks of exactly these constructed separations, for example in the scene in which singer Neta Elkayam speaks to her about the entanglements of Jewish Moroccan culture and Arabhood—a kind of conversation that Lachmann was probably not able have in his time.

In the introduction to *Orientalism*, Edward Said writes: "The scientist, the scholar, the missionary, the trader, or the soldier was in, or thought about, the Orient because he *could be there*, or could think about it, with very little resistance on the Orient's part."[33] We do not have a lot of documentation of Lachmann's experience in Jerusalem, but thanks to Ruth Katz's book *The Lachmann Problem*, we can reconstruct that he was not fully in accordance with Said's description. He was not there merely because he could be—as a Jewish scholar, he had been forced out of Germany; moreover, he faced plenty of resistance. As Katz writes, we have to imagine Lachmann as a "lone scholar having to missionize for his profession in an alien culture and in an impossible organizational context."[34] This "mission" was a difficult task since musicology was a relatively young and therefore still minor field. As the newly established Hebrew University did not yet have a music department, the members of the School of Oriental Studies needed to be convinced of Lachmann's project, but they only gave him the status of a Research Fellow, not a member of the teaching staff.[35] His efforts to establish a center for the study of Oriental music were of no avail, despite

32 Andrea L. Stanton, *"This Is Jerusalem Calling": State Radio in Mandate Palestine* (Austin: University of Texas Press, 2013), p. 20. Quoted by Hochberg, "Revisiting the Orientalist Archive," p. 40.

33 Said, *Orientalism*, p. 7.

34 See Katz, *The Lachmann Problem*, p. 16.

35 See the letter from Dr. Schlesinger, member of the Executive Council of the University, dated July 16, 1935, reprinted in ibid., pp. 125–126.

his support by the chancellor Magnes. On top of these difficulties, Lachmann faced many organizational difficulties[36] which, comparable to Goetz's situation, stayed partly opaque to him. From the beginning, Lachmann had to struggle for funding, which we can understand from his letter exchange with Magnes,[37] and until the end, he did not fit into the climate of the university with its Zionist agenda. It is telling that in a correspondence between Magnes and the administrator S. Ginzberg, the former called Lachmann one "of the stepchildren of the University"[38] while the latter suggested that such scholars are rather "in the nature of distant relations offered temporary hospitality."[39]

By 1938, Lachmann had gained support for his journal, but was suffering from severe health problems and since Germany cut off pension funds for Jews, he also lost his private income. On May 5, 1939, Magnes announced Lachmann's death to the scientific employees of the university, calling him "one of the refugees from Germany who found here a haven and a home" and will be kept "in memory in our hearts as if we were close family members,"[40] which reads in stark contrast to Lachmann's unsuccessful fights at the university. From the letters that Katz collected in the archive, we can understand that Magnes must have been the only one who actually kept Lachmann "in his heart." Moreover, he

It remains unclear why he stresses the fact that this is "a technical question—not a personal one."

36 See Katz, *The Lachmann Problem*, p. 127. The many letters, reprinted in Katz's book, discussing Lachmann's status and funding situation at the University must have stayed outside of his knowledge.

37 Magnes' letter to Robert Lachmann from January 1, 1935, reprinted in Katz, *The Lachmann Problem*, p. 95. Magnes tells Lachmann to ask his friends for donations until the university structure and its funds can be secured.

38 Magnes' letter to S. Ginzberg, February 11, 1937, reprinted in Katz, *The Lachmann Problem.*, pp. 168–169.

39 Ginzberg's answer to Magnes, February 12, 1937, reprinted inKatz, *The Lachmann Problem* ., p. 170.

40 Announcement of Magnes, May 9, 1939, reprinted in Katz, *The Lachmann Problem*, pp. 217–218.

praised Lachmann's connectedness to his research field in opposition to the other "Westerners": "through this expertise he was able to open to us Westerners the souls of those born and educated in the Orient, both Jews and Arabs."[41] The differentiation between Jews of the East and of the West, as well as the tension between self-occidentalizing and self-orientalizing shines through here, as the backdrop of Lachmann's struggle.[42] After his death, music vanished from the university's agenda and only in 1965, seventeen years after the foundation of the State of Israel, was the Jewish Music Research Center finally established.[43]

We read Lachmann's case—a German Orientalist and Jewish refugee in Palestine—as one that shows the gaps and cracks in the uniform image of the White male Orientalist as the superior figure. Instead, we understand him as a failing figure who tried to create an awareness for Oriental music across religious boundaries but whose vision stayed unsupported in an academic climate that was shaped by a heightened nationalism in the run-up to the foundation of Israel.

Conclusion: The Element of Chance in Failure

This time of heightened anti-imperial struggles and national movements in the 1930s in then still British-controlled parts of the world was the context in which both Hermann Goetz and Robert Lachmann left Nazi

41 Ibid.

42 On the historically changing positioning of Jews as White or non-White see for example Ulrike Brunotte, Anna-Dorothea Ludewig, and Axel Stähler, eds., *Orientalism, Gender, and the Jews* (Oldenburg: De Gruyter, 2015), which was accompanied by a workshop that challenged suggestions by Said and others that Orientalism is nothing more than a patronizing attitude and a "strange, secret sharer" of Western antisemitism. We are thankful to Nikita Dhawan for this important remark.

43 See Katz, *The Lachmann Problem*, pp. 236–237.

Germany and entered their respective research fields. Their experience and understanding of nationalism might have clashed with the kinds of nationalism they were confronted with in India and Palestine.[44] The tricky positionality of Orientalist experts but all-time outsiders, between strength and weakness, existing ambitions and lack of capabilities, wanting control and the need for cooperation and support,[45] is also described in the introduction of Maurus Reinkowski and Gregor Thum's anthology *Helpless Imperialists*. The authors state that even if empires were far from helpless, the imperial experience was significantly marked by the feeling of helplessness.[46]

Goetz and Lachmann did not arrive as the superior agents venturing out to measure and rule the "Other," as would be the Saidean image of the Orientalist, but they were in fact invited by their hosts to join institution-building processes that were part of the new nations in the making. Even if their academic thinking was located in the field of Oriental studies, their actual work experience in the "Orient," as shown in this essay, can be understood as the opposite of "European culture gain[ing] in strength and identity by setting itself off against the Orient as a sort of surrogate and even underground self."[47] While they thought they could continue their careers in India and Palestine, in practice

44 As sociologist Satish Deshpande writes, European notions of nationalism, such as Benedict Anderson's in *Imagined Communities: Reflections on the Origins and Spread of Nationalism* (1983), have not been very hospitable to the specificity of non-Western nationalisms. See Satish Deshpande, "The Nation as an Imagined Economy," in *Contemporary India: A Sociological View* (New Delhi: Viking, 2003), pp. 48–73, here pp. 49–51. Similar critiques have been voiced by scholars of Israel/Palestine, see for example Anna Bernard, *Rhetorics of Belonging: Nation, Narration, and Israel/Palestine* (Liverpool: Liverpool University Press, 2013).

45 See Maurus Reinkowski and Gregor Thum, eds., *Helpless Imperialists: Imperial Failure, Fear and Radicalization* (Göttingen: Vandenhoeck & Ruprecht GmbH & Co., 2013), pp. 7–8.

46 See ibid.

47 Said, *Orientalism*, p. 3.

they remained outsiders who were dependent on institutional hosts and never managed to get full access to their research field and the local networks they sought to be part of. To look at their experiences of struggle and failure helps us to understand that the relationship between the Oriental and the Orientalist is not always an easy opposition between silenced objects of study and dominant researchers. Especially if one wants to break away from this opposition, it seems important to us to investigate the details and differences between Orientalist scholars and to search for exceptions, maybe even possible allies. Just like in Jumana Manna's film, Lachmann becomes a kind of posthumous ally, someone who fought for establishing an archive that she as a Palestinian artist with a United States citizenship can dig out of the National Library in Jerusalem today, to build her own filmic archive journey through Palestine on top of it.

Given that Said described Orientalism as a praxis of the same sort as male gender dominance,[48] fighting against this system of domination ideally has to come from both sides of the oppositional divide that is to be overcome. Considering that Orientalist and patriarchal power dynamics are far from being overcome and that the forms of nationalism that Lachmann and Goetz encountered have continued to develop in different contexts and forms,[49] we as researchers who are socialized and (partly) trained in Europe might also want to ask ourselves more often if we actually fail to understand the ways in which phenomena travel and exist in different settings, carrying with them their own histories and meanings. Instead of using Orientalism and nationalism as easily transferable concepts that can be applied

48 See Said, "Orientalism Reconsidered," p. 103.

49 One would for example need to analyze the relationship between India's anticolonial nationalist struggle for a state independent of colonial rule and the current Indian Hindu-Nationalist government that violently tries to exclude minorities.

to an almost infinite number of contexts, we need to acknowledge their very different realities, but also how both are related to each other. An exploration of biographies of outsider figures like Lachmann and Goetz provides a counter-narrative to both Said's definition of the European Orientalist who needs the Orient as its non-resistant supposed Other, and Sheldon Pollock's analysis of German Orientalists who search for their "Aryan ancestors" in Asia during Nazi rule.[50] Said and Pollock had to leave these outsider figures out of their analyses, to be able to show the connectedness between Orientalism and Franco British colonialism and Orientalism and German nationalism respectively. We plead for taking figures like Lachmann and Goetz more seriously, not to undermine Said's and Pollock's important analyses but to come to a less homogenizing picture which is able to include struggling Orientalists who were excluded, who fought against resistance in their research field, and ultimately failed in their endeavors. While it might sound risky to search for allies in the field of Orientalism, which is mostly seen as the "enemy" because of the connections carved out by Said, Pollock, and many others, Manna's example shows us that it can be worth digging deeper. Finding allies in the middle of what was thought of as the enemy thereby becomes a way of undoing fixed constructions of us versus them that are at the heart of Said's description of Orientalism.

50 See Pollock, "Deep Orientalism?," p. 86.

"It takes a lot longer to build a city than it does to strike a target."[1]

Reversing Partition as an Art Practice

Akram Zaatari
interviewed by Rebecca Hanna John

Rebecca Hanna John: I am very curious to hear how you reflect on your work *Letter to a Refusing Pilot* (2013) today, nearly ten years after you showed it in the Lebanese Pavilion at the Venice Biennale. We could discuss it in relation to other projects that you were working on around that time, for example the lecture performance *A Conversation with an Imagined Israeli Filmmaker Named Avi Mograbi* (2012) in which you said: "Just as in prison one thinks of freedom, in wartime, thinking peace is inevitable. But we know that it is not simple to unmake history, to go back in time and unmake injustice, violence, occupation, and war."[2]

As you often mention, your photographic practice began not in an art school, but while documenting the

1 Hagai Tamir as quoted by Akram Zaatari (2012) from Avihai Becker in the *Haaretz* article "Why We Refused," (2002). The complete quotation being: "Who knows better than me, an architect, how hard it is to build a city? So at least, don't rejoice when you destroy houses. It takes a lot longer to build a city than it does to strike a target." Avihai Becker, "Why We Refused," *Haaretz,* September 25, 2002, https://www.haaretz.com/1.5098808?v=1651305074494 (accessed April 30, 2022).

2 The performance was turned into a publication: Akram Zaatari, *Conversation with an Imagined Israeli Filmmaker Named Avi Mograbi* (Berlin: Sternberg Press, 2012). This quote also stands at the beginning of the publication around *Letter to a Refusing Pilot* that accompanied the work and was distributed at the Lebanese Pavilion in Venice in 2013.

world around you during the Israeli invasion of Lebanon: You recorded the sounds of fighter jets and you photographed the explosions. But even if the previous quote and your work that we are discussing today is closely connected to this specific historical and geographical context, I was wondering if we can also discuss it in today's contexts of ongoing wars, for example Russia waging war on Ukraine as we speak. Looking at these instances of ongoing disaster, the aim to undo the course of history, to undo the violence and injustice that keep repeating not only seems difficult but also like an impossible task.

In both works, *A Conversation with an Imagined Israeli Filmmaker* and *Letter to a Refusing Pilot*, you take the viewer on a journey that looks at the situation that you observed as a young person from a later standpoint and from the eyes of the so-called enemy, the person at the other side of the border. In the case of *Letter to a Refusing Pilot*, you start to recover a specific story of an Israeli pilot who refused the order to bomb a target that was not a military one, but a school. Maybe you can tell us a bit more about the story of this refusing pilot and how he became the protagonist of your work for the Venice Biennale.

Akram Zaatari: Both works that you mention attempt to write a shared history between two enemy states. *Letter to a Refusing Pilot* might have started with the performance *Conversation with an Imagined Israeli Filmmaker Named Avi Mograbi*, because that was the first time that I told the story of this rumor that reached us in Saida, South Lebanon, in 1982: it was a rumor that there had been a refusal in the Israeli army, namely refusing to bomb the Saida Public School for Boys which my father had founded in the early sixties. Back then, my father wasn't affiliated with that school anymore, but worked for UNESCO. Nevertheless, this story reached us because his name as a founder was associated with it.

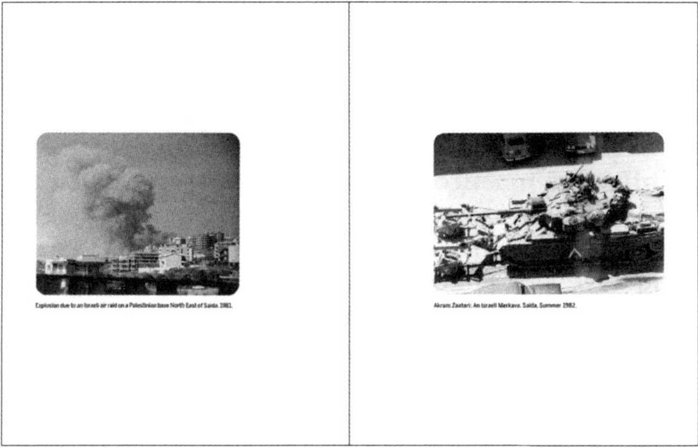

Fig. 1: Akram Zaatari, *A Conversation with an Imagined Israeli Filmmaker* (Berlin: Sternberg Press, 2012). Spread courtesy of the artist.

So, this rumor reached us slightly modified. It said that one of the members of the Jewish community of Saida, who had attended Saida Public School for Boys, left Saida at some point to go to Israel, entered the military and became a pilot, and that one day, when he was sent to fly over the school, and given orders to bomb it, he refused. But only after mentioning this rumor in my *Conversation with an Imagined Israeli Filmmaker Named Avi Mograbi,* I realized who this pilot was. It was through a doctoral student in History that I heard about the pilot Hagai Tamir.[3] When Seth Anziska came to Beirut for research in 2012, he came across the transcript of my conversation with Avi. He then urgently looked for me to tell me that this pilot exists, and that his name was Hagai Tamir. This is how I figured out that this story had reached us with a twist and that in fact Hagai had nothing to do with Lebanon. He is of Polish origin and

3 See also "Letter to a Refusing Pilot. Seth Anziska in conversation with Danielle Rose King," in *Ibraaz* 005 (July 2013), https://www.ibraaz.org/interviews/89 (accessed April 30, 2022).

had never set foot in Lebanon. He refused to destroy the school because he could tell, from his architectural training, that the building was either a school or a hospital. He had left the army sometime after 1973 to study architecture. He had built his own home and started an architecture practice but was still on reserve when the 1982 invasion started.

In my cinematic reading of the character, he is like Wim Wenders' angels in *Wings of Desire* (*Der Himmel über Berlin*, 1987) who wanted to change nature and develop a desire to become humans. They cross that threshold from angelhood to humanity. I like to see the pilot, Hagai Tamir, unwilling to take part in a war-making machine anymore, as someone who has crossed the threshold between military and civilian. His architecture studies turned him "human." When we met, he told me: "While studying architecture, I have learned how difficult it is to construct and how easy it was to destroy." As a soldier, it is so easy to destroy. He told me that other soldiers would see it as a competition and make jokes about who destroys faster. This is part of a language that is used in the army—in any army by the way. In published interviews with him, he talks about how safe the pilot is in a jet: You can destroy a whole city and not feel any bump. This attitude within the military made him realize that he belongs to a generation of pilots who were themselves the judges facing the target. And he gradually saw new values spreading in the army, striving towards bypassing any human reflection or skepticism in the larger machine of war. You just send a drone somewhere in the middle of the desert of Afghanistan, you look at it while sitting in Texas, and you press a button that kills people there. It strips killing of any possible guilt or questioning and turns it into what looks like a videogame because you are protected by a safe distance and do not deal with the repercussions of your assault. You do not even see the amount of destruction with your own eyes.

This is exactly what pilots like Hagai Tamir witnessed. They had been trained on values that are no longer applicable in today's army warfare.[4] I am saying this because you asked me about where *Letter to a Refusing Pilot* began. It might have begun while doing the conversation with Avi Mograbi. But it might have begun with me witnessing the Israeli invasion of Lebanon, which made it—for me as a young adult, back then I was sixteen years old—absolutely impossible to accept that leaders of another country would send their airplanes to destroy and to march into Lebanon without considering any human beings like them, like the Israeli citizens working and living on the other side of the border. I asked myself all the time: "How could these soldiers so easily return home a week later, hug their families and love their friends after they had just engaged with war, killed civilians, and tortured others in Lebanon, without feeling any guilt?" It is an innocent and a childish question that comes to mind. It comes to mind to every Ukrainian person who is forced to leave home today because of Russia's invasion, asking themselves: "Why are these Russians pushing me away from home? Do they not have families? Do they not have kids like me? Do they not have wives, lovers, friends, or parents living in a safe home?" These are simple and naive questions, but they are, unfortunately, obvious questions to ask when they have nothing else to say.

I was prepared to engage with this larger question: Is it possible to refuse an order coming from the most rigid and disciplined machine, the military? It is possible that you refuse a request at your place of work, but what does this mean when it is done in the context of war? Hagai clearly explains his motivations in an interview

4 Hagai Tamir finished his course in pilot school in 1968 and describes himself as belonging to the generation of "the lyric pilots," by which he means those who were raised on the traditions of European aviation which according to him were characterized by flying in an elegant manner. See Becker, "Why We Refused."

that he did with *Haaretz* in 2002. It took him so long, almost twenty years, to understand that by refusing, he is not betraying his country. If you love your country, you try to repress the thought that your country has produced aggression, has committed a crime. You ask yourself ten times before admitting that your country is responsible for aggression. And I am sure a lot of Russians are in a similar position today. They are about to admit that their country might have crossed the line of crime. They are not sure they want to admit it in public, because they do not want to be disgraced at home or accused of betraying their country. This is extremely sensitive at times of war. It is hard to admit refusal in the middle of war, especially in the context of the Israeli army, where soldiers have been given orders to eliminate Palestinian political leaders, as in the case of the killing of Yahya Ayyash in Gaza in January 1996—in a very similar way to the assassination of Osama Bin Laden by the US army, by the way. I am using the term "assassination" because there has not been a trial. Nobody has listened to this man, nobody caught him and brought him to justice. Nevertheless, there is still a military entity that decided to execute this man. And they looked for him and killed him. I am not defending him. He might have deserved to be caught and brought to justice. I am only saying that facing this kind of machine, people like Hagai Tamir say: "We do not want to execute illegal or inhuman orders." When he publicly spoke about his refusal, there was a wave of refusing orders in the Israeli military machine and he realized that he is part a community of refusing soldiers. Therefore, he accepted to be outspoken about it without fearing possible accusations of betrayal. Imagine, it took twenty years to accept the fact that it was okay to say "no" and that this is not a betrayal. On the contrary, you love your country, therefore you want to save it from committing a crime. I stress this notion because it is so important today to tell Russian soldiers: You are

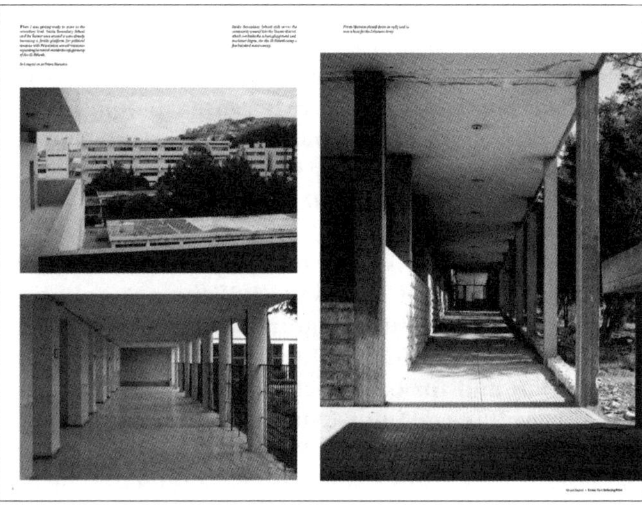

Fig. 2: Akram Zaatari, *Letter to a Refusing Pilot* (Venice, 2013), no page numbers. Published for the Lebanon Pavilion at the Biennale Arte 55 in Venice (June 1–November 24, 2013).

not betraying your country if you refuse an order. It is totally legitimate to say "no."

It is not a coincidence that I met Hagai Tamir, and I am very lucky to have encountered him, to have him in the register of my work because what he speaks of is universal, it can be applied to many situations. It is important for us to know that military machines have changed so much in the past forty years from the eighties until today, where we do killings everywhere in the world, using the army machine without any humans. *Letter to a Refusing Pilot* in a way praises the courageous act of refusal of a pilot and calls the world to hear him. Saint-Exupéry was also a pilot assigned reconnaissance missions in the French Army. Nevertheless, he produced books of great humanism. People who join the military are people like me and you. All of a sudden, the war erupts, and they have to take part in it. The questioning of having possibly engaged in a crime often comes late, after the fact. But *Letter to a Refusing Pilot* is also part of my ongoing digging in Saida's recent history. It is also partly looking at my personal history because what pushed me to learn photography were namely these events that surrounded our home in the late seventies and early eighties and that I did not apprehend as a young adult.

RHJ: You connect this act of refusing orders which turns into a refusal to kill innocent civilians not only with Hagai's experience in the military, but also with his experience as an architect. His refusal is a choice against destruction and for construction, one could say. Interestingly, Antoine de Saint-Exupéry, whom you just mentioned and whose book *Le Petit Prince* (1943) appears in *Letter to a Refusing Pilot*, was also a pilot and he also studied architecture in between.[5] And you also studied architecture!

AZ: Yes, I also studied architecture. Architecture education makes you already part of a community of people who think through design, architecture, and building, who think before building, who want a better life for their people. They may find themselves a minority in a larger context that praises war. In other terms, think of a queer person living in a very conservative society. When would that person cross the line and speak out loud of their desires? When do you come out? Someone like Avi Mograbi, for example, is another version of Hagai Tamir. He is confronted, on a daily basis, with convictions, statements, and acts around him in Israel

5 After having failed the final exams at a preparatory Naval Academy twice, Saint-Exupéry entered the École des Beaux-Arts as an auditor to study architecture for fifteen months, again without graduating, before in 1921 he started his military service as a basic rank soldier. After taking flying lessons, he was transferred to the French Air Force one year later, where he soon experienced the first of many aircraft crashes, a major one of which in 1935 is said to have inspired his 1943 story *Le Petit Prince*.

that he disagrees with. And these are coming from the army, the leadership and the society at large, namely hailing and supporting and legitimizing the continuing occupation of the West Bank. He is not in the army—so it may be easier for him to express his disagreement. I am interested in those situations when people do cross this threshold and stand up against the majority in their communities, aligning themselves with human values. I recently invited Avi Mograbi to be part of a one-day symposium at the Centre Pompidou called *Changing Hands*.[6] I showed an Egyptian film by Shadi Abdessalam called *The Mummy* or the *Night of Counting the Years* (1969)[7] and Avi asked me: "Why did you put me in this context?" I told him that the film is about a young man in Upper Egypt, around Luxor, who, upon the death of his father, learns that his tribe has been living from dealing in archaeological finds that they steal from the mountain. They clandestinely dig out, steal, and sell these finds to European travelers and local traffickers. When the young man realizes this, he refuses it, and he goes into the classical dilemma, like a Shakespearean or classical Cornelian conflict: "Do I hide the secret and keep it with my tribe and, therefore, protect my tribe? Or do I publicly express my disagreement, even if they accuse me of betrayal?" This is the question that I expect every individual today to ask themselves. It is the essential question, because yes, your tribe may go crazy and commit a crime. Do you want to blindly endorse those acts of your tribe—or not?

RHJ: It is a dilemma because saying "no" means risking to not have a tribe anymore.

6 *Changing Hands. Objects on the Move*, curated by Akram Zaatari, December 8, 2022, Centre Pompidou, https://www.centrepompidou.fr/en/program/calendar/event/M5odp1H (accessed December 6, 2022). The recordings of all the presentations can be accessed online.

7 The film was selected as the Egyptian entry for the Academy Award for Best Foreign Language Film at the 43rd Academy Awards, but was not accepted as a nominee.

AZ: And saying "yes" might mean to stigmatize your tribe with fascism and possibly crime. And, by tribe I mean your family, your political leaders, the political party you are part of; it can be your religious community, or your country, if it starts an aggression against civilians, against innocent people. And, of course, your family expects you, as a member of it, not to desert it. Your political leader expects you to do the same. When your country aggresses other countries, it is not going to expect that its own citizens oppose it and act to stop their country's aggression.

Letter to a Refusing Pilot is a film, indeed, is an art piece, yes. But I made it not only as an artwork, rather as a way to engage with the human face of this world. If there are several faces, I would always choose the human face, even at the cost of being criticized in your own place. We do not have any more room to choose other than humanity as a family. Very honestly. And I know it is very complicated. Your readers will start saying "but there are so many buts." Nevertheless, you need to start seeing things from a human perspective. When you see things from material, financial, power, or interest perspectives, you gradually drift away from the human perspective. *Letter to a Refusing Pilot* grounds itself in that position.

By the way, I always keep my most favorite books here. This is a book by Hagai Tamir's father.[8] I put it next to Albert Camus' book, which represents the core of my humanist position: No matter what happens, if everyone treats you as a thug, stand up for your values. Your human values are what is left. Camus wrote this during the Second World War at the height of Nazism. With the voice of Albert Camus, with the gesture of Hagai Tamir, and with my memories of Saida going through the Israeli occupation, I made this work against war.

8 Arnon Tamir, *A Journey Back: Injustice and Restitution* (Evanston, Ill.: Northwestern University Press, 1997). Translated by Ruth Hein.

RHJ: Is this book by Albert Camus that you were referring to the compilation of essays called *Letters to a German Friend*?

AZ: This one is *Resistance, Rebellion and Death.*[9] The first chapter here is a translation of what had been published in French as *Letters to a German Friend.*[10] In English, it hasn't been published as a stand-alone book. *Letters to a German Friend* is a collection of letters that Albert Camus published during the early forties, using a pseudonym in the French press.

RHJ: And that German friend was—in contrast to your "imaginary" filmmaker—an imaginary friend?

AZ: Yes.

RHJ: Speaking of imagination, I am also interested in how you chose the figure from *Le Petit Prince* as a character for *Letter to a Refusing Pilot*.

AZ: When I discovered *The Little Prince* as a kid, it blew my mind! My god, this imagination, this poetry, the simplicity and eloquence in evoking the basics of humanity!

RHJ: When the narrator in *Le Petit Prince* starts with a description of grownups and their inability to perceive important things,[11] he probably refers to what you also just described as an inability to be human?

9 Albert Camus, *Resistance, Rebellion and Death* (New York: Modern Library, 1960).

10 Albert Camus, *Lettres à un Ami Allemand* (Paris: Gallimard, 1948).

11 "Grown-ups love figures. When you tell them that you have made a new friend, they never ask you any questions about essential matters. They never say to you, 'What does his voice sound like? What games does he love best? Does he collect butterflies?' Instead, they demand: 'How old is he? How many brothers has he? How much does he weigh? How much money does his father make?' Only from

AZ: Yes, and this is exactly what is at the heart of Peter Handke's *Childhood Song*. This poem that was written for Wim Wenders' *Wings of Desire* refers to a time when the kid was a kid and did not mind doing this or that. But now that the kid is a grownup, it has become a complex person who needs to take into consideration the interests and realities of this and that. You lose your human virginity. You become a boring adult who is thinking of material things and the interests of that adult's tribe, country, of economic feasibility... etc. This is really how *Refusing Pilot* took shape: thinking of going back to childhood as a position (as an unformatted, as an early state when human subjects are not yet contaminated by interest, attraction to power, or anything else), thinking of uncompromising human values. I give tribute to all of those who, when in a conflict, would leave their tribe(s) and take refuge in humanity. Taking refuge in humanity is THE position to take in dark times like ours.

RHJ: While you asked how we can change the mindset of the majority through acts of refusal, I was wondering how these figures of refusal appear in the first place?

AZ: At the height of Second World War, Albert Camus had to publish under a fictitious name. But he could not not-publish those thoughts. He had to put them out because he believed in them. Hagai Tamir's refusal belongs to a different family of refusal. Hagai Tamir could not vocalize his refusal. He told the army that something went wrong and that he had to drop his ammunition in the sea.

I had asked Hagai to bring his photo albums to our first meeting. I looked carefully at his family history

these figures do they think they have learned anything about him." Antoine de Saint-Exupéry, *The Little Prince* (London: Egmont, 2002), pp. 15–16.

and I asked him if I could film him. He said no, but he accepted that I use only the parts of the story that he had evoked in the Israeli press. He did not want to give me more privileges than whatever was mentioned about his refusal in his own country. And I respected that.

When I made the film and I invited him to come to Venice to look at the installation, the moment was charged, at least emotionally. That was our second meeting. I met his wife Judith and a few of his friends. I had told him there was a seat dedicated to him in the middle of the Lebanon Pavilion, and that I would consider the installation as incomplete until he sits there.

Following our second meeting, the Israeli TV channel Channel 1 dedicated a debate to refusing army orders, taking *Refusing Pilot* as a starting point. A reporter went and interviewed Hagai upon his return from Venice and asked him about his refusal and the film. There, he said: "I still feel that I did not do what I should have done. I should have come out of my own bubble, not only in refusing that I engage with something like this myself, but I should have spoken out loud and clearly on the radio saying that this target should not be bombed." Saying something like this is a gift to any artist, to any political activist, because it proves that we as artists, within the very loosely defined art sphere, are sometimes able to do things that diplomats cannot do. And I am not saying that we achieved a lot. What we have achieved is only and simply planting seeds for the future. While looking at history, one day people would realize that Lebanese and Israeli individuals have been meeting and discussing shared history. This is really essential at war. Gaining mutual confidence between an Israeli and a Lebanese person means you have elevated yourselves above day-to-day politics, especially the politics of boycott. The idea of the boycott, whether it is BDS or Russia, or any kind of boycott, is blind.

RHJ: Do I understand it correctly that you would make a clear differentiation between boycotting and refusing?

AZ: Yes, they are two different things. Refusing an order is a single instance, where you say NO to a request that is addressed to you and that's against your personal ethics or beliefs in a context that is expecting you to obey. Boycotting is saying NO in advance to any offer from a specific party or community until that party or community changes positions seen as unethical or as an unjustified aggression or simply as illegal. Boycotting is a way to change an equation where individuals have leverage power. Refusing an order is simply not wanting to take part in an act that one sees as criminal. Therefore, refusing is a way to disengage from a collective hysterical or criminal act. This is why Hagai's refusal did not change history; the army sent another plane to bomb the school, and I mention in the film the day my father took me and my brother to take pictures of the school after it had been bombed.

Dealing with the politics of boycott is not at all easy. Think of Germany, where BDS is illegal,[12] but the calls to sanction Russia aren't. You could face difficulties if you

12 On May 17, 2019, the German Parliament voted with a broad majority in favor of a motion, formulated by the political parties CDU/CSU, SPD, FDP, and BÜNDNIS 90/DIE GRÜNEN, to label the international BDS movement as an entity that is unacceptable because it uses anti-Semitic argumentations and methods. See https://www.bundestag.de/dokumente/textarchiv/2019/kw20-de-bds-642892 (accessed December 6, 2022). The vote in favor of this motion has led to decisions, especially in the cultural sector, concerning who can be invited to publicly funded projects. Several initiatives voiced their critique towards the decision of the German Parliament, such as the *Initiative GG 5.3 Weltoffenheit* who published plaidoyer in December 2020, referring to article 5, paragraph 3 of the German Basic Law which guarantees the freedom of arts and sciences, see https://www.gg53weltoffenheit.org/plaedoyer/ (accessed December 6, 2022), and a group of activists called *Bundestag 3 for Palestine (BT3P)* who have sued the German Parliament, equally stating that its anti-BDS decision is violating the constitutional right to freedom of expression and that it hinders human rights work in Germany, see https://www.bt3p.org/en/home (accessed December 6, 2022).

are part of BDS, but not when you call or lobby for sanctioning Russia or call for boycotting its cultural products. If you are boycotting any contact between people from two enemy states, how do you imagine resolving their conflict? I do not believe in boycott because I want to use my mind. I want to be able to decide if I want to engage in something or not, each time. I am not part of any boycott. Otherwise, I would not have done *Refusing Pilot*, because I would not have allowed myself to seek a meeting with Hagai. I would not have talked to Avi Mograbi. We have changed each other since we have met and this is what humanism is. And I would not want to deny others that possibility of change.

RHJ: I think that is definitely a very strong takeaway from *Refusing Pilot* and your work in general: the strive towards unmaking not only history but also the differentiations between friends and enemies. Being confronted with so many images of war again and again, I am also wondering how, apart from engaging with people through speech, you think one can unmake these differentiations through visuals? What can be a visual method of dealing with war without repeating the violence, and with the aim to enable people to undo their perceptions of enemies?

AZ: My work is driven by emotions, not by the causes I support around me, and not by any burden of representation. I am not an activist. Despite the political situation plotted in *Refusing Pilot*, I do not try to promote my position. I mean, I promote it indirectly by making it visible through a narrative that looks like poetry. It's because the art sphere, for me, is not a court, where you debate a case. What I learned from Camus is that the tone with which you speak to the world is your imprint. Whether you use a still camera, or a moving camera, whether you use a *cinéma vérité* style or another style in a film, is really beside the point. And therefore, I cannot answer your question in a general way. There is no formula for making work. There is a position, where you come from. And all the rest is about your baggage, your training in seizing a situation and the complexity with which you can speak about the world. These are the key issues in making art work for me.

RHJ: But how did you find your poetry, your visual language?

AZ: In *Refusing Pilot,* there are three important visual axes. One is vertical: the camera starts from a floor and all of a sudden you are lifted up into the sky within seconds. This vertical axis is established from scene one. It is the axis that a bomb will take to go down from an airplane, too. It is also the axis that the kids take while going to the roof to fly their paper planes. I am interested in establishing the axes of my movements from the beginning. There is a circular movement somewhere in the middle of the film. It is almost like your belly button, your center of gravity. I see the sculpture by Lebanese sculptor Alfred Basbous that is placed in the middle of the garden of the school as its heart. It is the center of gravity around which the camera turns. That sculpture is the first art piece I ever saw in my life. And in the film, you see pictures of me standing next to it as a kid. The third axis is a horizontal one, expressed in the panning or straight tracking. And, of course, there is a seat, the cinema seat dedicated to Hagai. As you know, Israelis cannot come to Lebanon and Lebanese people cannot go to Israel. But I wanted to have Hagai figure in my installation. This is why I dedicated a cinema seat to him inside the Lebanese Pavilion. Have you seen any pictures of the Lebanese Pavilion?

RHJ: Yes.

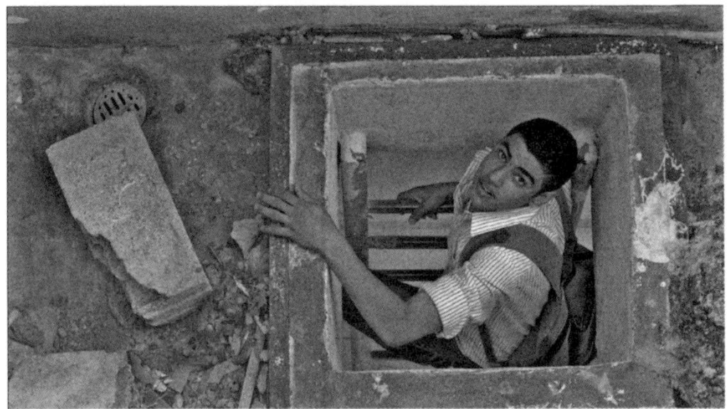

Fig. 3: Akram Zaatari, *Letter to a Refusing Pilot,* 2013, HD video, 34 min, film still.

AZ: There is a cinema seat that turns its back to the main film, this is an old seat coming from an old movie theater. And I told Hagai: "When you decide to come to Venice, I will send a photographer to take your pictures."

RHJ: On that seat?

AZ: On that seat, yes. The moment he sits on that seat is to me a metaphor of entering Lebanon. He is officially in the Lebanese Pavilion watching my photographs of 1982 unfold through a 16mm projection. His back faces the large cinema screen, and he is looking at a smaller screen showing a 16mm film which is an animation of the photograph of the first air raids that I took in my life using my father's camera. It is called Kiev, by the way, imagine! This is my first camera and "Kiev" is engraved on its viewfinder. It might have been made there, I presume, at the times of the Soviet Union. So, Kiev gave me the tool through which I documented the Israeli bombs falling in front of our house. That thought makes me want to cry today. I do not wish to see this happening in the world anymore.

The film is about refusing to engage in the destruction of the world and its civilization. It connects with architecture as the science of building, a discipline dedicated to the reverse of destruction. You become an architect to build. You do not become an architect to learn to excel in destruction. I always tell Hagai: "Your first architectural project is not the project that you built first, but your refusal to bomb a school. Is this not beautiful?" And I try to tell architecture students all the time: "Your mission is way beyond making interesting bedrooms and beautiful toilets. Your larger mission is to promote building as opposed to destroying." This is the film's mission basically. It is a portrait of a school addressed to someone who had refused to bomb it. Even when it was still bombed following his refusal.

RHJ: But his refusal changed things in history because there were more pilots that followed his example. As you said, he became part of a movement that became visible only later.

AZ: The refuseniks movement did not stop Israel from aggressing its neighbors continuously and expanding in size over the years. But it allowed us, on the other side of the border, to hear a minority voice. We were interested in refuseniks without them being interested in us. They were interested in ensuring the army's ethical conduct. But in the rare instances when a refusenik met people from the other side, it created, not an alliance, but some kind of link across a sealed border, call it—*rapprochement*—a coming closer between people who think in similar ways and who are not ready to submit to the blindness of boycott. I cannot be blind to their existence. I would want to establish a conversation. I would want to discuss. I would want to talk further.

RHJ: I wondered what would be different if you made a work around refusal today. After listening to you, I

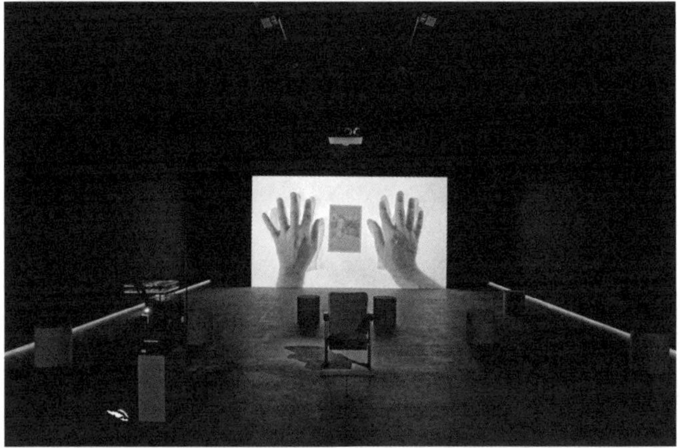

Fig. 4: Akram Zaatari, *Letter to a Refusing Pilot*, 2013, HD video and 16mm installation. Installation view: The National Pavilion of the Republic of Lebanon at the 55th International Art Exhibition – Biennale Arte, Venice. Photo: Marco Milan.

guess you would make it the same way as you did back then?

AZ: Absolutely. Whoever is unhappy with injustice in the world today needs to bet on shared fate. You cannot achieve peace through war. Many tried it in the history of humankind. They thought they could declare war to enforce peace. It's nonsense. More wars will not make the world warless. I mean, within a week, Europe has a war in its center! How did we get there?

If I were to do it again, I would do the film in the same way. This work has expanded beyond what it meant as a film, and because *Letter to a Refusing Pilot* started three years before it was made, namely with my conversation with Avi Mograbi. I still find both works stimulating today, and I am so proud of them because I succeeded in making my ethical position override my hesitations and fears. I had to silence all the fears in myself, believe in the work and act towards its completion with no fear.

Disappearance and Remembrance

In the Aftermath of Violence

On Being Present and Calling Into Presence

Diana Taylor in conversation with Sebastián Eduardo Dávila and Ulrike Jordan

Sebastián Eduardo Dávila/Ulrike Jordan: In the books that you have written throughout the past twenty-five years[1] there is a recurring topic: enforced disappearance, mostly in the Latin American context. In *Disappearing Acts* you already raise the sensitive question of how to position oneself, as a writer and a researcher, towards those disappeared and their families, which is a question we have been discussing as well, though from a very different context than the ones you are writing about. How do you think about the issue of disappearance and the question of positionality? In other words: How to relate to this form of violence that doesn't affect oneself directly?

Diana Taylor: The topic of disappearance has been with me my entire life. It is not that you think differently about it over time, but different dimensions and aspects come up when you think about it in relation to the specific cases that you are working on and the people you are working with. Although for us Latin Americans and Latin Americanists it is a constant issue, I think it is for everybody. We just have to understand our history in a different way so that we know that this is so. Who had and has to disappear so that the powerful can have the

1 See Diana Taylor, *Disappearing Acts: Spectacles of Gender and Nationalism in Argentina's "Dirty War"* (Durham, N.C. and London: Duke University Press, 1997); Diana Taylor, *The Archive and the Repertoire: Performing Cultural Memory in the Americas* (Durham, N.C. and London: Duke University Press, 2003); Diana Taylor, *¡Presente! The Politics of Presence* (Durham, N.C. and London: Duke University Press, 2020).

life they think they deserve? Is it Native Americans? The poor? Migrants? It is very dangerous to believe that violence is only taking place elsewhere. We take comfort in this belief but it's wrong. When I am in the United States for instance, Mexico seems like the most violent place on earth, and when I am in Mexico it feels the other way around. This way violence always seems to be displaced. So, when I am writing or speaking about violence "elsewhere" it is with a sense of responsibility, of disquieting mutuality. Are my tax dollars paying for the military equipment that the United States exports to conflict areas? Is my lack of awareness or attention contributing to the assaults on minoritarian communities? Are my choices about where to send my children to school or go on vacation further cementing Anglo-European privilege and self-centeredness? Are my eating habits contributing to the everyday devastation of animals and our environment? I may not think I "experience" violence, but my role as citizen and consumer helps perpetuate it.

UJ/SED: Your chapter "Tortuous Routes: Four Walks through Villa Grimaldi" in your recent book *¡Presente!* is but one example of your engagement with practices of connecting violence and its victims with the very places where violence took place. This relates both to official memory sites like Villa Grimaldi, that functioned as a detention and torture center during the Augusto Pinochet dictatorship in Chile, but also everyday places. In your account of your recurring visits to Villa Grimaldi, you describe the different ways in which memory is evoked and remembrance is activated therein: through the differing accounts of a survivor, an educational center, and in information panels. You also mention how you experience the place anew during each visit. With regard to the significance of the place itself we wondered whether you think these sites can transmit information *as sites*, and what role a guide or witness/survivor plays in order to understand their significance and history.

DT: This is one of the questions that keeps me going back to that place. I keep swearing to myself I will never go back, but I do. One of the reasons has to do with what you were mentioning earlier, the positionality of those who write about violence without being directly affected by it, which is something that I brought up in *Disappearing Acts*. Those are central questions for me. I begin the chapter with an account of the torture survivor and now guide Pedro Matta who started speaking to me in English during his tour. When I told him I am from Mexico he changed languages. He had an audience in mind, but I was not that particular audience. That made me wonder: who are these places for? Who is being asked to do what in these spaces? The first time I met Matta, I realized he is a very compelling guide. He begins the tour in a very objective manner and then gets more and more personal. He really draws you in. There is a moment where he breaks down and cries, it is very moving. As a performance studies scholar I was very interested in that as a performance as well as a form of testimony. Telling his testimony again and again, he becomes a sort of professional survivor. There is something very suspect about this, because we do not have categories for what he is doing. His telling oscillates between a performance, which is supposedly not truthful to what he is actually feeling, and the heartfelt account of a survivor. This oscillation is repeated again and again during each tour. How to understand this? Maybe as both/and—it is a performance, and it is testimony. As a survivor of torture, in my view, Matta compartmentalized his experience so he could continue to live. I think that is a way of containing the trauma, a way of managing it without having it crush him. By consciously reenacting the experience of violence as part of the "tour" he decides when and where to engage the brutal memories rather than re-experience torture as traumatic flashback, for example, every time anew. I kept going back to Villa Grimaldi, because I was trying to understand how to understand, as it were. Can I understand by being there, with this person? Or does the place itself help me understand? Will I ever understand?

One of the most interesting visits was when I was there with one of the other survivors, Teresa Anativia. We had gone to other places where she had been detained, such as the Estadio Nacional where they had tortured and killed protesters and dissidents after the coup in 1973. She pointed out the exact spot where certain terrifying acts of violence took place. In Villa Grimaldi, she told me, she was trying to remember, there were no spatial markers left. What was once the elegant nineteenth century Villa Grimaldi had become the torture center. Then, to destroy the evidence, it had been torn down by Pinochet's family, who planned to build condominiums there. The buildings had been destroyed and Anativia could not figure out where she was. She told me something remarkable: the survivors who had gathered in Villa Grimaldi when it was recuperated as a memory site did not recognize each other. As prisoners, they had never seen each other. They had always been blindfolded. So years later, when they met again, they closed their eyes and spoke. And then they knew, they recognized who they were. She said that they hugged each other almost in silence and with their eyes closed. It was like a "reunión de ciegos," an encounter among blind people. I asked her what she felt being back there. And she said: "Nothing. This is not the place," because it had been so transformed. And then she said: "But my bones hurt." Her body knew.

SED/UJ: There is a similar sentence in *¡Presente!* that we found very revealing: "The torture site is transitional, but torture itself is transformative."[2] So if the places where violence took place may change over time, the effect that violence has on the body irreversibly transforms it, it leaves a mark on it. Needless to say, this ten-

2 Taylor, *¡Presente!*, p. 185.

sion between the bodily experience of violence and the traces that violence leaves in space is present wherever something like torture or disappearance has taken place, be it an official military building, a street, or a desert.

DT: The ways in which certain sites become memorial sites and others don't depend on multiple factors. Horrible things have happened on every square inch of our earth. Why decide to commemorate this and not that? Why out of the 800 torture centers that existed in Chile does Villa Grimaldi hold its iconic status? Or why ESMA,[3] for example, in Argentina? Why Auschwitz as opposed to all the other places in which Nazis exterminated human beings? This tendency to memorialize, to encapsulate, to single places out from the rest—as if that was possible—is interesting. Because you cannot separate it out. In Argentina, but in Chile too, the sites of terror were everywhere: in department stores, in schools, in garages. The idea of containing memory in specific sites like museums and statues is also a way of detaching remembrance from our everyday lives. It makes us, again as citizens and consumers, feel safely out of the picture, and thus not responsible. Parts of these official attempts to memorialize are also real attempts to forget.

UJ/SED: There was a very similar discussion about the Memorial to the Murdered Jews of Europe in Berlin. Critics made the point that by building a centralized memorial the German people would be liberated from actively remembering the many instances and places of violence and terror of the Shoah.

A question that comes up for us in relation to your accounts of the visits at Villa Grimaldi is whether you think the sites where (state) terror took place need some

3 During the military dictatorship in Argentina between 1976 and 1983, the Escuela de Mecanica de la Armada (Higher School of Navy Mechanics) served as a clandestine detention center, where around 5,000 so-called subversives were tortured and murdered.

sort of activation by survivors, or others that feel responsible for giving an account of what has happened, in order to become meaningful sites of remembrance? Can they function as sites in their own terms, or do they need other forms of presence and interaction to enable moments where one can really commemorate or put oneself in relation to the history of the site?

DT: In one of my books I wrote "trauma lives in the body, not in the archive."[4] Our pain is in our bodies and so to remember and to be able to acknowledge what has happened is something that takes place in our bodies and not in archives. However, official memory sites also function as archival places, and this is an important function of course, an access point to the past. For example, I was not alive at the time of some of the worst lynchings of Black people in the United States or Mexicans in the Southwest United States in the nineteenth century. I came to the United States in 1980. But I know those histories because I have read about them, because there is archival material, because there are songs like *Strange Fruit* by Billie Holiday and many other artistic representations. The same way that there are many accounts about the Shoah. There is a lot about Pinochet's Chile. There is a lot about Argentina during the dictatorship and so forth. If you know that and then go to a place, you are bringing what you think you know there and then that gets transformed over time. The archive enters into interaction with the body. That is what I am trying to do in that chapter in the *¡Presente!* book: it is an account of how all those repeated visits actually changed me. They changed me and they changed what I knew or what I had thought I knew over time. In my first meeting with Matta I said: "I am from Mexico, this has nothing to do with me." And at the end of my last meeting with him, where I volunteered to translate his tour from Spanish

4 Taylor, *¡Presente!*, p. 201.

into English, I understood how much it had to do with me. I understood that in a way, I am a professional witness. In the book it reads "He [Matta] might be a professional survivor, but I am not a professional witness. And, yet, of course, I am."[5] It's that acknowledgment that hurts me and that gets me so angry. Through his language I have absorbed his story in my own body. So it is also my story now, like the Dori Laub observation that "listeners become co-owners" of the story. The goal of all of these sites is to make us co-owners of these histories, in effect saying "Yes, this is also your history. You have inherited this history." While we are not responsible for what happened there, then, we are responsible for how we act on that knowledge in the here and now. Do we perpetuate the violence implicitly or explicitly? Or do we do everything in our power to move towards a more just and sustainable world? The fact that we were not there at the moment that the violence happened in any one of these sites does not mean that we are not coparticipants in these traumas.

SED/UJ: There is a double movement at many points in your texts; the simultaneity of presence and absence, of being there and not being there. And in a way it is inherent to the practice of writing as well. On the one hand, to write means to make something visible, but it can also serve to hide that which is left unwritten, for example the perspective of victims or survivors in official historical accounts. In this way, it is an exposure, but it can also serve as an instrument of violence. How do you think about the limits of writing, for example in relation to what you call the repertoire? The repertoire brings to the fore practices other than written texts, in your own words in *The Archive and the Repertoire*: "performances, gestures, orality, movement, dance, singing—in short,

5 Ibid., p. 200.

all those acts usually thought of as ephemeral, nonreproducible knowledge."[6]

DT: The "repertoire" as I define it transmits social memory, cultural identity, and attitudes that get passed on through bodies. How did the survivors of Villa Grimaldi recognize each other? Through the sound of their voices. They heard each other through whispers. They heard the screams of the torture sessions. They knew and transmitted much that then goes on to form part of the official, archival record. Trauma, too, lives in the body and is transmitted through behavioral issues, "reenactments," flashbacks, nightmares, and other forms of repeats, experienced in the here and now. How do we communicate or understand if we side-line the acts that are the repertoire? Silencing voices and testimonies means disappearing an invaluable source of memory and knowledge. This embodied form of transmission is crucial, and not just for communities in which meaning-making does not pass through print culture.

Let me go back to what I meant by collective trauma that concerns most of us in our countries—certainly in Germany, certainly in Guatemala, certainly in Mexico, certainly in the US and certainly right now in Canada, where they are in a state of national mourning, because they are finally beginning to understand the nature of the violence that their citizens committed against Indigenous people. They are finally beginning to assume responsibility, which has never happened in the United States by the way. They have never owned the brutality of slavery either. These things that get transmitted are all part of the repertoire. They are part of us. They are part of the way that we interact with people, of the struggle of coming to terms with what happened before we were born, and in the societies which we were born into.

6 Taylor, *The Archive and the Repertoire*, p. 20.

In regard to writing, I remember trying to think through all the different kinds of writing about disappearance, about the writing that the officials do, the "Nunca más" reports in Argentina, the writing that survivors of disappearance do, then the fictionalized versions. There are many different ways of writing and trying to write through. Some are confessional and some are more reparative, trying to work through some aspects of that trauma. Some are more artistic in the sense that they are trying to reach out to those who do not know what happened and get them involved to become co-participants of these traumas. Writing helps us to a certain degree to communicate. But it absolutely cannot communicate everything the bodies do. In other words, bodies have the capacity to transmit memories and knowledge, for example of traumatic events from the past, in a different way than written or spoken accounts. They exceed narrative. And so there are aspects that get transmitted through the body that cannot be transmitted through text.

UJ/SED: We would like to shift the conversation to the question of representation, which is often at stake when speaking about disappeared people. The families of the victims or friends or activists have to re-invoke the presence of the disappeared, obviously, because the people themselves cannot be there anymore. They are absent. In *Disappearing Acts*, on the one hand, you mention these representations of the disappeared as being very fragile and difficult, because in a way, you have to repeat or re-invoke a certain form of violence when you describe what has happened to them. On the other hand, there is a necessity and urgency of speaking about that violence in order to raise awareness and make political demands. There is a fragile tension between these two aspects. You used the terms "acuerpar" (roughly translatable as "to make it part of your body," or "to put a body alongside someone else's") and "hermanarse" ("becoming siblings") in your book *¡Presente!*, which you describe as

strategies of learning from a situation by living through it and building trust with each other. But you also say that there are limits to these strategies. How are these practices of connecting affected by different degrees of involvement?

DT: These are strategies that I have learned through different practices. In theater acting, an actor takes on a part, and can "acuerpar" (give body to) the character. This is a technique in which you yourself can become this other person. But that is not what I mean when I want to accompany someone, emotionally or politically. I am not them, and I have not experienced their loss or pain. When I started working with the Mothers of Plaza de Mayo in Argentina,[7] walking around the Plaza de Mayo demanding that their disappeared children be brought back alive by the military—I understand this as "social drama" as Victor Turner and Richard Schechner called it.[8] These are national dramas, international dramas. It is not something that is aesthetic and limited to the stage. Social actors, such as "mothers," make a scene on a national stage, metaphorically. And if we care it's about some kind of empathy. Empathy is very hard to write about, because it is usually misunderstood. People think about it in terms of taking on somebody else's feelings. Some people say it is about appropriating somebody else's sorrow. I do not see it that way at all. And there are some major biologists who think the same way, as for example Frans De Waal.[9] I turned to

7 "Madres de la Plaza de Mayo" is an organization formed by mothers during the Argentinian dictatorship with the original aim to reclaim the appearance of their children, detained and disappeared by the state. After the dictatorship, they keep fighting for the legal prosecution of the perpetrators of these crimes against humanity.

8 See Victor Turner, *From Ritual to Theatre: The Human Seriousness of Play* (New York: Performing Arts Journal, 1982) and Richard Schechner, *Between Theater and Anthropology* (Philadelphia: University of Pennsylvania Press, 1985).

9 See Frans de Waal, *The Age of Empathy: Nature's Lessons for a Kinder Society* (New York: Harmony Books, 2009).

them because I think the answer I am looking for when thinking about "acuerpamiento" goes more along what these biologists are saying than what critical theorists say. For instance, if you have a dog or a cat and you are sick the animal comes and stays there with you. The animal knows that there is something going on and wants to comfort you. It is not feeling what you are feeling, but it can sense your need for comfort. Animals, and therefore we as animals, have this capacity to sense what another animal is feeling. So the feeling of being with these women who had lost their children and who were out on the street was incredible, and I felt I could sense their pain and injury in some way. Seeing it mobilized for social justice at the same time was transformative for me. So "acuerparnos" means "I am putting my body alongside yours, I will follow you in the protest movement." When I write about my work with migrant populations on their migrant trail it means "I am walking beside you." "Hermanarnos" is to say "you are like my brother or my sister." It is a quality of care; "I care what happens to you." It is not identical to me putting on a role or me being you. It is not identification. Those two things allow for the fact of difference. I am a very privileged person: I live and work in New York and I can fly down to Guatemala if I want to. I am not walking on that migrant trail. But these practices and strategies allow me to walk beside others and care about what happens to them. So it is more of an ethical position.

SED/UJ: When thinking about places or the topography of violence, ethical positions are equally relevant. We can of course go on describing and say that places always need mediation, because they do not speak for themselves. But we can also urge ourselves and each other to take on that mediation; we can ask ourselves if we do want to make these places speak, and how to do so. And of course we know that there are limits to our acts. In this sense, not only the figure of the co-walker but the very practice of walking along makes sense to us, as an activity with an open end. We cannot forget however the privilege that this decision entails, but that should not keep us from walking along.

DT: Yes, without negating these other realities. In *Epistemologies from the South*, Boaventura de Sousa Santos distinguishes between two sides of an abyssal line.[10] On the one side, there are those (humans and nonhumans) who have been disappeared or violated through acts such as torture or dispossession, and on the other side there are those of us who haven't suffered that. I am not from the side of the line (in this case that of the Mothers) who have suffered disposseśion. But my thinking, like Santos', is on their side of the line. So I make a distinction about where my politics and my ethical commitments are. Are they on the side of the dispossessed—the women and men who are getting tortured? Or the migrants who undertake a death-defying terrible journey to offer their loved ones a safe future? I have to accompany, that is my ethical responsibility, and it is our responsibility as academics and I would argue as citizens. To go back to an earlier point: I may not be responsible for the violence that created these brutal situations, but I am responsible for doing everything I can to put an end to the brutality. We have an obligation to stand up and to take sides. This is part of what I mean with being "presentes." I quote Hannah Arendt who said that Plato was the first to distinguish between those who *know* and those who *do*.[11] I want to break down that distinction, because in fact, you cannot separate the knowing from the doing. Ignorance is also a kind of doing, it is a decision that one makes. To say "I do not want to know" is to say "I do not care." My academic work is part of my doing, and as such cannot be sepa-

10 Boaventura de Sousa Santos, *Epistemologies of the South: Justice Against Epistemicide* (London and New York: Routledge, 2016).
11 Hannah Arendt, *The Human Condition* (New York: Doubleday Anchor, 1959), p. 223.

rated from the work that I am doing with the communities I work with: with the Mothers or with the migrants or with artists like Regina Galindo and others. Therefore, to do research cannot be separated from the task of walking and talking along these actors and communities. This understanding of doing is also relevant for the most basic definition of performance, namely as a doing.

UJ/SED: We were wondering about the specific status of art, and of practice, in the art practices you dealt with, for example by Regina José Galindo. How do these practices relate to activism, and to theory?

DT: Art depends on or is always in the realm of the imagination. You have to envision something else, something that does not exist. Therein lays the potentiality of art to have an impact on life. It is this ability to imagine things otherwise, to transform, that makes artistic practices so important. If we cannot imagine a world that is different or relationships that are different, how can we do anything different? The work of Regina Galindo is a great example. In her performance *Earth* that I analyze in *¡Presente!*, she puts her fragile body on the edge of a pit that is being dug out by a huge excavator. What she makes visible with this seemingly simple performance is the historical violence of biopower, from the times of the Conquest and coloniality to the present practice of neo-liberal extractivism.

SED/UJ: Yes, watching it is almost a physical experience, because you feel the vulnerability, the exposure of the body. It is a very strong work that operates on many levels, on a very immediate physical one but also on the symbolic level by evoking such a powerful image. An image that refers to the practice of dumping people into mass graves during the Internal Armed Conflict in Guatemala, but that may also evoke other contexts because of some generalizable elements: the pit, the naked body,

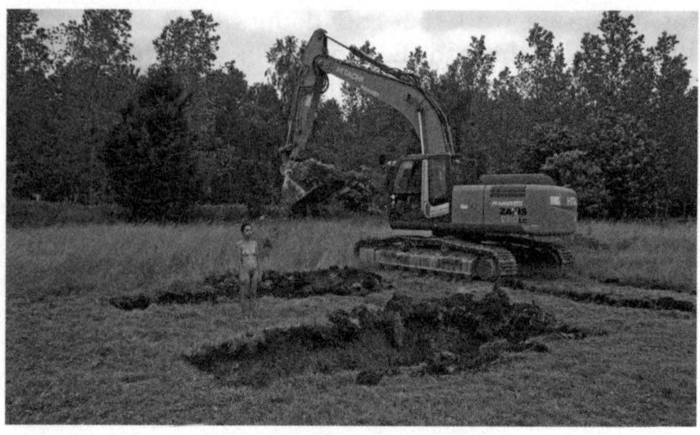

Fig. 1: Regina José Galindo, *Earth* (Les Moulins, 2013), performance, courtesy of the artist.

the digging machine. Using one of your terms, these different elements are part of a scenario.

When trying to compare or relate different contexts that do not seem to have a direct connection at first, we found the notion of the scenario instructive. As we understand your use of the concept, it is not about establishing causal correlations between different places, nor about applying one term onto them, top-down, but about bringing them together as scenarios, making unexpected and structural connections visible that you would not see otherwise. How did you come up with this concept, and have you also experienced its limits as a tool for understanding entanglements?

DT: When I started writing about the scenario, everything was talked about in terms of narrative. Accounts of torture or trauma for example were seen as narratives. I could not sit with that, because I thought that the narrative couldn't do justice to what happened to the bodies involved. A narrative is basically a description through words. It leaves out a lot of things that are absolutely essential. Scenarios are "plots" but they are enacted, not told. Scenario, as I define it, is "an act of transfer, as a paradigm that is formulaic, portable, repeatable, and often banal because it leaves out complexity, reduces conflict to its stock elements, and encourages fantasies of participation."[12] So when I talk about "discovery acts" by Christopher Columbus and others, I try to think about all those bodies that the narratives of discovery leave out. To leave them out is a form of disappearance. It is very easy to narratively disappear things or humans: "people watched from the sidelines" for example. People? What people? Men? Women? Indigenous people? These are issues that you have to take more seriously if you are actually thinking about bodies and space. The concept of scenario originally came from the *Commedia dell'arte*, where the plot, and the list of things that *had* to happen were pinned to the back of the curtain on the stage. Everything else was improvised. Scenarios account for these different elements, but they allow for improvisation and different endings and humor and all of these subtexts. In theater you can communicate without saying anything. It is not in the text or the narrative but in the bodies. It seemed to me that scenarios allow us to see a lot more in terms of what I was referring to with the repertoire and the communicative capacity of bodies than a narrative. A narrative is already scripted, it eliminates a lot of options and choices. You could put different scenarios together, you could put a conquest scenario next to a scenario of national liberation.

UJ/SED: So scenarios are not just an analytical category but refer to very concrete contexts of historical violence. We also wondered about the risks of bringing different scenarios together, for example by means of comparison. Is it possible to compare violent acts that have taken place in very specific social and historical contexts?

12 Taylor, *The Archive and the Repertoire*, p. 54.

DT: I think it is very risky to do comparative work. I prefer the idea of connective work rather than comparative work. For example, you cannot compare what happened in Argentina and Chile and Mexico during the seventies and eighties using the same parameters—concluding for instance that Pinochet "only" killed around 3,000 people and in Argentina they killed 30,000. Because Pinochet tortured one out of eight Chileans. So the terror tactics of each context were very different and you cannot compare them. But they are connected because they were all part of Plan Condor that was devised in the Escuela de las Americas as a way to "fight communism" in the seventies.[13] Plan Condor was put together in the sixties. Guatemala and Nicaragua were basically also destroyed in this battle against communism, so these strategies were hemispheric. The CIA was involved. In the case of Brazil, if an Argentinian "subversive" was found, he would be sent back to Argentina, because like Argentina, Brazil was also involved in Plan Condor. These were all connected histories. They may have had different effects in different places but the politics and the connections are very clear. This is how I would approach the issue, rather than simply comparing these countries. Why did we have dictatorships in Brazil, Argentina, Chile, Uruguay and many other countries throughout this whole zone during this period? This was a strategy to make sure that communism was defeated, and anybody who supported it even intellectually was going to be disappeared.

SED/UJ: Moving from the question of the perpetrators and the state terror to the side of the protest against it, your notion of traumatic memes provides a useful model to grasp how certain forms of protest are related,

13 Plan Condor was a political campaign implemented by right wing dictatorships in Latin America and backed by the United States. It encompassed repressive operations against political opponents including their assassination.

neither in a genealogical sense, nor in a direct mimetic one. You point out that it's impossible to devise a certain point of origin, and yet these forms reappear in different contexts. Could you tell us a little bit more about how you conceptualize this? How do these traumatic memes, as you call them, operate?

DT: The difference between memetic and mimetic came to me when I was thinking about a photograph I saw of the Mothers in El Salvador. They were using very similar forms of protest as the Mothers in Argentina so I asked them if they knew about the Mothers of Plaza de Mayo and they said no. So how do these things get transmitted? I realized it is not mimetic. If they had seen the Mothers in Argentina walking around it would have been mimetic: I am going to do the same. But the transfer had taken place by means I could not see or identify. There was no trace of how the Central American Mothers had come up with the same strategy of the scarves, placards, and photographs of their disappeared children. I asked Central American librarians to help me: where is the connection between these Mothers at this time and the Mothers in Plaza de Mayo? The only thing that we could come up with was that maybe the women had heard about something on the radio. So how do those ideas travel? They do so as memes. When you see these memes you know what they are. For example, photographer Susan Meiselas gave me a photograph of a mother holding a small photo of her son from Kurdistan in her hand. You do not know where it is necessarily, but you know what it means.

UJ/SED: It is interesting to see how certain forms of protest bear similarity across different global contexts, as they grow out of a very concrete political necessity. In the German context, in response to a series of right-wing terrorist murders, the families of the victims and activists have employed strategies of saying their names and telling their histories in order to make their individual existence visible and not focusing only on the perpetrators. They are commemorating them as the individuals they were, insisting that their lives are not expendable as they are very often perceived in Germany's racist climate.

DT: It is so important. Those practices have traveled everywhere, they are contagious, #SayHerName in the US and in Mexico the Ayotzinapa 43 protests.[14] I think that you are right that the focus on the families and on the individuals who have been lost is so much more productive. That does not mean you do not have to go after the perpetrators. But you have to get public opinion on your side, and on that of the survivors. And that is what the Mothers were able to do. It is the Mothers who were able to change public opinion in Argentina. The fact that these unarmed, middle-aged women were out on the streets in 1977, at the height of the Dirty War, was crucial. All the "guerrilleros" were either underground or had left the country or were dead/disappeared. But the Mothers kept going out and the only thing that protected them was their "vulnerability," the fact that they were mothers, that they were unarmed. It is very powerful how they are using their bodies and these familiar relationships. "These are our kids" they say. And yet the socialization of families and motherhood goes beyond narrow notions of kinship—you do not have to be family to be concerned or engaged. I think that made a huge political difference and it did change public opinion.

14 #SayHerName is a social movement that started in 2015 to protest police brutality committed against Black women in the United States. Ayotzinapa 43 refers to the 43 students from a college in Ayotzinapa (Guerrero, Mexico), who were forcibly disappeared in 2014 by the local police in collaboration with organized crime while they were traveling on a bus to take part in the commemoration of the massacre of students committed by the state in 1968 in the Plaza de las Tres Culturas (Mexico City). After their disappearance, the number 43 has become the symbol for the protest against these crimes.

Marivi Véliz

Feeling Presences: Regina José Galindo's Acts of Becoming Someone Else, Something Else

Necropolitics That Fall Upon Women's Bodies

Patricia Samayoa was a well-known feminist, who worked for fourteen years at the Women's Office of the municipality of Guatemala. She was in charge of coordinating several programs, which frequently meant visiting dangerous neighborhoods. Minutes before her death on June 3, 2014, she quickly ended what became her final phone call because she was afraid of being assaulted and robbed while using a mobile phone in the streets. She then entered a pharmacy in the city's downtown where the security guard shot and killed her. The accident shocked society, particularly feminist organizations, and artistic and intellectual groups, who quickly expressed their anger because of the lack of media coverage and the police's inefficacy. After assassinating Patricia, the security guard remained entrenched in the pharmacy for several hours and continued to shoot aimlessly even when the victim's friends and family, the police, and members of the security company that employed him had already arrived at the scene. Patricia Samayoa had been exiled in Costa Rica during the 1980s, the cruelest years of the civil war in Guatemala (1960–1996), and later returned to the country where she began working with women affected by poverty and violence. Having survived the apparently most hazardous periods of violence during the war and the steady threat that working within violent communities involves, she ended up being violently assassinated by a security guard who later stated he thought that she was an attacker. The pharmacy's attendants noted that the guard had seemed nervous the entire day. He was later revealed to be schizophrenic and, since 2012, a patient at the National Psychiatry Hospital. How could a security company have employed someone with that type of mental disorder?

In order to become a private security guard in Guatemala, every candidate is supposed to take a course and understand the legal framework regarding private security companies as well as have general knowledge about human rights, basic use of arms, and take psychological exams. Most of the security companies, however, are not legally registered, and the government seems to have no control over who is employed by these private security companies nor over the weapons they use. Shield Security, the employer of the guard who murdered Patricia Samayoa, was later found to force their employees to work twenty-three-hour shifts without any breaks. Moreover, it only had twelve supervisors for 45,000 guards and did not control the number of arms in their employees' possession, as well as committing many other irregularities. The majority of the security guards do not have basic employment benefits and often pay for the required training course—if taken at all—out of their own pockets, in order to gain employment.[1] The judicial process initiated by Patricia's daughter, Andrea Carrillo, has sought to condemn these practices, at the

1 See Marco Antonio Avendaño, "Vivir con temor de quienes protegen: Las anomalías de la seguridad privada,"September 12, 2020, *Ciclos de Actualización para Periodistas*, https://cicloscap.com/vivir-con-temor-de-quienes-protegen-las-anomalias-de-la-seguridad-privada/ (accessed June 22, 2022).

same time pointing out that they are embedded in state-promoted necropolitics.

Achille Mbembe proposed the concept of necropolitics, not to reject the notion of biopolitics as the administration of life, but to show its underside as the state's power to put to death, particularly as it becomes transnational, and defends enclave economies over a rights-assuring national sovereignty. These enclaves are, following Mbembe, mainly tied to mineral extraction and are the privileged spaces for war and death *par excellence*. Around them, armies, private militias, and private security firms emerge with a strong link to the state, which often turns itself into a war machine, as in the case of Guatemala. Therefore, the power of the state is not only or any longer oriented towards inscribing the body via disciplinary mechanisms but towards an economy of control carried out through massacres and the spectacle of dead bodies.[2] Lastly, what drives Carrillo's lawsuit is the intention to blame the state for such practices, which disproportionally affect women's bodies. In order to reach her goal, she has sought to elevate the trial to the International Criminal Court.[3]

Feminist anthropologist Rita Segato has argued that this type of international court is a fundamental tool for women who seek justice and to prove how contemporary violence preys on female or feminized bodies like never before. Segato highlights that women's bodies are the first and the last realm of colonization and, as such, the recipients of all forms of violence.[4] The work of Guatemalan performance artist Regina José Galindo has developed mainly around this topic. For more than two decades, she has focused on power relationships, with

2 Achille Mbembe, *Necropolitics* (Durham, N.C.: Duke University Press, 2019), pp. 66–87.

3 Personal interview between the author and Andrea Carrillo, August 30, 2020.

4 Rita Laura Segato, "Femigenocidio y Feminicidio: Una Propuesta de Tipificación," *La Revuelta*, 2011, http://www.larevuelta.com.ar/pdf/Femigenocidio-femicidio-Segato.pdf (accessed March 7, 2022).

performances that impugn the normalization of necropolitics. To this end, she uses her body as if it were the body of any female victim. In so doing, Galindo's artwork also points towards other knowledges, other epistemologies that the modern state systematically erases.

Feeling Presences

Patricia Samayoa was Galindo's friend and inspired the performance *Presence* (2017), a series of *actions* that took place in Guatemala City's downtown between March 6 and 12, 2017 and ended in the art space Casa Encendida, Madrid, Spain, a month and a half later, in April 2017. Each time, in *Presence*, Galindo stood silently wearing the clothes of an assassinated woman, assuming her name, which was in the title of the performance that day, and sharing the story of her death through an exhibition leaflet available at the entrance to the galleries (when set in galleries) or distributed by collaborators, mainly women (when in public spaces). In total, the performances called thirteen assassinated women into presence, whose legal cases remain unsolved and, therefore, whose killers remain unpunished. Either in a private or in a public space, the action was always the same.[5]

Since the conception of this project, Galindo was clear about her purpose. She wanted to explore if a performance could also serve as a sort of séance in which the presence of the assassinated women could sensorially be brought back. Such a task took more than the thirteen days during which Galindo assumed the identity

5 I analyzed it based on the artist's documentation on her website "Regina José Galindo," https://www.reginajosegalindo.com (accessed June 22, 2022), some additional photographs that Galindo sent me, and interviews or email conversations with both the artist on August 25, 2020 and other people involved in the performance in Guatemala: Andrea Carrillo, AumRak Sapper on September 6, 2020, Bernardo Euler on August 29, 2020 and Silvia Trujillo on September 4, 2020, as well as in Spain: Cristina Rodríguez on September 2, 2020.

of each of the women. Once she finished the research process and gathered the garments needed to perform, she began taking part in ceremonial processes with the female *Ajq'ij* (Mayan Daykeeper) AumRak Sapper. They *summoned* the murdered women that would be felt in the performances, asked them for permission to perform and for several days performed a *limpia* (cleansing) of their clothes using smoke.[6] Not unlike dancers who rehearse or repeat some movement or performers who train their bodies, she carefully opened her senses in order to receive and channel the energy of the summoned women. This process lasted until the beginning of every performance session.

Each day, before performing, the artist placed a small altar with a fire nearby, yet outside of the visual frame of the performance's main scenario. While performing in Guatemala, a friend of the artist, who is knowledgeable in Mayan rituals, helped her maintain the fire and offerings until each performance was finished and, afterwards, put it out. The production of *Presence* and the performance itself involved many people who were moved and interconnected by the experience. Henceforth, I propose that this performance should be understood as a long ritual that includes heterogeneous moments within and behind the scenes, and which surpasses the understanding of presences as an intersubjective relation by establishing a sensorial relation to the unknown. The fire in Galindo's performance contributes to transforming smells, sounds, and sometimes blurring vision, thus generating a sensorially charged atmosphere that the artist expands when performing in front of the audience. In *Presence*, the invisible yet real network of sensations that made up the incorporeality of the corporeal performance, the virtuality that intercon-

6 Cleansing here is connected to its spiritual meaning in Spanish and Portuguese; in both languages it means to liberate someone or something from bad energies.

nects everything, helps bring the energy of the deceased women into the scene, making them present. The performance links the sensorial stimuli with the names of the deceased and thus addresses their presences as real. Consequently, presence in this performance is not about the tension between present and absent bodies, but about the incorporeal network that unifies them.

Following philosopher Peter Pál Pelbart,[7] I argue that Galindo re-installs abjected existences, by publicly displaying the abjection to which these women were relegated.[8] That is, the performance *Presence* achieves its presence by the *mise-en-scène* of the preternatural made sensible.[9] Pál Pelbart, expanding on Étienne Souriau's ideas, states that things, beings and entities, must be installed in order to exist. "Establishing refers less to creating for the first time and more to establishing something 'spiritually', guaranteeing it a 'reality' of its own."[10] He welcomes the creation of an art that accounts for the multiplicity of actors in the universe. By appropriating the uses of ceremonial fires, reaching people on the fringes of society and performing as if she were one of the victimized women, Galindo establishes not only their abjected existence, but also things, beings that dwell within non-rational practices such as cleansing the clothing and asking the fire for permission. In

7 Peter Pál Pelbart, "Por uma arte de instaurar modos de existência que 'não existem'," *Como (...) Sobre Coisas que Não Existem*, exhib. cat., 31 Bienal de São Paulo, São Paulo 2014, pp. 250–265.

8 Following Judith Butler, I use the term "abjected" to refer to the majority of the dead women embodied by Galindo in *Presence* as bodies outside the domain of the "subject" because of their exclusion and illegibility. See Judith Butler, *Bodies that Matter: On the Discursive Limits of "Sex"* (New York: Routledge, 1993), p. 3.

9 Preternatural refers to the intervention of angels and demons in the material world, in Fabián Alejandro Campagne, "Witchcraft and the Sense-of-the-Impossible in Early Modern Spain: Some Reflections Based on the Literature of Superstition (ca. 1500–1800)," *The Harvard Theological Review* 96, no. 1 (2003), p. 33.

10 "Instaurar significa menos criar pela primeira vez do que estabelecer 'espiritualmente' uma coisa, garantir-lhe uma 'realidade' en seu gênero próprio." Translated by the author, original quote in Pelbart, "Por uma arte de instaurar modos de existência que 'não existem'," p. 250.

so doing, she traces back to the invisible forces that expunged these women's bodies and obliterated them.

When Galindo began this performance series, she conducted research and reached out to the Fundación Sobrevivientes [Survivors Foundation], a non-profit organization that supports women, children, and teenagers who are victims of gender and family violence in Guatemala by providing them with legal and psychological support. Through this organization, she gained access to many stories and, randomly, to certain objects belonging to the victims of violence. However, she needed to contact either their family members or those closest to the murdered women in order to explain the project to them, get their permission and collect clothing, a task for which she hired two producers. Those closest to the victims shared their feelings, memories and personal stories, and also chose the clothes that Galindo should wear during the performance. According to Bernardo Euler,[11] one of the producers, at first he thought that Galindo's encounter with the disconsolate family members could be an intrusion into their privacy. He thus decided to accompany the artist when she met the three people that he had previously approached. Euler recalls that breaking the ice was extremely hard. These family members had not talked about their losses and the circumstances around their relatives' deaths for years. But finally, they were able to speak, cry, and communicate the feelings that their loss left them with. Consequently, the very production of the performance initiated a path towards healing. Galindo reached out to people in pain, listened to their stories and took care of them in ways that the state had not.

Once Galindo gathered the garments, she prepared the ceremony along with the *Ajq'ij*, who told her that she was scared. Sapper, the *Ajq'ij*, had never worked in circumstances like this one and had no idea what might

11 Interview by the author.

happen. However, she remembers that after all the offerings were given to the fire, the first sign that she received was a feeling of happiness. The abjected finally mattered, their lives were celebrated. Galindo folded the clothes and together with Sapper distributed them around the fire. The artist also brought a framed photograph of each victim, as well as printed copies of the stories of the death of each one, which she would later distribute while performing. She placed them on the top of the clothing and embellished them with *ruca*, copal, cinnamon, bougainvillea petals and bay leaves. Then she read each of their stories and both Galindo and Sapper silently meditated. They summoned each of the dead women through evoking love and companionship, aiming to reconnect them to the joy and cheer of life.[12] The fire seemed to power these connections.

Although Galindo grew up in an urban *ladino* family,[13] she states that she was aware of the Mayan ceremonial fires since she was young and she consciously wanted to include fire in her preparations for her performance. In the Mayan cosmovision, fire is the great purifier, destroyer, revealer and transformer. It evokes the sun and it is in itself an offering.[14] Galindo's purpose, however, was not reclaiming a pre-Hispanic tradition nor a contemporary Mayan ceremony but initiating a sensorial communication with these women that ultimately would allow her to perform in their names. In doing so, she employed and reinforced techniques she knew of but had never consciously practiced. She knew that

12 Interview by the author.

13 *Ladino* refers to the racially mixed population that adopted the cultural patterns of White people. They speak Spanish and dress in western clothing. The term became more popular than mestizo during colonial times because it erased the ethnic roots that at that time also included African people or Afro-descendants. See Arturo Taracena, "Guatemala: Del Mestizaje a la Ladinización, 1524–1964," in *Antología del pensamiento crítico guatemalteco contemporáneo*, ed. Ana Silvia Monzón (Buenos Aires: Clacso, 2019) pp. 517–544.

14 See *Popol Wuj*, trans. Luis E. Sam Colop (Guatemala: Cholsamaj, 2008), note 211.

she would again work with *things* that she could not control.[15] After the first conversations with the victims' closest family members, the artist realized that the performance would be about endurance, about feelings and emotions. She would allow herself to trust her body's senses because only through them could she channel the presence of these women. She intended to act as if she were a medium, and as Jonathan Searle considered,[16] intentionality is a direction that produces a reality. The artist's embodiment of the thirteen deceased women rather than proving the existence of spirits shows the outcome of sensorial communication.

–Galindo–Paredes–Trujillo–and–Many Others–

After experiencing *Presence* on the day that the artist embodied Iris Yesenia Paredes, who was dismembered by neighborhood *mareros* (Central American gang members), feminist activist Silvia Trujillo pointed out: "There is a certain distance between her body and ours and yet her presence is lacerating, it stabs like a dagger that is inserted little by little into the guts, and brings the person who wields it, every time closer. It is her, but at the same time, she is another woman. There is pain, I can feel it. There is time, but frozen. There is oblivion and homage."[17]

15 "Things" refer here to the non-rational. See André T. Lepecki, *Singularities: Dance in the Age of Performance* (New York: Routledge, 2016), p. 29.

16 See "John Searle on the Philosophy of Language: Section 4," *YouTube*, March 15, 2008, https://www.youtube.com/watch?v=CFX0wz86bMw (accessed April 21, 2022).

17 "Hay cierta distancia entre su cuerpo y el nuestro y sin embargo, su presencia es lacerante, punza como una daga que se introduce poco a poco en las entrañas, y coloca a quien la empuña, cada vez más cerca. Es ella pero a la vez es otra. Hay dolor, puedo sentirlo. Hay tiempo, pero congelado. Hay olvido y homenaje." Translated by the author, original quote in Silvia Trujillo, "Regina José Galindo: Presencia contra el olvido," *Esquisses*, March 8, 2017, http://www.esquisses.net/2017/03/regina-jose-galindo-presencia-contra-el-olvido/ (accessed April 25, 2022).

The performer's "lacerating presence" referred to by Trujillo could be understood along the lines of Peggy Phelan's argument that the performer disappeared becomes something else,[18] which in this case is death. In that way, performance places the experience of death closer to us, the beholders, who, unable to embody it, end up feeling the tension between presence and absence. This tension is a network of affects, things that relate the performer's body to the others' bodies in the space that Trujillo metaphorically identifies as a dagger for its capacity to penetrate the skin. The performer, as in Trujillo's gloss, wields the dagger, commanding the action by putting her body on the line directly aiming at the beholders' senses. Everything is on her and everything is triggered from her body to the extent that she stages the act of becoming somebody else, something else. "She is the artist, the artwork; her body is the mannequin, the raw material, the image,"[19] adds Trujillo. The performance is not reduced to intersubjective links; it exposes the links themselves. That is, it is not only about Galindo that day embodying and transferring Iris Yesenia's presence to Trujillo or others in the audience, but about the force of pain as an agent of connection and becoming something else; an image, a material. By staging this felt intensity, it brings the absent woman into a corporeal present, the presence of a nowness where the bodies of the performer and beholders are also an encounter through osmosis, in/ex-corporations, sensations that transpire on the skin. All of these exchanges could be seen as a narration of the real, a corporeal archive full of presences that interconnects living systems, affects that in Galindo's performance take the name of assassinated women.

18 Peggy Phelan, *Unmarked: The Politics of Performance* (London and New York: Routledge, 1993), p. 150.

19 "Ella es la artista y ella es la obra, su cuerpo el maniquí, la materia prima, la imagen." Translated by the author, original quote in Trujillo, "Regina José Galindo."

The event of recognizing these incorporeal yet real presences in their own unknown nature is what Pál Pelbart considers to be the basis of the art of establishing existences. This process encompasses imperceptible beings, substances that make up the multiverse, planetary entities, zombies, minoritarian subjects, all of them beings-in-becoming. More than a solemn institutional ceremony, "it is a process that raises what already exists to its own level of splendor and reality."[20] To that end, this process does not seek to convert beings into objects with fixed identities, but to establish them in their own nature and state. Artists, clairvoyants, thinkers, singular (strange) subjectivities can propitiate this process since it is a collective practice that involves those who "see" intensities, the power of forces that interact in a specific moment.[21] Galindo's work in *Presence* is aligned with this process because in order to bring the thirteen women's lives back, the artist must connect with the imperceptible, align communication with her nervous system, and allow the virtual presences to take over and express themselves through her body. While Galindo's performance is focused on assassinated women, the process of re-establishing them before and while performing has an ancestral Mayan knowledge in which fire is a central entity that *speaks* and reveals what is conveyed by the symbolic. The artist explored and learned from the spiritual practices of a Mayan Daykeeper, fellow artists, and two producers who helped her contact family members of the deceased as well as, in some cases, be part of their grieving process. This aspect, the grieving, provides the performance with an approach to pain, deploying those painful feelings in preparation for the artist to just feel without the fear of being affected by

20 "[...] um processo que eleva o existente a um patamar de realidade e esplendor próprios." Translated by the author, original quote in Pelbart, "Por uma arte de instaurar modos de existência que 'não existem'," p. 250.

21 See ibid., p. 262.

something unknown. Indeed, as the artist has declared, *Presence* is the first performance in which she allowed herself to show her emotional reactions, which seemed to respond more to the space, the fumes, the smells from the altar; the involvement of people in grief within the audience than to the women's stories.

Galindo trained herself not to act as if she were one of the women she embodied, but to expose herself to a space symbolically charged by a woman who had been brutally killed and remained as an example of gender and social injustice.[22] Consequently, the performance focuses on feeling the intensities that affect the body when present, and in that way becomes an act of channeling multiple presences. More than seeing the women, Galindo summons their presence through feeling, stripping it of the symbolic. Thus, *Presence* is an act of awareness and recognition of the myriad human and non-human presences that neutralize the binary absence-presence.

Pál Pelbart's argument that not only mediums, but thinkers, artists and freaks could serve as conduits to other existences, resonates with the term *open sensibility*. Galindo recounts that she always thought that this sensibility contributed to her becoming an artist. What artists, thinkers and mediums appear to have in common is an acknowledgement of the body as a sensorial organ, that is, a source of non-rational knowledge. An open sensibility could take on different shapes, all dealing with the virtual, the felt, the elusive, that which transitions from one state to another. When Galindo

22 Despite the fact that the law against feminicide and other forms of violence against women was approved by the Guatemalan Congress in 2008, until 2018 only one in six cases was condemned. See Carmen Quintela, "Guatemala: los crímenes que no se nombran en el país de la impunidad," July 21, 2020, *Agencia Ocote*, https://www.agenciaocote.com/blog/2020/07/21/guatemala-los-crimenes-que-no-se-nombran-en-el-pais-de-la-impunidad/ (accessed May 31, 2022). All the statistics related to violence against women considerably rose during the Covid-19 pandemic lockdown.

started preparing for *Presence*, she knew that she would be utilizing her own—already open—sensibility and would feel unknown presences and existences. Ultimately, by embodying the pain suffered by the women involved in the performance, the artist intervenes in their transition to death, enabling all that which cannot be seen or reproduced again to be felt. Therefore, the performance stages the resonance of these women's lives, acknowledging the continuum of material transformations. It restores these women's existences by creating a community where they were present again. Moreover, *Presence* traces a trajectory of feminine alliance. Starting with the memory of Galindo's maternal grandmother, continuing to the Mayan Daykeeper, the firekeeper, the honored women, and the audience, it weaves an expansive network, mainly made up of women, although not restricted to them, yet enough to highlight feminine energy. I am also included within this network. It informs and situates my research and the *place* where I am writing from.

Public Grieving

On March 8, 2017, International Women's Day, forty-one girls (aged 14–17) died in a fire at the Hogar Seguro Virgen de la Asunción [Virgen de la Asunción Safe Home],[23] because the police guarding the doors refused to open them to let the girls escape the inferno. Many people gathered in front of the National Palace of Culture, a governmental building in Guatemala City, and

23 This "children's safe home" is a public entity created to protect orphaned children from violence and sexual abuse. However, for years, its authorities have been accused of being the perpetrators. In fact, several of the girls who died in the fire were pregnant. Survivors Foundation, the same institution that initially helped Galindo, represents many cases against Virgen de la Asunción Safe Home, before and after the fire tragedy.

began chanting "It was not the fire, it was the state."[24] The National Palace of Culture and the gallery where Galindo performed are relatively close and that allowed some people to stop by to experience the performance that became part of a funerary ritual. On that same day, Galindo was performing Dorita, who was burned by a group of bandits that broke into her house. The final minutes of Dora Alicia Secaira—Dorita—parallel the girls who were burned alive at the Virgen de la Asunción tragedy. Dorita's presence turned into those forty-one young girls, who, like her, were burned. They were also connected by memories linked to a deep pain, a feeling that some people could embody thanks to Galindo's performance. According to Silvia Trujillo, if the feminist movement in Guatemala has organized to report feminicides and violence against women, and has put the topic on the media's agenda, "*Presence* was an experience that went through the body of those of us who stopped by."[25]

Reverberation of Silences

While *Presence* was still a work in progress, Galindo was contacted by Asociación Mujeres de Guatemala (AMG) [Guatemalan Women's Association] in Madrid, Spain. The association is directed by Mercedes Hernández, a Guatemalan lawyer and expert in feminicide who combats violence against women. She asked Galindo to talk about her body of work, and Galindo commented on the piece that she was currently performing and offered to perform at the event, before the conversation. The artist explained that one of the women that she had selected was Mindy Rodas, who was murdered, presumably by her husband, before traveling to Spain, where she wanted

24 The chanting against the state recalls the reaction to the disappearance of 43 students from the Ayotzinapa Rural Teacher's College in Iguala, Mexico in 2014.

25 Translated from interview by the author.

to restart her life. Coincidentally, the Association's team knew the case very well since they had been involved and had even bought the plane ticket for her. Galindo closed *Presence* wearing Mindy's dress in the inner patio of La Casa Encendida, where about two hundred and fifty people congregated. As on the previous occasions, she prepared the altar, made her own ritual before starting, and silently stood still for two hours. When the performance was about to end, a woman stood up and took the artist's hand, which was repeated by other women that held hands together creating a circle, while others touched her feet. According to Cristina Rodríguez,[26] a Guatemalan cultural manager based in Madrid and who collaborated with Galindo, the resulting image recalled something religious; people in the audience cried. Once two hours had passed, Galindo freed her hands and exited the space. Rodríguez heard somebody from the audience say "these were the most agonizing minutes of silence in my life." People were crying without clearly understanding what was happening.

Presence initially began with the support of an alliance of anti-gender violence activists, which continued expanding as the performances kept occurring. As if it were a natural effect of the activist network's power, the assassinated women came back virtually in the performances and really mattered. To some extent, this effect could be also linked to Samayoa's legacy, having dedicated her life's work to protecting women against violence and in doing so, expanding their community. Similarly, Galindo follows Samayoa's legacy by using her piece as a means to create a feminine constellation that reconnects those who have passed with the ones still alive. All of them become part of an ancestral collective memory, which has been activated through fire, the language of the senses and the rituals of silence. In the performance, the loss of Patricia, Iris, Dorita, Mindy,

26 Email conversation with the author.

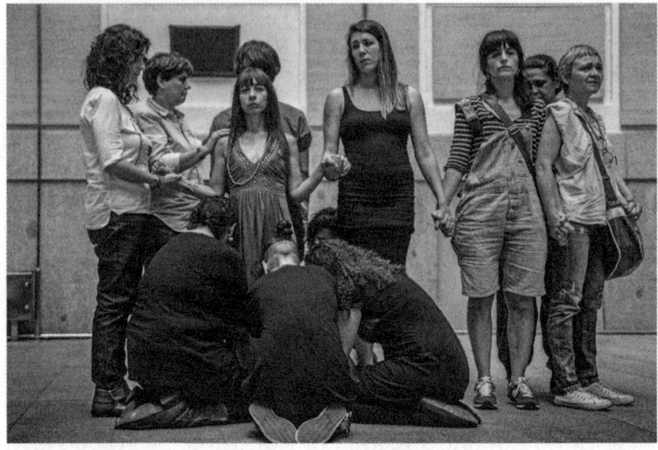

Fig. 1: Regina José Galindo, *Presencia* (Madrid: Casa Encendida, 2017), performance, photograph: Francisco Magallán, courtesy of the artist.

Saira, Florence, María de Jesus, Sandra, Karen, Kenia, Flor de María, Velvet and the Franco family became a ceremonial process that allowed the artist to re-establish their presence. By highlighting their loss, the performance values what is absent and invisible yet real. Thus, the piece creates a privileged scenario in which feelings, emotions, sensations and affects trigger the presence of these thirteen assassinated women. It is through the unknown but felt world that affects the body that *Presence* reinstitutes the lives of female victims of violence and injustice, and along with them ways of healing that seem to work in tandem with some Guatemalan feminist organizations such as the Red de Sanadoras Ancestrales [Ancestral Healers' Network]. Its aim is to bodily delve into the multiple oppressions that have silenced corporeal expressions and subjectivities.[27] In doing so, this female network, as in

27 See Claudia Korol, "Guatemala: Feminismo comunitario y recuperación de saberes ancestrales," *Nodal. Noticias de América Latina y el Caribe*, January 11, 2020, https://www.nodal.am/2020/01/gua-

Galindo's performance, unveils the multiplicity of ways of living.

In the interview that I conducted with Galindo when researching this piece, she mentioned that silence was key for her performance. Through silence, she felt the audience's presence and established her own. In Madrid, silence turned into an energy that took over the space and marked instants of profound intensity. Indeed, this experience highlights a unique moment in Galindo's career because it places her as a static actress in front of a relatively stable audience. But her actions were minimal, she breathed and avoided eye contact. By standing still, focused and silent, she believed her body became a ticking bomb. Her muteness became more powerful than if she had screamed loudly. That is why silence is an act of resistance.[28] It penetrates bodies, turns "excorporations" and incorporations into a type of prelinguistic exchange underpinned by the visual that moves the meaning of words and sense-making.

A prelinguistic state is intimately linked to the bodily language and performance that emerges in *Presence*. The performance relates to the archaic by reducing the visual experience to the performer's body which, during the event, turns into many bodies as in a spiritual séance. Consequently, the idea of silence as resistance appears to involve an ancestry that is not only tied to femininity, but also to ritual and performance. In this context, *Presence* could be seen as a scenario that neutralizes the social relations of power. The performance's ritual tries to suspend, through silence, that which subjects contemporary bodies to a cultural system that alienates their sense of interconnectedness. In the light

temala-feminismo-comunitario-y-recuperacion-de-saberes-ancestrales/ (accessed June 5, 2022).

28 When I asked Galindo what silence is in her work, her first answer was "resistance." Then she elaborated, adding: "silence is awareness, control, a way of holding the space, and a non-confrontational manner of being in the fight."

of Latin American performance art tradition, Galindo traces back, actualizes, and exhibits the painful forces that subject the body to the control of dominant powers.[29] She transforms her anger, her sorrow, her grief, and the social and cultural material that make up her own flesh. She heals herself while unveiling the violence that incites gendered cultural constructions on the body. Using her body as a proxy, Galindo puts herself in the victim's place and, as in an exercise of augmented reality, expands the time in which power relationships act over her, threatening her physicality or conditioning her physical and sensorial responses. Throughout this process, she embodies these abjected others, unintelligible before the law, like the thirteen assassinated women who were at the origin of *Presence*. Galindo, the deceased and absent "performers" that were made present, and the audience, meet in a space of abjection that many people do not want to see and acknowledge, and which therefore remains silenced. Once there, the artist consciously works on a corporeal state that turns silencing into silence, repressions into agency, and the resistance to forgetting into a ritual that brings back absent presences.

29 See Judith Butler, "Forces and Fluids: Regina José Galindo," in *Prince Claus Awards Book*, ed. Fariba Derakhshani and Barbara Murray (The Hague: HRH Prince Claus and Institute of Social Studies, 2011), pp. 46–47.

Pınar Öğrenci

Purple Panic: 43[1]

For the children of Ayotzinapa, Tlatelolco, Gezi, Ankara, Suruç, Sur, and many others beyond borders ...

Mexico City's sidewalks are full of cracks not only because of earthquakes but also jacaranda trees. The jacaranda tree that can be found all across Mexico City is an invasive species, which is overpopulated and doesn't allow other plants to grow.[2] The roots are outside of the earth where the vast body of the tree meets the ground, cracking the cemented sidewalks, enveloping the roads, almost occupying its surroundings. Meanwhile, Jacaranda is also a testament to the city's history and—with its roots—a witness to the collective memory both over and under the earth. Could it have witnessed and objected to the history of the city, which once consisted of islands over the lakes and the bridges connecting them, until

1 *Purple Panic: 43* is the name of two days of public interventions and performance by Pınar Öğrenci with jacaranda flowers at Mexico City's public spaces and ended at Plaza de las Tres Culturas, Tlatelolco, Mexico City, on April 26, 2015. The lecture performance *Purple Panic: 43* took place on January 30, 2019, at District, Berlin and a shortened version of the lecture has subsequently been published in Andrea Caroline Keppler, Katharina Koch and Dorothea Nold, eds., *Revolt She Said. Dekoloniale und feministische Perspektiven auf 68* (Berlin: District Berlin/alpha nova & galerie futura, 2019), pp. 34–45. The text has been slightly revised for publication in this book.

2 Mark A. Davis and Ken Thompson, "Eight Ways to be a Colonizer; Two Ways to be an Invader: A Proposed Nomenclature Scheme for Invasion Ecology," *Bulletin of the Ecological Society of America* 81, no. 3 (2000), pp. 226–230.

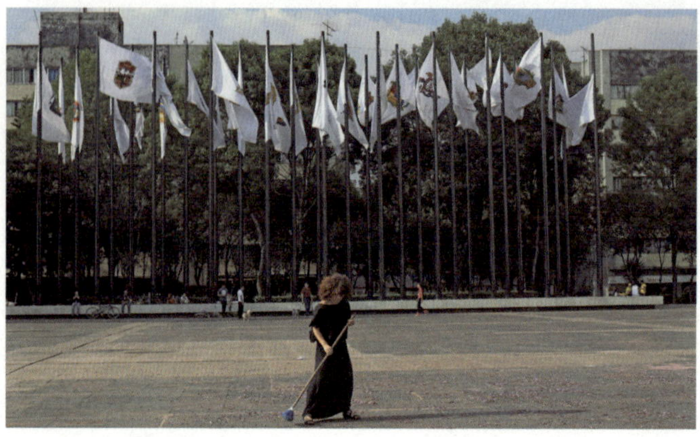

Fig. 1: Pınar Öğrenci, *Purple Panic: 43*, performance on Tlatelolco Square, Mexico City, 2015. Photo: Jose Luis Arriaga.

the lakes dried up when it was occupied by the Spanish? Could this be the reason why it objects? Could it be suffering while enchanting people with its tropical beauty? Jacaranda is an invader, it's never docile…

Jacaranda has its own specific term called "Purple Panic." Purple Panic is a term for student stress during the late spring used by students in Queensland, Australia. "Purple" refers to the color of jacaranda flowers, while the "panic" refers to the pressure of completing assignments and studying for the final exams. They say: "If you have not started seriously studying for the final exams by the time the jacaranda blooms, it is too late. Forget the exams!" That's why the jacaranda is also known as the exam tree.

It is impossible to think of schools, students, and teachers without thinking about Ayotzinapa in Mexico. 43 students from the Ayotzinapa Teaching School were on their way to Iguala to protest against the discrepancies in school funding by the government when they were stopped by the local police on the evening of September 26, 2014. The police fired on the 43 unarmed students. The following kidnapping was a collaboration between the state and the mafia. The 43 students were never heard from again. The students had planned to continue to Mexico City for the commemoration of the Tlatelolco Massacre, which took place on October 2, 1968. From the late 1960s to today, such killings became common practice in Mexico, as the government together with drug cartels killed and disappeared thousands of students, teachers, women, journalists, and others.

The families who did not see the bodies of their children still believe they may be alive. The roots of the policy to completely destroy young people with oppositional views can be traced back to the student movement of 1968. What had happened in Mexico in 1968, exactly fifty-one years ago? Mexico's student movement came about in a political climate that was dominated by the Institutional Revolutionary Party (PRI), which had come to power in the 1940s. The party saw itself as the embodiment of the Mexican Revolution. In 1964, the most conservative candidate, the former interior minister, Gustavo Díaz Ordaz from the PRI, was elected as the next president.

The '68 movement emerged in response to a routine instance of police brutality against youth that was also, in their estimation, part of the regular violence of Mexico City's modernization. Spectacular preparations to host the Summer Olympics that year highlighted not only how much the physical form of the city had changed since the 1940s, when capitalist urbanization intensified, but also the underlying social contradictions and fissures. The so called "Mexican Miracle," however, was still a leap of faith for most citizens, who didn't profit from the expansion and chafed against its authoritarian core. Despite the government's claims of urban integration and national unity, Mexicans were governed as distinct populations with different and delimited social, economic, and political mobility based on class, ethnicity, and gender.

The Venezuelan playwright José Ignacio Cabrujas, commenting on his country's oil boom and collapse in the 1970s and 1980s, compared the national territory to an encampment that evolved into an oversized hotel. Within this hotel, citizens are treated as guests, and the state acts as a manager, although in permanent failure when it comes to guaranteeing their comfort.

Cabrujas continues:

> To live (...) is to pretend that my actions are translated into something (...) something that clashes with the rule of the hotel, given that when I stay in a hotel, I do not try to transform its accommodations, or to improve them, or to adapt them to my wishes. I simply use them.[3]

A hotel is a compelling metaphor for modernizing authoritarian states like Mexico: although featuring some alluring amenities, it is never intended to become a home, and so the roles of host and guest are never supposed to be reversed.

Jacques Derrida theorized the politics of hospitality. He argues that most hospitality is conditional, hinging on populations and sovereignty, limits and borders, and calculations of risk and management of resources. Derrida's work focused on the experience of foreign immigrants and refugees; but how does hospitality apply to citizens estranged in their own homeland?

Derrida admits that unconditional hospitality is impossible, as it requires the host to give up his home to the stranger. In unconditional hospitality everything is offered without even asking the stranger's name. "Name" for Derrida, refers not only to individual identity but to the quantifying and managing of citizens as populations. Derrida's thinking can be developed to

3 Interview with José Ignacio Cabrujas, in *Heterodoxia y estado: Cinco respuestas* (Caracas: Estado & Reforma, 1987), cited in George F. Flaherty, *Hotel Mexico: Dwelling on the '68 Movement* (Berkeley: University of California Press, 2016), pp. 14f.

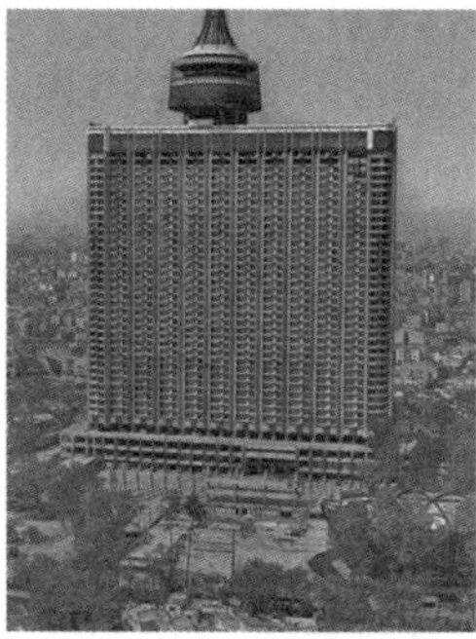

Fig. 2: Hotel de Mexico: Ely Eduardo G. Rojas, www.monografias.com.

take into account the estranged status of citizen-guests in Mexico and other places in the global South.

The Hotel de Mexico was to be the largest and most sophisticated hotel in Latin America, built for the influx of tourists anticipated for the 1968 Olympics. The 207 meter hotel tower was to feature 1,512 guest rooms, seven restaurants, thirteen bars, six reception halls, a shopping mall, a gym, a pool, and parking for 2,000 cars. However, the hotel was never completed. The fifty-storey concrete shell loomed over its low-slung neighborhood for three decades. It was a potent landmark because of its incomplete monumentality and the corruption accompanying its construction. The architect Juan José said: "It's like watching a child grow up. One feels almost duty bound. But this child should have left home by now!"

And finally, in 1994, the hotel shell was retrofitted as the World Trade Center, heralding a new era: a post-NAFTA (North American Free Trade Agreement), neoliberal Mexico. The Hotel de Mexico serves as a case study for what was truly Mexico's largest hotel: a single party authoritarian state that claimed the role of absolute host and treated most of its citizens as mere guests, with only limited rights and few alternatives.

Thousands of leftists, including leaders of the '68 movement, students, workers, and intellectuals were arrested, tortured, raped, murdered and "disappeared" at Lecumberri prison in Mexico in the 1960s and 1970s. The Palacio de Lecumberri, otherwise known as *El Palacio Negro* or *The Dark Palace*,[4] was built in 1900 as a prison, made to look like a palace from the outside. Originally designed to accommodate 800 prisoners, by the 1970s it detained some 4,000 inmates, living in overcrowded cells under abject conditions.

Perhaps the most striking feature was its watchtower, thirty meters in height, located in the central, circular courtyard. From this perspective guards could supervise the seven segments of two-storey wards called *crujias* that radiated from the watchtower at the center of the courtyard. The watchtower recalled Jeremy Bentham's panopticon, the late eighteenth century prison prototype that took its name from a hundred-eyed monster in Greek mythology. For Michel Foucault, prisons that sought to discipline bodies were forms of punishment. He understood designs like the panopticon to enact regimes of compulsory visibility.

José Revueltas, who was one of the leaders of Mexico's established Left, describes the geometry of the prison as follows:

> Diabolical incident of the mutilation of space, triangles, trapezoids, parallels, oblique or perpendicular segments, lines and more lines, bars and more bars, until finally obstructing any movement of the gladiators upon the diagram of this colossal defeat of liberty at the hands of geometry.[5]

For Revueltas, the prison is a microcosm of degraded democracy. The Palacio de Lecumberri was a copy of Mexico City, with comparable geographic, social, eco-

4 *Lecumberri: The Dark Palace*, is the title of a documentary about the prison directed by Arturo Ripstein in 1977.

5 José Revueltas, *El Apando* (Mexico City: Ediciones Era, 1982 [1969]), pp. 54–55.

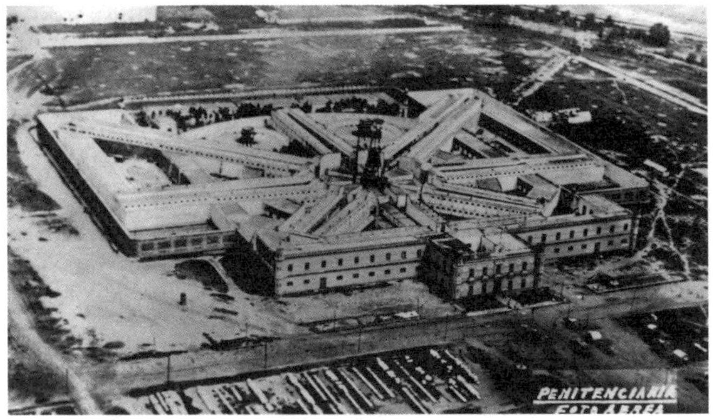

Fig. 3: Palacio de Lecumberri, Aérea Mexicana, www.rozanamontiel.com.

nomic, and ethnic continuities and divides. Indeed, prisoners understood Lecumberri's design in urbanistic terms, referring to the open-air *crujias* as neighborhoods and the passages in between them as streets.

And finally, in 1976, Lecumberri was transformed into the national archive. This archive contains photographs of marches and protests, lists of victims, fingerprint records, cartoons, propaganda banners, police reports, interviews, and activists' political profiles from the '68 movement.

By the end of August 1968 more than one hundred thousand people were marching in the student demonstrations, sometimes several hundred thousand. By their mobilization in the movement, young women challenged traditional concepts of their proper place within Mexican society and the movement itself. On August 2, 1968, The National Union of Mexican Women published a condemnation of the government's actions:

> As Mexican women, as mothers, as sisters, as wives we express our indignation, our pain, and our protest before a situation that through its course in these past days has become worse. This gravely unstable and disruptive cli-

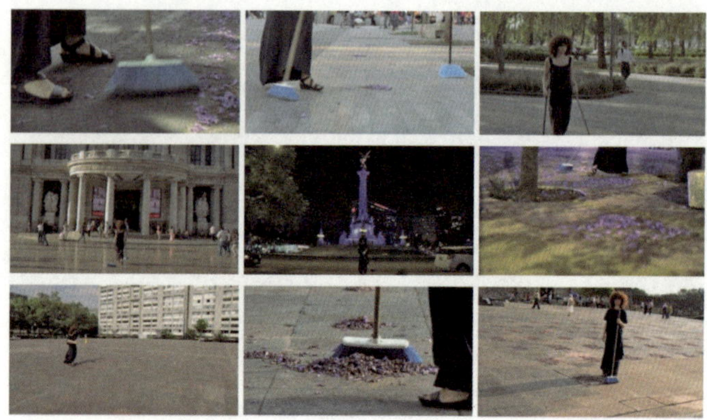

Fig. 4: *Purple Panic: 43*, performance in Mexico City, April 24–26, 2015, video stills, director of photography: Jose Luis Arriaga.

> mate has intensified (...). Mothers, Mexican women: We call on all of you in our country to hold your own protests and support the various outstanding groups, defend our children for the return to normal life.[6]

On September 18 at 10:30pm, the army surrounded the UNAM (The National Autonomous University of Mexico) campus with soldiers and armored vehicles, raided, evacuated and closed the buildings, rounding up hundreds of students, academics, and university officers and arresting them. There were over a thousand people imprisoned.

The violence was escalating. On October 2 the government and the National Strike Council had a meeting. After this meeting, the council was going to announce a ten-day hunger strike for political prisoners until the opening day of the Olympics. The rally to announce the plan was to be at a place called Tlatelolco.

6 *Excelsior*, August 2, 1968.

The Tlatelolco Massacre

> Where were you? And you, where were you? And you were where?
> Where were you and? Where were you? Where, where, damn, where
> did you die?[7]

If a single place could tell the history of Mexico, its conquests, its slaughters, its ambitions, defeats, victories, and aspirations, it would be Tlatelolco. Tlatelolco was one of the thriving commercial hubs, and a market center in the capital city Tenochtitlan during the Aztec Empire. When the Spanish colonizers invaded the Aztecs, the last rebels gathered here. A catholic monastery was then built in the middle of the ruins.

In the 1960s, the Mexican government added its own presence in this spot of conquest and destruction: a high-rise accommodating the Ministry of Foreign Relations and a huge, sprawling, middle-class housing project made up of long concrete blocks. The pre-Hispanic ruins and colonial architecture were to serve as the cultural core of the housing complex, to display material culture as official national culture. Through the windows of the houses people could observe first-hand the state's orchestration of Mexico's indigenous and colonial past under the banner of the modern, the "three cultures in harmony." As they call it, "Plaza of Three Cultures": Aztec, Spanish and Modern Mexican culture.

Tlatelolco's inhabitants were displaced first by the Revolution and then by failed land and agricultural reforms. It was also a margin to which the city's poor and disenfranchised were pushed by capitalist urbanization. After the Revolution, Tlatelolco served as a hub for the national railroad network that drove the country's integration and modernization as well as waves of rural

7 Jorge Aguilar Mora, *Si muero lejos de ti*, 1979.

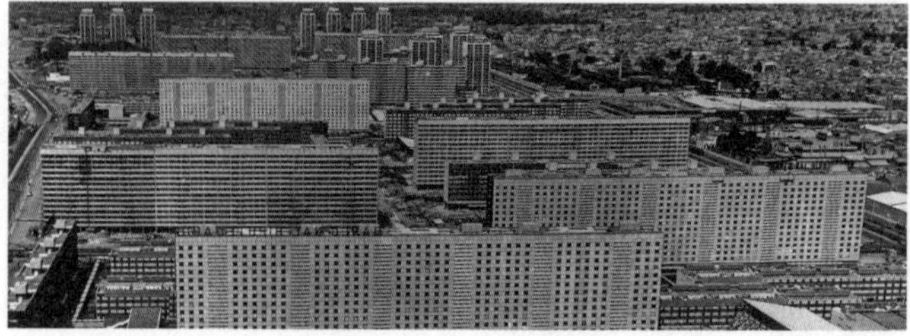

Fig. 5: The Nonoalco Tlatelolco housing estate in Mexico City, designed by Mario Pani, 1964. © Armando Salas Portugal.

migrants. It was filled with neglected housing, cantinas, and cheap hotels as well as persistent smoke and ashes from passing locomotives and nearby industry. The Tlatelolco neighborhood was cleared of its proletarian and often militant residents and redeveloped as a massive public housing complex named Nonoalco Tlatelolco by architect Mario Pani in 1964. Those residents were part of a larger population living in improvised housing throughout the city (*colonias proletarias*) referred to as "parachutists" by the press, and they were displaced to offer 70,000 government employees modern apartments.

The rally to announce the strike was scheduled to begin at 4:00pm. Myrthokleia González Gallardo, a National Strike Council delegate from the Polytechnic Institute, went to the rally despite the fact that her parents asked her not to go; they feared something terrible would happen. Progressives in Mexico were just beginning to think about women's rights, and Gallardo was one of only nine women among three hundred delegates.

> As I approached the square with the four speakers I was going to introduce (...) we were warned to be careful, that the army had been seen nearby (...) There were workers,

> students, and families coming into the plaza, filling it up. We didn't see any soldiers in the plaza.[8]

They went up to the third floor balcony and started their speeches. A few minutes after 6:00pm, a helicopter hovering overhead dropped a flare. It was a signal to the members of the presidential guard and a group of paramilitaries trained to provide security for the Olympics, who were also present but in plain clothes. Snipers positioned on the top of the buildings around the plaza shot at the people below. Suddenly everyone down in the plaza started to fall to the ground. And then men with white gloves and automatic weapons appeared, they wore white gloves to recognize each other.

The crowd ran towards the space between the church and the apartment blocks, but it was blocked by the soldiers. They tried to run into the church, which was supposed to be open at all times, but the massive sixteenth-century doors were barred and snipers were shooting from the domed roof. It was a perfect trap.

Margarita Isabel, an actress who lived in the complex, reported that she was chased by soldiers:

> When I got to the corner, I ran down the street to my building as fast as my two legs would carry me, dashed up the stairs to my apartment, and locked myself in! About five seconds later, I heard the downstairs door open, but those two dumb bastards never dreamed they'd be confronted with so many apartments inside my building. From outside it looks as though there are only two or three apartments, but once you're inside, it's a labyrinth, like an Antonioni film—you know?—a real maze, with forty apartment doors or so, and you lose your mind if you don't know your way around.[9]

8 Myrthokleia González Gallardo, cited in Mark Kurlansky, *1968: The Year That Rocked the World* (London: Vintage, 2005), p. 341.

9 Margarita Isabel, cited in George F. Flaherty, *Hotel Mexico*, p. 210.

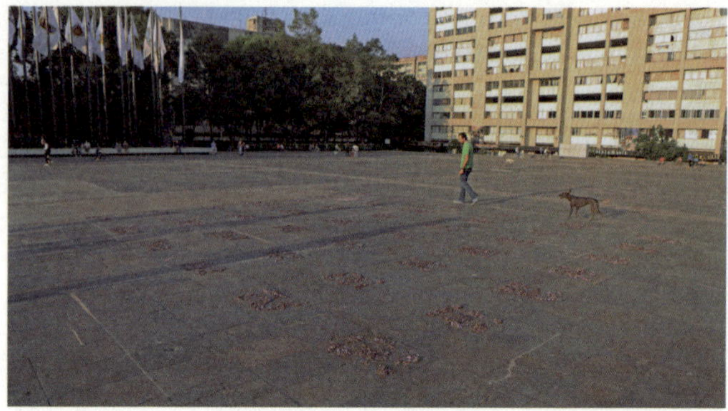

Fig. 6: Pınar Öğrenci, *Purple Panic: 43*, performance on Tlatelolco Square, Mexico City, 2015. Photo: Jose Luis Arriaga.

Middle class residents of the complex came to the student's aid in several locations, hiding them in their apartments, tossing garbage, stones, or scalding hot water out of windows in order to distract the authorities.

Nearly a thousand people were arrested overnight. The state would argue that participants of the '68 movement fired first—and that the army responded in self-defense. The television simply reported that there had been a police incident. The *New York Times* reported "at least 20 dead," whereas *The Guardian* reported 325 dead.

Rosario Castellano's poem comments on the early-onset amnesia of the mainstream media's reporting:

> By dawn the following morning the Plaza has been swept clean.
> The lead stories in the newspapers
> Were about the weather.
> And on television, on the radio, at the movie theaters
> The programs went on as scheduled.[10]

10 Rosario Castellano, cited in ibid., p. 213.

If Lecumberri offered the state a readymade national archive, then Tlatelolco offered the narrators of the '68 movement a place where they could show that the state's violence could take many forms and that it was routine rather than exceptional. As Jorge Aguilar Mora pleads "Where were you? And you, where were you?" on the night of the Tlatelolco Massacre, insisting that event and place are inseparably linked.

Nonoalco Tlatelolco's design, financing, and construction were informed by modernization's double impulse: creation and destruction. Apartments that were advertised as the epitome of modern domestic hygiene were quickly turned into smoke-filled bloodied holding cells on October 2. The relationship between the built environment and violence at the core of this reclamation is not casual. Buildings can physically register violence; many of the apartment blocks at Nonoalco Tlatelolco still exhibit damage from October 2. The Tlatelolco Massacre revealed that architecture—which embodies social, economic, and political structures—stands on unsteady ground when it's built on routine violence.

After the massacre on October 2, the student movement dissolved. The Olympics progressed without any disturbances locally. The massacre and the use of extreme violence by the government, however, are never forgotten. The massacre of the 43 students in September 2014, or their disappearance, are the direct consequences of the justice that has never been achieved for the Tlatelolco massacre. While the Mexican state has become a laboratory for state violence, or state-supported violence, it has not been held accountable for the killings and disappearances. However, the Mexican people do not give up their demand for justice for many violent episodes, including Tlatelolco and Ayotzinapa.

Sebastián Eduardo Dávila and Ulrike Jordan

A Psychiatric Clinic, a Monastery, a City and a River

On the (Artistic) Legibility of Disappearance in Topography

What can be seen at locations that were scenes of political violence, where people were forcibly disappeared or tortured? In Berlin, where we are writing this text, this question presents itself particularly with regard to places such as the present-day Topography of Terror. From 1933 onwards, with the rise of the National Socialist regime, this centrally located site served as the headquarters of the Gestapo, and later that of the Reich High Command and the Security Service of the SS High Command as well. It was here that the persecution and murder of Jews, Roma, homosexuals, communists, and people with disabilities were planned and organized, and where the Gestapo tortured political opponents during interrogation. After the buildings damaged during the war were demolished in 1950, the site was used as storage space for a construction waste recycling company in the 1970s and later as a track for driving practice. It was only in the mid-1980s that a memorial site was established here on the initiative of local citizens, in recognition of its historical significance. Although the institution bears the word topography[1] in its name, one

1 For an introduction to the concept of topography in relation to violence, see Pamela Colombo and Estela Schindel, "Introduction: The Multi-Layered Memories of Space," in *Space and the Memories of Violence: Landscapes of Erasure, Disappearance and Exception*, ed.

only learns about the history of this particular place by walking through the area to the rear of the site. Along a narrow path, small informational signs explain in a succinct, matter-of-fact tone which buildings stood where and how the area was used after the end of the war. There is very little to actually see. Trees and shrubs have overgrown much of the site, and there are only a few places where one can still make out the concrete slabs of the race track, where people practiced driving until the 1980s. The area is surrounded by a simple fence that runs along the street. Towards the end of the walking path, one arrives at the former Gestapo prison, the outlines of which are marked on the gravel. Here, too, the description on the informational sign is terse and factual. There is very little written about what exactly took place here, about the desperate suicides of the detainees, for example, or the torture in the interrogation rooms.

It must have been a conscious decision on the part of the planners to stay with simple descriptions of the site's function on the signs, we think to ourselves during our visit. Maybe the only way to deal with such a contaminated site is to leave it as a rubble-filled wasteland overgrown with trees, because it is impossible to convey the magnitude of the terror that was planned and carried out there. Maybe the emptiness itself is more powerful than any informational sign could be?

And yet the question of what could possibly be said at a location such as this, and what the location itself conveys, comes up in our conversation. The sober demarcation of the structures which no longer exist requires prior knowledge in order to be able to assess the scale of violence which took place there. At the same time, this demarcation fails to translate the speechlessness expe-

Pamela Colombo and Estela Schindel (Basingstoke and New York: Palgrave Macmillan, 2014). Taking into account the so-called spatial turn, the authors understand topography as directly and indirectly shaped by violent relationships, but also as shaping these relationships, and as producing subjects.

rienced in the face of the crimes that were committed. The location remains silent, it reveals nothing. We, the visitors, are the bearers of history. Is it even possible for a place to speak? What constitutes the expressive quality of a physical location, in particular when the traces of the buildings in which the violence took place no longer exist? And even more so, when the bodies of those who experienced such violence are no longer there, and can no longer be? Should the stories that are bound to this place, as well as to these bodies, not be remembered and retold over and over again?

Such questions arise in particular in locations where the disjuncture between the scale of violence and its (ill) legibility in present-day topographies becomes palpable; a present that Saidiya Hartman describes as the future of the past in her hope of underscoring the continuity of slavery until today.[2] In *Lose Your Mother*, she describes her frustrating attempt to approximate the history of enslaved people, to go beyond mere factual knowledge of these people and places, through an encounter with their physical, material, and possibly spiritual remains in the confines of the dungeon of Cape Coast Castle in Ghana—a fort where people were imprisoned for the transatlantic slave trade. When materiality alone is unable to render the histories of those enslaved, the author is compelled to compensate for the absence of the latter through imagination and projection onto the space. This attempt, nevertheless, remains itself incomplete; Hartman describes how her project of adequate witnessing as a descendant of the enslaved often fails. The prison itself does not speak, there is nothing to see, and yet the author returns there again and again.[3] The

2 See Saidiya Hartman, *Lose Your Mother: A Journey Along the Atlantic Slave Route* (New York: Farrar, Straus and Giroux, 2007), pp. 110–135.

3 Here one is reminded of Diana Taylor's repeated, although different, return to Villa Grimaldi, a former detention and torture center in Chile, as described in Diana Taylor, *¡Presente! The Politics of Presence*

following pages are devoted to four artistic practices which attempt to give visibility, or even a presence, to victims of violence, as well as to their family members and friends, through situated practices, opposing the state's and society's refusal to commemorate certain victims. In doing so, they call attention to concrete places, histories, struggles, and their protagonists. The processes of mourning and elucidation are negotiated through the mediums of film, installation, and performance, activating a different kind of witnessing.

A Former Monastery in Antigua Guatemala

[…] And so,
shed no tears.
You know that here the rain is always abundant so why swell the earth any further.
You should rather take advantage of its humidity and plow it deeply,
sow all the seeds you bring and wait attentively.
You may feel my breath in one of the germinations.[4]

Luis de Lión's untitled poem, written in 1984, ends with this appeal. That same year he was imprisoned by the military in Ciudad de Guatemala, tortured for twenty days and then executed.[5] His body has not been found to

(Durham, N.C. and London: Duke University Press, 2020), pp. 175–202. See also the interview with her in this book, pp. 159–177.

4 "Así pues,/nada de lágrimas./Vos sabés que aquí la lluvia siempre es abundante y para qué/hinchar más la tierra./Mejor aprovechá su humedad y arala profundamente,/sembrale todas las semillas que traigás y esperá atenta./Puede que sintás mi respiración en una de las germinaciones." Author's translation, original quote in Pedro Boche, "A 31 años de su desaparición forzada, Luis de Lión, enemigo de Estado: Autoridades de Guatemala no cumplen el acuerdo firmado hace más de una década," *Mapeo de la Memoria,* November 24, 2015, http://mapeo.memorialparalaconcordia.org/article.php?id=103 (accessed June 10, 2022).

5 See Simón Antonio Ramón, "El día que desaparecieron al escritor Luis de Lión," *Prensa Comunitaria,* May 15, 2022, https://www.

this day, and thus de Lión is still considered to be missing. In the poem, he seems to prepare his audience for this very eventuality, as if he knew that he would not live much longer. This is conceivable given the fact that he was a socially and politically engaged poet in Guatemala during the harshest years of the Internal Armed Conflict; he was well aware of the risk. He implores his readers not to mourn his absence, but rather to seek his presence and life ("my breath") where it will inscribe itself materially, namely in the earth. Here, the "reading" of his absence is expressed as the outcome of planting and harvesting, which evokes the subsequent work of mourning and the fight for truth and justice on behalf of his relatives and friends.[6]

Isabel Ruiz, who died in 2019, also chose to stay in Guatemala during this time. She was an artist and a good friend of de Lión. She commemorated him twenty-four years after his imprisonment with the performance *Matemática Sustractiva*. Day and night, she drew a total of 45,000 lines with white chalk on the orange-red wall of the Cooperación Española [Spanish Cooperative] Education Center in Antigua Guatemala, which is housed in a former Catholic monastery founded in 1582.[7] Ruiz's drawing was done in the context of an exhibition on those who were disappeared during the war in Guatemala, the number of which is estimated to be as high as 45,000.[8] Line by line, Ruiz traced a long thread, or

prensacomunitaria.org/2022/05/el-dia-que-desaparecieron-al-escritor-luis-de-lion/ (accessed June 10, 2022). The family learned that he had been shot after the publication of the military log, or Diario Militar, in 1999.

6 Every year, on the anniversary of the period when her father was tortured, Mayarí de Lión celebrates the Festival Jornadas de la Memoria Luis de Lión.

7 "Historia," *Centro de Formación de la Cooperación Española en La Antigua Guatemala*, https://www.aecid-cf.org.gt/index.php?option=com_content&view=frontpage&Itemid=225 (accessed June 10, 2022).

8 See *Los Desaparecidos: Horror Vacui*, exhib. cat. (Antigua, Guatemala: Centro de Formación de la Cooperación Española, 2008). For the background and status of this number, see Diane Nelson, *Who Counts? The*

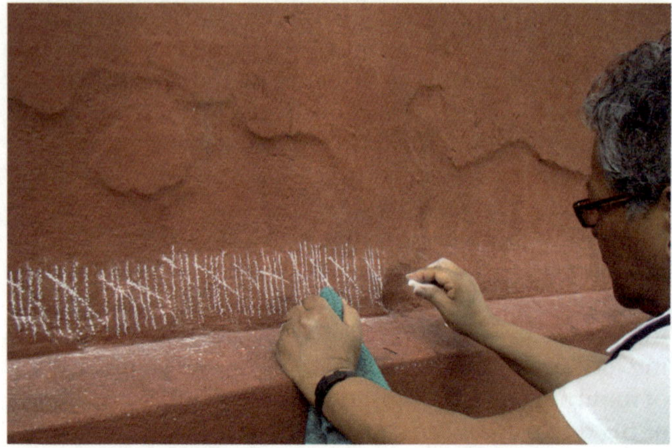

Fig. 1: Isabel Ruiz, *Matemática Sustractiva* (Antigua Guatemala: Cooperación Española, 2008), performance, photograph: Francisco Morales Santos, courtesy of the photographer.

perhaps a web, between her own mourning and the suffering of thousands of disappeared people, their family and friends. In the process, the disappearance of her friend provided the impetus for the commemoration of both him *and* everyone else, a commemoration and an act of mourning that is achieved, but not completed, through this physically exhausting, repetitive act. As Judith Butler describes,[9] mourning is characterized by loss, repetition, and an uncertain course and end, but in this case the body is also missing. How to mourn someone who has died without the fundamental, material evidence of their death, without the most manifest of what remains of them? This challenge is faced by the loved ones of people who have been disappeared;[10]

Mathematics of Death and Life after Genocide (Durham N.C. and London: Duke University Press, 2015), pp. 79–85.

9 See Judith Butler, *Precarious Life: The Powers of Mourning and Violence* (London and New York: Verso, 2004), pp. 21–23.

10 Diana Taylor examines attempts to spatially and physically locate the loss of those who have disappeared in various Latin American contexts. See Diana Taylor, *The Archive and the Repertoire: Performing Cul-*

they are also captured in the web drawn by the artist, spoken to by the lines she draws—but not only them. The poet Francisco Morales Santos, who is also Ruiz's widower, recounts that during Ruiz's performance, she was insulted by people passing by, some of whom even threatened to arrest and kill her.[11] Why?

One reason for this anger could be the historical and religious significance of the former monastery. Historical in this case means colonial. The structure stands among many other buildings and ruins as a monumental testimony to the colonial era in a city that was a regional center of power between the sixteenth and eighteenth centuries, and which today is considered a tourist hub of the country. With her performance, Ruiz thus marks a building that, like many other buildings in Antigua, forms part of the national heritage and is listed as a historical monument. It is precisely there that she makes reference to a bloody period that occurred only a short time ago, thus marking the continuity of colonialism into the postcolonial present. In no small measure, the labeling of Indigenous communities as enemies of the state by the military during the war can be traced back to their status in colonial society.[12] At the same time, the threats made against the artist reflect the collective unwillingness or even inability to acknowledge the war crimes at all, let alone to come to terms with them. *Matemática Sustractiva* intervenes to counter this, because even if no one could count all the lines, nor know exactly what they represented, their steady accumulation as well as their sheer presence must have been impressive. So many lines here cannot possibly

tural Memory in the Americas (Durham N.C. and London: Duke University Press, 2003), pp. 161–189 and Taylor, *¡Presente!*, pp. 127–152.

11 Conversation between Sebastián Eduardo Dávila and Francisco Morales Santos in Ciudad de Guatemala, September 2021.

12 Compare Marta Elena Casaús Arzú, *Genocidio. ¿La Máxima Expresión del Racismo en Guatemala? Una Interpretación Histórica y una Reflexión. Cuadernos del Presente Imperfecto*, no. 4 (Guatemala: F&G Editores, 2008).

represent anything good. If one takes the title of the work seriously, the lines stand for what is gone, their accumulation is at the same time a subtraction, their presence absence. Every individual stroke is intended to represent a disappeared person, to replace their body. In its vulnerability, the artist's drawing body points to the precariousness and incompleteness of these representational functions. That 45,000 is a necessarily estimated number makes things all the more difficult.

And yet for a limited time these lines were read, by exhibition visitors, tourists, and other passersby who encountered them on the exterior of the former monastery, with anger, curiosity, fright, and perhaps sadness. If the presence of the disappeared could be gleaned from the lines drawn on the wall, or in the sense of Luis de Lión, from the seeds that germinate in this tilled field, is not for us to answer. The scale of violence and suffering, however, cannot be captured through these acts of drawing and reading, just as it cannot be captured in a monument or an archive. The performance *Matemática Sustractiva* differs from static monuments and archives because of the visible presence of the body in it and the transience of the lines, which were probably slowly washed away by the rain. In the days following the performance, they gradually began to blend into each other, their white color mixing with the orange-red wall. They ceased to be symbols, transforming themselves into a material layer, into a kind of patina that remained neither visible nor completely removed. With its open process, the performance resembles the search for the disappeared, their presence and their traces in the space; a search that is everything but finished. In this way, it too becomes an act of mourning.

A Psychiatric Clinic in Deir Yassin / Kfar Sha'ul

Unmade Film is not an unfinished film, but rather a multifaceted collection of photographs, sound pieces, workshops, drawings, and installations created over several years. With this work, Uriel Orlow makes an attempt to approach a complex place where various histories of violence and trauma overlap. Horrible stories are inscribed into the stones here, as one passage in the work tells us. If the stones could speak, they would tell about the violence they witnessed. But they remain silent, and thus an active uncovering is needed of the history of this place, which initially appears as the site of the Kfar Sha'ul psychiatric clinic west of Jerusalem. Opened in 1951, many of the first patients were survivors of the Shoah, who suffered from the trauma they experienced in the European extermination camps. One of these patients was the artist's great-aunt, an Auschwitz survivor who emigrated to Palestine at the end of the war. She suffered a nervous breakdown in the late 1950s and spent the last thirty years of her life in the clinic. When Orlow's family visited Israel from Switzerland during his childhood, they often came to see her there.[13]

The clinic is not located in one contiguous building, but is made up of several smaller, old limestone houses scattered around the site. These are the remaining houses of the Palestinian village of Deir Yassin. In 1948, right-wing Israeli militias perpetrated a massacre there, killing over a hundred residents and forcing the rest to flee the village. In the following years, the name of the village became synonymous with the forcible expulsion of Palestinians from their land, and references to it were

13 See Uriel Orlow and Andrea Thal, "A Conversation about Unmade Film," in Uriel Orlow, *Unmade Film*, exhib. cat. (Jerusalem: Al-Ma'mal Foundation for Contemporary Art, Paris: Centre Culturel Suisse, Zürich: Les Complices*, Southampton: John Hansard Gallery, 2014), pp. 151–168, here p. 155.

sometimes made as open threats,[14] which led many Palestinians to flee their villages in the months that followed, fearing a massacre like the one in Deir Yassin. The massacre has occupied a central place in Palestinian memory ever since, but no explicit reference to it can be found at the site itself.[15] The only witnesses are the silent buildings that house the clinic.

Orlow tries to approach this location, one where different experiences of violence and traumatic memories are overlaid, through different formats, without simplifying the complexity of the various narratives or narrowing them down to a singular linear account. The project thus adopts the structure of a film that will never be completed, leaving the individual parts to exist on their own.[16] The individual elements of the work expose varying layers of trauma that are separated in time and condensed in space in strange ways. *The Voiceover* takes the listener on an imaginary—because it was not possible to create it on site—audio tour through the former village, in which the present and the past are intertwined. The buildings in the village, including homes, mosques and bakeries, are described in terms of their architectural characteristics and their role as the scene of a massacre, as well as their present use as a psychiatric clinic. *The Script* compiles a list of the various symptoms that trauma victims often suffer from, for example

14 See Ariella Azoulay quoted in Hanan Toukan, "Continuity from Rupture: Deir Yassin's Absent Presence," in Orlow, *Unmade Film*, pp. 20–26, here p. 23.

15 See Orlow and Thal, "A Conversation about Unmade Film," p. 156.

16 The elements are: *The Reconnaissance* (Wallpaper image, audio, sandbox, 2012–2013), *The Voiceover* (8-channel audio, dimming light, 30′, 2012-2013), *The Staging* (HD video, silent, 10′, 2012–2013), *The Storyboard* (Drawings, booklet 28 x 22 cm, 16 pages, 2013), *The Score* (Audio with video, 15′/audio in five parts, 45′, 2013), *The Script* (Series of 60 pencil drawings on paper, 21 x 29,7 cm each, 2013), *The Stills* (Archival pigment prints, 36 x 36 cm, 2013), *The Production Photographs* (C-type prints, dimensions variable, 2012–2013), *The Props* (Glass bottle with olive oil, cigarettes, chocolate, dimensions variable, 2013), *The Closing Credits* (16mm film, 7′, 2013–2014), *The Proposal* (Lecture performance, 45 min, 2013).

aggression, concentration and sleep disorders, personality changes and skin rashes. The terms are written in pencil in Arabic, Hebrew and English on sheets of white paper, defying any clear attribution to a particular history of suffering, even though they are taken from medical records at the Center for Victims of Torture in Ramallah. It becomes clear from the several interviews Orlow conducted with Palestinian psychologists, which are printed in the *Unmade Film* catalog, that the issue of trauma is not one that pertains only to the past.

In the interviews, the psychologists describe how the ongoing psychological stress caused by living in a continuous state of emergency under Israeli occupation can hardly be subsumed under the diagnosis of post-traumatic stress disorder (PTSD). Rather, one needs to think about it as Continuous Traumatic Stress Disorder.[17] Astrid Schmetterling makes clear through her analysis of *The Storyboard*, a collection of children's drawings, how closely connected the experience of the Nakba is to the situation of many Palestinians today. In a workshop at the Dar Al-Tifl Al-Arabi School in East Jerusalem, students drew the story of the founding of the orphanage, which is located at the same place. Palestinian Hind Al Husseini founded it in 1948 after the Deir Yassin massacre to house the orphaned children of the village. Schmetterling observes that one of the students' drawings shows modern day Israeli missiles striking the village, presumably evidence of the students' own traumatic experiences.[18]

The Staging, a video with tableaux vivants, approaches memory through the body and its inscribed experiences. During a workshop in Jerusalem and Ramallah

17 See "Continuous Trauma: A Conversation Between Uriel Orlow and Yoa'd Ghanadry," in Orlow, *Unmade Film*, pp. 61–75, here p. 64.

18 See Astrid Schmetterling, "Uriel Orlow's Unmade Film: A Multidirectional Archive for Palestinian and Israeli Traumatic Memory," in *Infinite Record: Archive, Memory, Performance*, ed. Maria Magdalena Schwaegermann and Karmenlara Ely (New York: Brooklyn Arts Press, 2017), pp. 136–143, here p. 139.

modeled on the approach of Augusto Boal's *Theater of the Oppressed*, participants came up with various images whose messages are ambivalent. Scenes of a handshake seem to suggest a form of reconciliation, while others, such as that of a man with his foot on the body of someone lying on the ground, or that of a woman weeping over a body also lying on the ground, suggest painful or conflictual encounters. But rather than referring to concrete events, the scenes seem to open up to a range of associations in their indeterminacy. The presence of bodies in varying constellations, and the at times intense interactions of the participants, contrast with the sense of emptiness and abandonment conveyed by the photographs of empty chairs in the courtyard of Kfar Sha'ul, titled *The Stills*. Heedlessly scattered across the grounds, the chairs seem to refer to a twofold absence: that of the displaced and murdered Palestinian villagers and that of the Shoah survivors of Kfar Sha'ul, who had no place in the society of the newly founded state of Israel. Orlow explains that although the memory of the Shoah was and is a central part of Israel's national self-image, the traumatized survivors of the death camps often did not fit into the image of a modern state looking optimistically to the future, and were thus relegated to the margins of society.[19]

That Orlow leaves the work fragmentary and does not develop a coherent film out of the various elements is also the refusal of a linear cinematic narrative. By trying to think history spatially rather than temporally in *Unmade Film*, he allows for the superimposition of the historically specific painful memories onto this place to become visible. These memories become tangible both on a concrete spatial level and on the level of psychological trauma, which in the case of Palestinians persists

19 See Orlow and Thal, "A Conversation about Unmade Film," p. 155. Here Orlow refers to Idith Zertal's book *Israel's Holocaust and the Politics of Nationhood* (Cambridge: Cambridge University Press, 2005).

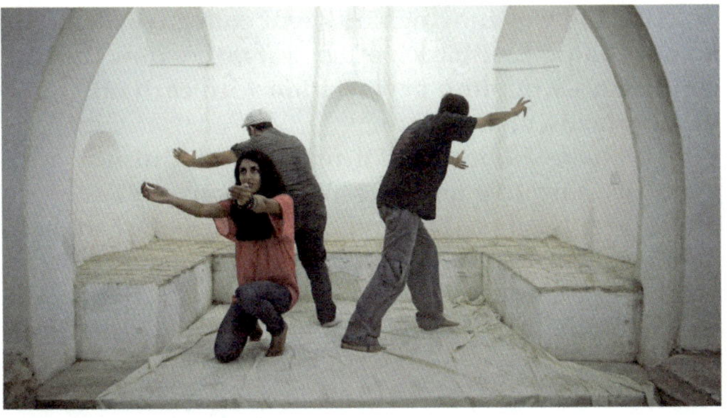

Fig. 2: Uriel Orlow, *Unmade Film: The Staging* (HD video, silent, 10′, 2012–2013), film still, courtesy the artist. All Rights Reserved, DACS/Artimage 2022.

to this day. The aim is not to create an equalizing relationship between the two. The experiences of violence do not compete with each other, the pain of one cannot be relativized by that of the other. In the case of Deir Yassin/Kfar Sha'ul, the repression of the pain of the Shoah survivors prevents the memory of the massacre in Deir Yassin. According to Orlow: "What does it mean when one trauma conceals another, in other words, when one trauma's immanent incapacity for remembrance becomes the obstruction of memory for another?"[20] Thus, talking about this location is only possible if one understands history as an open process in which remembering one thing also makes possible the memory of the other, instead of obscuring it. In *Multidirectional Memory*, Michael Rothberg outlines how, during the era of decolonization, the memory of the Shoah was linked to the articulation of other accounts by victims of racism and colonialism, and how different collective memories have mutually influenced each other. He proposes the concept of multidirectional memory to

20 See Orlow and Thal, "A Conversation about Unmade Film," p. 155.

describe the way in which different collective identities do not compete with each other, but rather how they are continuously put into new relation with each other in a malleable discursive space.[21]

In *Unmade Film*, the film remains "unfinished business," its narrative and memory unresolved. The work offers no explicit reading and rejects cinematic catharsis. As a result, a space for multidirectional memory is created in two senses. On the one hand, in relation to the concrete physical place where different memories overlap and are "stored" in the stones of the buildings. And on the other hand, in relation to the politics of memory regarding suffering and violence, where two different and incomparable traumas, which are nevertheless complexly entwined, can be placed in relation to each other. Or, as Orlow himself puts it, "I am not trying to find a solution for these contradictions, but a way to be with them."[22]

A Flower Stand, a Tailor Shop and a Snack Bar in Nuremberg

"How can you film a crime scene so that it can simply be a place? A place that looks, across the street, at the city," reads a passage in the film *Tiefenschärfe* (in English *Depth of Field*), by Mareike Bernien and Alex Gerbaulet.[23] The place is Nuremberg, or more precisely, three places in this city. A flower stand located on the side

21 See Michael Rothberg, *Multidirectional Memory. Remembering the Holocaust in the Age of Decolonization* (Stanford: Stanford University Press, 2009), pp. 4–5. He continues, "The model of multidirectional memory posits collective memory as partially disengaged from exclusive versions of cultural identity and acknowledges how remembrance both cuts across and binds together diverse spatial, temporal, and cultural sites." (p. 11).

22 Orlow and Thal, "A Conversation about Unmade Film," p. 168.

23 *Tiefenschärfe / Depth of Field*, (dir. Alex Gerbaulet and Mareike Bernien), Germany 2016–2017, 15′.

of a street, a tailor shop, and a snack bar located at the entrance to a supermarket parking lot. It was at these locations that three people were murdered by the right-wing terrorist group National Socialist Underground (NSU). What does a place reveal about the events that took place there? What does it mean to look at the city from these places, a city that seems to resist remembering and mourning?

Tiefenschärfe opens with a long shot of an underpass. Traffic rushes by uneventfully in both directions. Almost imperceptibly, the image tilts slightly to the left before tilting horizontally again. This is followed by a cut to a wooded area, the low rumble of traffic can still be heard in the background. Although this mundane scene can probably be found a thousand times over in Germany, this is not just any road running through a forest. This is where Enver Şimşek was shot dead at a flower stall on September 9, 2000. Şimşek was thirty-eight years old then, and had built a career with a wholesale flower business. He was the first victim of a series of racist attacks and murders that claimed the lives of nine people of Turkish and Greek origin, as well as a German police officer, between 2000 and 2007. The investigating authorities and the media falsely implicated the victims' friends and family, and constructed links to organized crime. Only in 2011 did the far-right group expose itself and the murders were finally acknowledged as racially motivated acts.

Just as the authorities refused to investigate right-wing terrorism as a motive, Nuremberg seems to have difficulties commemorating those who were murdered at the places they were killed, to mark the fact that people died violently at these places and to mourn these deaths.[24] "A tailor shop, an empty warehouse, a memorial" is how

24 The inability of broad sections of the German public to feel empathy and mourn the lives of those who were killed is analyzed by Deniz Utlu in his article "On Behalf of Grief and Anger. Against an Economy of Remembrance" in this book, pp. 239–257.

Bernien and Gerbaulet refer to the store on a street corner where the owner Abdurrahim Özüdoğru was murdered on June 13, 2001. "The fact that a tailor was murdered here is something everyone knows and have never heard about" says an off-screen voice. The blinds of the shop windows are closed and windows with lowered shutters are reflected in the glass. The only indication of the crime—in the form of a cardboard sign—becomes the object of struggle for interpretive hegemony. The word "Nazis" has been scratched out and written over with a marker. A similar scenario is to be found at the location where İsmail Yaşar was shot dead in his snack bar in the parking lot of a supermarket on June 9, 2005. Without showing us the images, the narrator's voice tells us that here, too, the writing on the memorial plaque has been crossed out, and a piece of graffiti reading "NSU lebt" (NSU lives) has been hastily crossed out not far from the scene of the crime. The city's amnesia reveals itself as willful denial and aggression, in which the victims of the murders are not only ignored, but where there are repeated attempts to actively prevent their remembrance.

Tiefenschärfe does not show us iconic views of Nuremberg, but rather sober shots of the crime scenes and their surroundings. The locations are unmarked, and the camera wanders across facades to empty balconies and windows, underpasses, doorways and front yards. There are hardly any people in the images, the city seems quiet and uninhabited. These are everyday scenes of a city that was rebuilt in the 1950s and 1960s after the destruction of the war, tidy and car-friendly. Nothing in these images seems to point to the murders; rather, there is a mute orderliness that helped produce an image of German normality in the post-war era, at a time when a return to normality was actually impossible.

The seemingly neutral images of the city keep tilting, however. The camera rotates the shots of a backyard with garages or a storefront with windows, turning

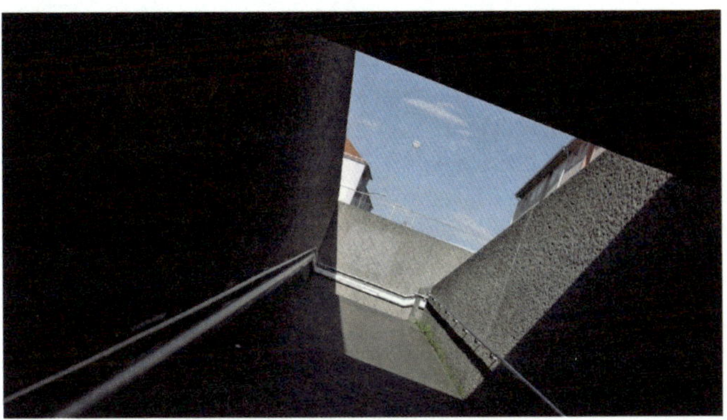

Fig. 3: Alex Gerbaulet and Mareike Bernien, *Tiefenschärfe / Depth of Field* (HD video, 15′, 2016–2017), film still, courtesy the artists.

them upside down. While the images turn, the narrator describes the murder investigations, which inverted the perpetrators and the victims. Before the NSU's self-disclosure, the authorities had primarily investigated the victims' communities. Frequently, ties to drug trafficking and organized crime were fabricated and indications of right-wing terrorism were ignored. This resulted not only in the victims' relatives having to mourn the sudden loss of their parents and partners, but also their subjection to suspicion on the part of the authorities and the resultant social stigmatization. This pattern of ignorance and a structural lack of empathy was perpetuated in public opinion,[25] with the loss of migrant life being considered, as it still is, as not deserving of mourning. The situated knowledge possessed by migrant communities was ignored.[26] Early on, relatives pointed to the

25 See Ayşe Güleç and Johanna Schaffer, "Empathie, Ignoranz und migrantisch situiertes Wissen. Gemeinsam an der Auflösung des NSU-Komplexes arbeiten," in *Den NSU-Komplex analysieren. Aktuelle Perspektiven aus der Wissenschaft*, ed. Juliane Karakayalı, Çağrı Kahveci, Doris Liebscher and Carl Melchers (Bielefeld: transcript Verlag, 2017), pp. 57–79.

26 See ibid., p. 58, footnote 2.

connection between the murders and attacks scattered all over Germany and to racism as the motive for the crimes. Yet their expertise was not taken into account during the investigations, and any witness statements that did not conform to the established explanatory framework were disregarded.

The film's frame tilts horizontally again when the narrator mentions the demonstrations that relatives of the victims organized in Kassel and Dortmund in 2006, which demanded that the murders be recognized as a series of racist crimes and that they finally be solved. In this act of collective empowerment, in which grief was articulated together with the demand for explanation and the recognition of the underlying racist motives, the image seems to momentarily "straighten out." Even though the demonstrations went largely unnoticed, the sociologist Çiğdem Inan sees a space that opens up in these moments of expropriated mourning, in which sadness and the affective can become a political resource for change[27]—beyond a classical understanding of emancipation as the "reclamation of autonomous subjectivity."[28] In *Tiefenschärfe,* Bernien and Gerbaulet plumb the refusal of recognition, and mourning as a gesture of solidarity, through a spatial approach to the crime scenes. The shots of silent streets and corners, which stand in stark contrast to the violence that continues to be denied to this day, are also images of a society that continues to refuse to come to terms with the NSU complex on a comprehensive political and societal level.

Nuremberg is a historically fraught location. It was here that the Nuremberg Laws were passed in 1935,

27 See Çiğdem Inan, "NSU, rassistische Gewalt und affektives Wissen," *ZRex – Zeitschrift für Rechtsextremismusforschung,* no. 2 (2021), pp. 212–227, here p. 223, https://doi.org/10.3224/zrex.v1i2.02.

28 Çiğdem Inan "'Diesmal nicht' Zur Enteignung der Trauer," *Texte zur Kunst,* no. 126 (June 2022), https://www.textezurkunst.de/126/cigdem-inan-diesmal-nicht/#id30 (accessed June 29, 2022).

codifying the anti-Semitic and racist ideology of the National Socialists into law. It is where the National Socialist Party (NSDAP) rallies were held until 1938, on the specially constructed and monstrously sized National Socialist Party Rally Grounds. At one point in the film, one can see parts of the site's remaining buildings, discernible only by their massive stones. Cars drive past the remnants of the former main grandstand. The nearby SS barracks are now the headquarters of the Federal Office for Migration and Refugees. The camera pans across the roof and onto the brick facade with its windows framed in gray stone. It refuses the monumental lines of sight that would result from long shots and instead opts for seemingly banal angles that present the normality of that which cannot possibly be normal and yet has apparently long since become so.[29] Much like the NSU crime scenes, this site appears to be an arbitrary location, the history of which has been rendered indiscernible and is only revealed through the narrative voice. In between these shots, the image of a wall with the outline of a smashed Reich eagle and swastika flashes repeatedly, like past patterns encroaching on the present.

A River in Western Colombia

The bodies literally appeared in the river before those who found them knew how, where and why they had been thrown into the water to begin with. The first bodies were spotted on a small path known as Beltrán, on the banks of the Cauca River in the municipality of Marsella, in western Colombia.[30] They were followed by hundreds of either intact or mangled, tortured and

29 Today, the Nuremberg Folk Festival and the Rock am Ring festival, along with other events, take place on the site.

30 Hereafter, reference is made to Anderson Paul Gil Pérez, "Los muertos de Beltrán en el Río Cauca como Manifestación de la Violencia en

decomposing bodies, found by residents and particularly by fishermen over decades until today, but with increased frequency in the 1980s and 1990s. Occasionally they were carried north with the currents, repeatedly to the same spot. Sometimes they were retrieved from the water by organized residents with the aim of documenting them and having them identified by forensic organizations and relatives of the disappeared, but also to bury them. The accumulation of bodies and the criminalization of those who "fished" them out of the water made these activities much more difficult. This is how Beltrán and Marsella came to symbolize the extent of the violence experienced by the people of Colombia during the Internal Armed Conflict. And yet it was simply the place where the bodies appeared; it was there that they became testimony to the violence to which they had been subjected. Many of the bodies could be traced back to the so-called Trujillo Massacre, a series of individual murders and mass killings perpetrated in communities more than one hundred kilometers south of Beltrán between 1986 and 1994 by drug cartels in collaboration with state officials, with the intention of terrorizing the population and driving them from their territories.[31] During the fight against the guerrillas, people who were not involved were also brutally tortured, murdered and thrown into the river in order to make not only them, but also the perpetrators and the scene of the crime invisible, as well as to send a message to the people living along the river. The paradoxical operation of making identities and traces disappear while at the same time making violence visible with the aim of terrorizing people is particularly striking here, but

Colombia," *Revista Conjeturas Sociológicas* 6, no. 17 (2018), pp. 143–159.

31 See Gonzalo Sánchez et al., *La Masacre de Trujillo: Una Tragedia que no Cesa. Informe del Centro Nacional de Memoria Histórica* (Bogotá: CNRR-Grupo de Memoria Histórica, 2011), pp.17–31, 52–64.

not unique in the history of Latin America.[32] Choosing this long, wide and murky river as a flowing mass grave affects not only those who lose their loved ones in the river, but also all others who become witnesses to this loss by finding their bodies in the same place that constitutes their livelihood.[33] This is particularly the case for the local fishers.

It was when fishing, of all things, that artist Gabriel Posada first saw a body "floating" in the Cauca, as a child during an outing with his father.[34] This experience became the driving force behind his many-year series *Magdalenas por el Cauca,* which he initiated in 2008 in collaboration with artist and poet Yorlady Ruiz. The first painting Posada did was a portrait of an anonymous woman carrying a photograph of her son, who had disappeared, on a several meters long canvas. The painting was mounted on a raft the artists built themselves, which then floated in the Cauca River near Cartago, south of Beltrán. The portrait was accompanied by the artists and other participants, who sailed alongside it in their own boats until the raft disappeared into the horizon with the current. In the years that followed, Posada and Ruiz made contact with other communities that had both lost loved ones and discovered, recovered, and buried bodies from the river. They changed and expanded their series to include many more portraits of victims, their mothers, and also other witnesses,

32 See for example Diana Taylor's discussion on the visibility of public abductions during Argentina's "Dirty War," in Diana Taylor, *Disappearing Acts: Spectacles of Gender and Nationalism in Argentina's "Dirty War"* (Durham N.C. and London: Duke University Press, 1997), pp. 98–109.

33 See Isabel Cristina Zuleta, "Los Ríos de Colombia: Lugares de Vida, no de Muerte," in *Cartografía de la Desaparición Forzada en Colombia: Relato (Siempre) Incompleto de lo Invisibilizado*, ed. Fidel Mingorance et al. (Human Rights Everywhere, 2019), p. 112.

34 The following refers to a personal conversation between Sebastián Eduardo Dávila, Gabriel Posada and Yorlady Ruiz on Zoom, June 2022. See also "Magdalenas por el Cauca," https://magdalenasporelcauca.wordpress.com (accessed June 10, 2022).

using a range of techniques and materials, installed on increasingly stable rafts that they built with techniques adopted from the people living along the river. Whereas the first *Magdalena*—in Spanish, weeping women are referred to as "Magdalenas" in reference to Mary Magdalene—was intended to represent the disappeared and their families throughout Colombia due to its non-personal but recognizable nature, the other portraits took on more personal meaning for the surviving relatives and witnesses of actual people and their deceased bodies. Further witnesses joined the process alongside the family members.

One of the portraits was of María Isabel Espinosa, an inhabitant of the foothills, a poet, and a conscious witness to hundreds of bodies in the Cauca River, to which she maintains an ambivalent relationship. In her poems, the river appears both as an accomplice, because it materially decays and spatially displaces the bodies, and also as a witness, and thus itself a victim of violence.[35] As an autonomous agent, the river thus oscillates between the status of perpetrator, victim, and witness, interfacing with drug cartels, paramilitaries, state officials, witnesses, family members, and, last but not least, the victims. Its physical ability to contain and transport bodies gives it this agency, bringing together two paradoxical qualities: ingestion and movement. Unlike a cemetery or a mass grave, it does not merely receive the bodies, but moves them over hundreds of kilometers into the Magdalena River and finally into the sea, or simply to its banks along the Beltrán Path. This is made possible by the materiality of flowing water, as opposed to solid earth. On the one hand, this rendering visible serves the perpetrators, who hope to convey a threat through the corpses. On the other hand, the possibility of recovering,

35 See Freelance Producciones, "RASTRO PÚRPURA,"*YouTube*, November 13, 2012, https://www.youtube.com/watch?v=2RqJvqr02Ik (accessed June 10, 2022).

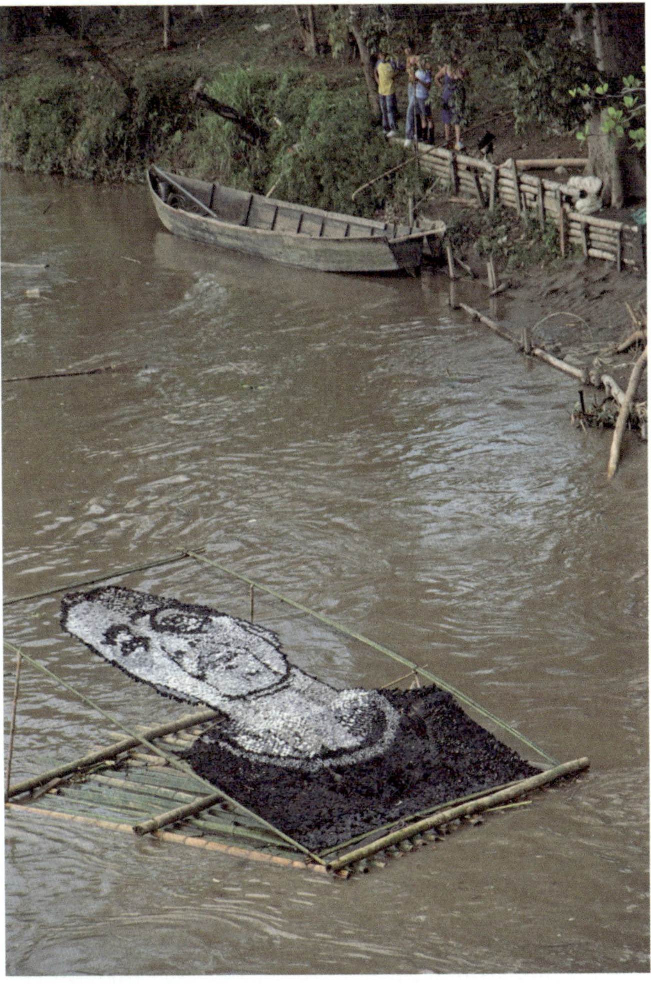

Fig. 4: Gabriel Posada and Yorlady Ruiz, from the series *Magdalenas por el Cauca* (Cauca River, 2008), intervention, photograph: Gabriel Posada, courtesy of the artists.

identifying, and burying the bodies from the river runs counter to their attempt at anonymization and, to a certain extent, terrorization.

With their series *Magdalenas por el Cauca,* Posada, Ruiz and the other participants engage with the material and spatial nature of the Cauca River in multiple ways.[36] Because those who are portrayed are most often crying, the materiality of water is transformed into a medium of mourning in a way that transcends the disappearance of bodies. Metaphorically, the tears of the "Magdalenas" mix with the water of the river that swallows their portraits as well as the bodies of their loved ones. Then there are the materials used, which come from the area around the river itself, such as the pieces of clothing salvaged from the water for the portrait of María Isabel Espinosa, as well as the logs for the rafts. The residents themselves became conscious witnesses by collecting the pieces of clothing and weaving them into the portrait of Espinosa. Together with the surviving relatives, they participate in the work of collective mourning through their traditional techniques of crocheting and raft-building. Furthermore, the visibility of the portraits afforded by the raft's kinetic engineering stands in stark contrast to the standard practice of concealing the bodies and body parts in bags, thereby keeping them as invisible as possible.[37] Because of its powerful current, the Cauca itself also refuses to fulfill this function by freeing the bodies from their bags. The *Magdalenas,* which appear monumental in size, are only visible for a short distance before taking their own course, independent of the boats accompanying them, eventually disappearing with the flow of the river towards the

36 For a similar examination of the specificity of a river as a site of disappearance, as well as the role of art as a medium of memory, see Estela Schindel, "A Limitless Grave: Memory and Abjection of the Río de la Plata," in Colombo and Schindel, *Space and the Memories of Violence,* pp. 188–204.

37 See Sánchez, *La Masacre de Trujillo,* pp. 58, 179, 231.

sea. It is in their farewell to the bereaved, while surrendering themselves to the river, that they come closest to the victims of violence. Their journey re-enacts these disappearances, but differently.[38] From the beginning, their journey is embedded in a process of mourning, marked by an unresolved ending and the lack of explanation from the state, but also by the will, particularly of the inhabitants of the river banks and the artists, to bear individual and collective witness to the violence.

Rendering Visible, Remembering, Mourning

The artistic interventions by Isabel Ruiz, Uriel Orlow, Mareike Bernien and Alex Gerbaulet, Gabriel Posada and Yorlady Ruiz deal with how violence has inscribed itself into space in varying ways. In doing so, the question of how these violent acts can be made legible in the present arises as a first consideration. With the specificity of their particular contexts in mind, their interventions are attempts at making the forgotten or neglected victims of violence visible again. As such, they intervene in the processes of mourning and remembrance and thus in the political and historical work of reconciliation, which is often undesired and obstructed by the state, as well as by society. Their sometimes direct, and at other times indirect—filmic, for example—material inscriptions into the topographies of disappearance often coincide with efforts to center the work of the victims' families and friends, as well as to commemorate the victims, whom they seek to give presence to in an attempt to resist the logic of the state that often is the driving force behind their disappearance and erasure.

38 Compare Ileana Diéguez, *Cuerpos sin Duelo: Iconografía y Teatralidad del Dolor* (Córdoba: Ediciones DocumentA/Escénicas, 2013), pp. 200–203.

These artistic practices reveal the tensions inherent in the relation between topography and past acts of violence. While the physical location remains and these past events have virtually sedimented themselves there, the bodies of those who experienced the violence are absent and can no longer attest to it. As a result of the temporal differences between place and past events, the artists are compelled to uncover this sedimentation of violence and loss through an engagement with the physical locations. This is done either directly on site or through other mobile or even fluid media, underscoring both the sedimentation of history and the processual nature of mourning. In her durational performance, Ruiz gives her own body a central role in an individual and collective mourning process that continues until today. Orlow investigates the spatial overlaying of violence through various means of activating the memory of this superimposition and allowing its multidirectionality to manifest. By means of a cinematic site visit, Bernien and Gerbaulet reveal the disjuncture between the racist violence that took place and the reluctance to mourn the victims. In *Magdalenas por el Cauca*, Ruiz and Posada respond to the movement of water that puts violence into motion as opposed to sedimenting it, by transposing the images of the bereaved, victims, and witnesses onto the river and letting them flow, both literally and metaphorically, as an open process of mourning.

As different as the artistic processes and political contexts are, they are all acts of making suppressed histories and absent bodies visible. They go far beyond a mere pointing out however. By directing attention to the victims of violence and their relatives and friends, and by thematizing their losses in varying degrees of public space, the works also actively intervene in processes of mourning and remembering. The incompleteness of mourning is not merely reiterated, but artistically translated and politically transformed. Memory is not neutral, but rather is always subject to conflicting politics of remembering, forgetting, and ignoring, as is demonstrated in the work of Ruiz, and Bernien and Gerbaulet. Grief that has been expropriated through violence and denial often results in some lives not being considered worthy of mourning. These artistic practices propose forms of remembrance and mourning that render present and give space to the lives that have been lost. This is not simply about making loss visible, however. Rather, through mourning, the awareness of being interconnected and interdependent is materialized. The understanding of the vulnerability of existence as a political resource that is activated in the works goes hand in hand with the collective responsibility for each other's physical lives.[39]

Translation: Angela Anderson

39 See Judith Butler, "Violence, Mourning, Politics," in Butler, *Precarious Life*, pp. 19–49, here p. 30.

Deniz Utlu

On Behalf of Grief and Anger

Against an Economy of Remembrance[1]

I The Impossibility of Commemoration

In November 2011, an explosion revealed that a Nazi terrorist organization, the so-called National Socialist Underground (NSU), had been murdering migrants, or people perceived as migrants, throughout the Federal Republic of Germany for the past ten years. This came as a shock to most people, albeit for different reasons. Many people working in the fields of migration politics, the arts or academia felt the need to find ways to commemorate what had happened. What was missing was a form of commemoration that could have fulfilled this need. Perhaps it is more accurate to speak in the plural, in fact. The different reasons for being shocked generated the need for different forms of commemoration, some of which were in contradiction to each other or even mutually exclusive.

I myself attended various events, and there was always something wrong with one form or the other. When one of these commemorative events used the strategy of silence, against the prevailing silence, some said:

1 This essay was first published in November 2013 as part of the Rosa Luxemburg Foundation's publication series *Standpunkte* (13/2013) and has been slightly revised for its publication in Azar Mortazavi, Tunay Önder and Christine Umpfenbach, eds., *Urteile. Ein dokumentarisches Theaterstück über die Opfer des NSU mit Texten über alltäglichen und strukturellen Rassismus* (Münster: Unrast Verlag, 2016), as well as for its English translation in this book.

"Speak, don't be quiet, there has been silence for too long." An auto convoy was considered inappropriate; in the case of a petition, there was apparently disagreement on "certain points." The need to do something remained unsatisfied, even though so much was being done. I understood this as the inability to commemorate. Everyone's objections were justified, because there is no right way to remember when the discursive framework is wrong.[2]

I did not know Halit Yozgat, Enver Şimşek, Abdurrahim Özüdoğru, Süleyman Taşköprü, Habil Kılıç, Mehmet Turgut, İsmail Yaşar, Theodoros Boulgarides or Mehmet Kubaşık. I wanted to mourn them, and be with myself and with those who had been killed. However, my grief was entangled with the struggle for a place in this society, for an appropriation of history, for a negotiation of the discourse. I did not want to engage with the murderers and the society that produced them as I grieved. I wanted to focus on myself and on those who had been killed. This proved to be impossible.

II Grief as a Political Space

In her speech at the official state commemoration of the NSU murders, Semiya Şimşek, daughter of the murdered Enver Şimşek, said: "We didn't have the chance to mourn in peace." The entire three minutes and forty-eight seconds of Semiya Şimşek's speech belong to the few minutes of what I consider to be *commemoration*. I read her words in the newspaper and heard friends talking about her and watched her speech

2 In the German text, this sentence ("Es gibt kein richtiges Gedenken im falschen Diskurs") reads as a reference to a well-known quote in Adorno's *Minima Moralia*: "Es gibt kein richtiges Leben im falschen" ("wrong life cannot be lived rightly"). See Theodor W. Adorno, *Minima Moralia: Reflections on a Damaged Life*, trans. E. F. N. Jephcott (London and New York: Verso, 2005 [1951]), p. 39.

many times on the Internet. It seemed as if the constellation of speaker, content and audience had never been as opportune as it was during these three minutes and forty-eight seconds.

The victims can no longer speak. They cannot accuse. They cannot forgive. It is precisely this fact that makes commemoration necessary and impossible at the same time. Every speech, every expression of condolence runs the risk of becoming a space for the projection of one's own ideas, or of being instrumentalized for political interests, because of the indirectness of the experience.

Semiya Şimşek did not express her condolences or speak on the basis of what she had only indirectly experienced. Her speech was intensely political, without allowing for its political instrumentalization. Semiya Şimşek spoke from a place of emotional grief and the loss of a loved one, someone who was needed. From this position, a space opened up where her voice could be heard. She was political in a *human* sense in her speech. In her book *Undoing Gender*, the philosopher Judith Butler argues that loss and grief reflect the significance of others for us; indeed, our own being is invariably defined by our relationships to others. Violence against specific people based on their alleged belonging to a particular group arises when the mere existence of these people in the fabric of society represents an untenable contradiction with the perpetrators' conception of the world and of themselves. What does it mean when someone's murder does not trigger grief or at least empathy for the grieving relatives? What does this say about our understanding of the human, about what a human is?

In reference to the reactions of politicians and police after the excessive violence against asylum seekers in the early 1990s, Guido Gebauer, Bernhard Taureck and Thomas Ziegler remarked in their 1993 appeal for a culturally integrative society: "One cannot help noticing that asylum seekers in Germany are no longer treated as human beings with rights."[3]

And what happens to someone for whom an event is merely a political scandal, or simply a political event, when they suddenly experience it in the form of emotional grief over the loss of a person? Should this not unsettle their notion of what constitutes humanness?[4]

The term *emotional grief,* adopted here from Judith Butler, may seem redundant at first as it constitutes a pleonasm, because grief already implies emotionality. However, because grief as an affect has been instrumentalized in public discourse and in an economy of commemoration to such an extent that its expropriation takes place, it is meaningful and necessary to counter it specifically with the concept of emotional grief. Semiya Şimşek's speech undermined this expropriation. Her speech was meant as a commemoration to strengthen those who were themselves victims of this terror, or who could potentially be, and to unsettle everyone else's understanding of humanity. I think that only emotional grief opens a space in which not only rights and political positions can be reconsidered, but also the ontological and epistemological foundations of our society and our understanding of humanity.

A reordering of positions and understandings based on emotions would permeate all levels of our being, including our image of ourselves and of others, our desires and perception, and our understanding of the world. In short, our positioning in relation to everything we have experienced and done up to this

3 Bernhard Taureck, Guido Gehbauer, and Thomas Ziegler, *Ausländerfeindschaft ist Zukunftsfeindschaft – Plädoyer für eine kulturintegrative Gesellschaft* (Berlin: Fischer Verlag, 1993).

4 "I think that if I can still address a 'we,' or include myself within its terms, I am speaking to those of us who are living in certain ways beside ourselves, whether in sexual passion, or emotional grief, or political rage." Judith Butler, *Precarious Life: The Power of Mourning and Violence* (London and New York: Verso, 2004), p. 24.

point.[5] A form of commemoration based on emotional grief could make possible what Seyla Benhabib refers to as the "cultivation of an expanded way of thinking."[6] Differences would be acknowledged, and common human dignity would be respected. The question of how societal constellations can be changed in such a way that emotional grief opens up a political space, instead of being misused by symbolic politics, is an important one. The fear of facing consequences is perhaps one reason why the father of the murder victim Halit Yozgat was prevented from speaking at the official state commemoration ceremony.

III The Voice of the Others

The Berlin newspaper *Tagesspiegel* reported that the father of murder victim Halit Yozgat was initially not scheduled to speak at the official state memorial ceremony. According to *Tagesspiegel*, it was only after İsmail Yozgat threatened to take the stage anyway, and thanks to the mediation of Barbara John, the ombudswoman for the friends and family of the NSU victims, that he was allowed to give his speech after all.[7]

The organizers certainly had many justifications for the fact that Halit Yozgat's father's speech was not included in the initial program. Citing formal reasons is one method of silencing the voice of others, one that is as efficient as it is hypocritical. Efficient, because it

5 See Judith Butler, *Frames of War: When is Life Grievable?* (London and New York: Verso, 2010).

6 Seyla Benhabib, *Gleichheit und Differenz. Die Würde des Menschen und die Souveränitätsansprüche der Völker im Spiegel der politischen Moderne*. Speech at the award ceremony of the Leopold Lucas Prize on May 8, 2012 (Mohr Siebeck: Tübingen, 2013).

7 See Armin Lehmann, "Barbara John verhinderte Eklat," *Der Tagesspiegel*, February 24, 2012, http://www.tagesspiegel.de/politik/gedenkveranstaltung-fuer-nazi-opfer-barbara-john-verhinderte-eklat/6249896.html (accessed May 14, 2013).

seems to be only about the how and not about the what. Hypocritical because the what is restricted by the how, when it should not be. Formal reasons are as effective as the standardization of language in academia. Some of the ground-breaking authors in the field of colonial studies, such as Frantz Fanon, have managed to break out of an epistemology that is unable to register and thus reproduces inequalities through form and method, by employing a language that is atypical, perhaps even inadmissible, for academic writing. As a result, Fanon's dissertation *Black Skin, White Masks*—today a foundational work of critical research on colonialism and racism—was not accepted for formal reasons.[8]

There are countless formal reasons that could be cited in order to justify the exclusion of a speaker from such a large, high-profile and supposedly representative media event. It could be that it didn't fit into the schedule because of the elaborate program already in place. Maybe the program had already been sent out, the deadline for the announcement had passed, or a translator was not included in the budget. Or the ratio between victims' relatives and political representatives, or between women and men on stage would no longer have been right—there are many possible reasons.

There is often a consistent pattern underlying formal explanations when it comes to the speech of the *others*. Several writers and academics—shaken after the disclosure of the NSU—who began to research and write their first articles, received only two answers from their editorial departments and professors. First, the topic of right-wing extremism was not suitable for ratings. Second, they would not be able to be *objective* about the issue because they themselves had a connection to migration. In *Plantation Memories*, Grada Kilomba is confronted by

8 Frantz Fanon, *Peau Noire, Masques Blancs* (Paris: Éditions du Seuil, 1952).

the statement that her work is interesting, but not academic. Such comments function …

> like a mask, that silences our voices as soon as we speak. They allow the *white* subject to place our discourses back at the margins, as deviating knowledge, while their discourses remain at the centre, as the norm. When they speak it is scientific, when we speak it is unscientific; universal / specific; objective / subjective; neutral / personal; rational / emotional; impartial / partial; they have facts, we have opinions; they have knowledge, we have experiences.[9]

It is thus all the more remarkable that İsmail Yozgat delivered his speech after all. However, the *voice of the other* was tamed in the process of translation. The journalist Mely Kiyak published her own translation of the speech in her column in the *Frankfurter Rundschau*, commenting on the translation of the memorial service:

> So now it says everywhere that the Yozgat family is asking "for spiritual support." Mr. Yozgat neither mentioned nor asked for such a thing. They received support in Kassel-Baunatal. Kassel-Baunatal and not, as it reads everywhere, "my hometown Kassel-Baunatal"; the translator thought she had to add things here and there. Maybe she thought that Mr. Yozgat's words were not substantial enough. He did not greet any of the "distinguished guests" and certainly not "our Chancellor Angela Merkel".[10]

The *unforeseen speech* was *lost in translation*, its content changed, it was less irritating, it sounded submissive, just as hierarchy demands when a Turkish-born

9 Grada Kilomba, *Plantation Memories. Episodes of Everyday Racism* (Münster: UNRAST Verlag, 2008), p. 28.

10 Mely Kiyak, "Lieber Ismail Yozgat!," *Frankfurter Rundschau*, February 25, 2012, https://www.fr.de/meinung/lieber-ismail-yozgat-11333160.html (accessed May 14, 2013).

owner of an internet cafe addresses the German chancellor. There are cracks in the system, however. Yozgat's speech slipped through one such crack and made its way into the *Frankfurter Rundschau*. For me, this speech was a moment of commemoration. It faced an obstacle-laden path before it could manifest in the form of a commemorative act. I attribute these hurdles (with reference to Althusser) to a "bureaucratic-racist state apparatus."[11] A set of bureaucratic rules, the adherence to which is always institutionally tracked, and the non-adherence to which is penalized. For example, no-parking zones, orderly accounting, adherence to deadlines, and so on. This bureaucratic apparatus is racist in structure because there is a ranking of rules in the bureaucratic regulatory framework that often conforms to ideologies of inequality (albeit in the rarest of cases explicitly, intentionally, or even consciously). The rules themselves can also be discriminatory, such as the *Secondary Labor Market Access* clause (Section 39 of the Residency Act), which requires companies to prioritize German citizens in hiring if they have the same qualifications. The *bureaucratic-racist state apparatus* goes further than this, however. Meaning that even if a regulation itself is not discriminatory, there is a tendency to interpret it in such a way that it has a discriminatory effect, in this case a racist-discriminatory effect. Even when it depends on the interpretation of those involved—civil servants, prosecutors, judges, etc.—there is still a structural problem, because the interpretation, so the hypothesis goes, is consistently and not merely occasionally racist.

In his structuration theory, sociologist Anthony Giddens sees a recursive relationship between structure and agency. The actions of the actors are what create the structures that constrain them while at the same

11 Louis Althusser, "Idéologie et appareils idéologiques d'État. Notes pour une recherche," *La Pensée*, no. 151 (1970), pp. 3–38.

time giving them the possibilities to act.[12] The investigation surrounding the NSU murders is an example par excellence of how the bureaucratic-racist state apparatus functions. Through the memories of her father, his murder, and the ensuing years during which her family was suspected by investigators of being connected to his death, Semiya Şimşek reveals in passing that her father had a longer history with the bureaucratic apparatus, one that began long before his death and which continues until today. Şimşek describes how police officers regularly checked to see if her father had a permit for his flower stand, and how they prevented him from doing business during the process. She describes a scene in which her father refuses to pack up his stand, and then the police confiscate all of the flowers: "The merchandise needed to be 'seized,' is how the officers referred to it in their report. 'Exceeding the legally permitted sales hours, not having a permit in accordance with the Federal Highway Act, unauthorized extension beyond the area allocated for use with a special permit.'"[13] It seems that those responsible weighted the bureaucratic regulations in such a way that the work of the (*Turkish*) florist was made more difficult.

The investigation into the murder of Enver Şimşek was different. An imprisoned drug dealer had testified that Şimşek had been transporting heroin excipients. The police pursued this claim for years, even though a simple, routine fact check would have proven the inconsistency, or in other words, the falsity, of the testimony. In this case, however, the bureaucratic regulations were weighted in such a way that a fact check did not take place—perhaps because the officers thought it was obvious that a Turkish florist could also have been a drug

12 Anthony Giddens, *The Constitution of Society: Outline of the Theory of Structuration* (Berkeley and Los Angeles: University of California Press, 1984).

13 Semiya Şimşek, *Schmerzliche Heimat. Deutschland und der Mord an meinem Vater* (Berlin: Rowohlt, 2013), p. 33.

courier. Meanwhile, the police had confiscated bank statements and invoices during a search. They noticed that not everything had been correctly taxed and initiated proceedings: "This was the result of the investigation into the murder of Enver Şimşek" writes his daughter, "they looked for his murderer and found tax debts."[14] The weighting of rules, whether for a speech or a murder investigation, is not merely a *glitch*, because they systematically turn out negatively for the same constituencies.

The bureaucratic apparatus, regardless of whether some want it to be or not, is racist. Some of the reasons for this can certainly be found in people's socialization (school as an ideological state apparatus) and in media discourse (the information apparatus). The devastating influence the media can have is illustrated in this statement from Wolfgang Cremer (the first director of the Federal Intelligence Service) regarding his investigation of the perpetrators of the June 2004 nail bomb attack in Cologne's Keupstraße, who we now know were members of the NSU: "I admit that I considered right-wing extremism, but I was dissuaded by reports in the media about organized crime."[15]

Countless examples of the bureaucratic-racist state apparatus are to be found. Why did the Munich Higher Regional Court choose such a small courtroom for the NSU trial so that at first there was no room for the Turkish media, and then after a new seat lottery, the most important German media outlets in terms of the formation of public opinion were excluded, including the *Süddeutsche Zeitung*, the *FAZ* and *Die ZEIT*? For the proceedings against the Red Army Faction (RAF) in 1975, dedicated buildings were constructed.

14 Ibid., p. 173.

15 Protocol no. 24 of the 2nd parliamentary NSU investigation committee, October 10, 2012, p. 76, https://dserver.bundestag.de/btd/17/CD14600/Protokolle/Protokoll-Nr%2024a.pdf (accessed July 19, 2022).

IV Regarding Careful Consideration

Despite the many hurdles, İsmail Yozgat made himself heard. Many people have been empowered by this, because their perspectives found their way into the dominant discourse through his perspective, at least partially. And yet İsmail Yozgat's demand remained unfulfilled. His son was shot and killed in his internet cafe at Holländische Straße 82 in Kassel. İsmail Yozgat fought his way to the microphone, to audibility, and made a request to the chancellor and the entire nation. He said that what they wanted was not money, but that they wanted Holländische Straße to be renamed Halit-Straße. But his request was met with resistance in Kassel. "What a memorial should look like and where it should be needs to be grounded in a broad community consensus," and must be "carefully considered,"[16] wrote the daily newspaper, quoting Jürgen Kaiser, the mayor of the city of Kassel. In response, İsmail Yozgat said to the *taz*: "It is a disgrace that they are still discussing whether the street should be renamed or not. Would the authorities continue this discussion if it had been their son who had died in their arms in this street?"[17] In other words, what İsmail Yozgat was asking was: To what extent is it conceivable for *those in power* to think of the person who was murdered as a human being? No one who understands the grief of a father who lost his son, particularly in this way, would *carefully consider* in this situation. It needs to be asked why it is that *those in power* are unable to put themselves in this position. It is not because the pain is unimaginable, because that would imply attentiveness. The life of the victim is too distant, shrouded by stigma, beneath which the person is barely recognizable. No one would deny that someone

16 Timo Reuter, "Kassel sperrt sich gegen 'Halit'-Straße," *taz*, March 16, 2012, https://taz.de/Neonazi-Morde/!5098207/ (accessed July 18, 2022).

17 Ibid.

was killed. But why is violence against some groups of people less terrible than against others? Because they are less likely to be perceived as human beings? Is this not precisely this devaluation that İsmail Yozgat is rightly so outraged by? Is Holländische Straße (*Dutch Street*) too good for a Halit?

Using Judith Butler's terminology, Halit's life is not *grievable*, or not grievable to the extent that a street should be named after him. There is an expropriation of grief that takes place when it is met with *careful consideration*. Consideration can be a (micro-)economic mechanism with philosophical roots in utilitarianism. The benefit of addressing the murder would then be weighed against the benefit of maintaining a positive understanding of oneself and the world. In this case, a microeconomic calculation poses the following question: How much of my understanding of myself and the world am I willing to trade for *minimal extra confrontation* with the murder? I will call this phenomenon the *marginal rate of commemoration*. Provided that one proceeds from an individual and not from a collective rationality, one estimates the confrontation to be of little value. This confrontation could situate oneself, and one's position in society, in relation to this murder; and one would have to think about accountability, and possibly about (historical and societal) guilt. In the short term and on an individual basis, the costs appear to be relatively high. The benefits in the short-term could include improved relationships, the alleviation of social (neighborhood, for example) conflicts. On the other hand, the maintenance of one's self-image and understanding of the world would have to be accorded a higher value at first, because it provides stability, at least in the short term, and keeps us functional in our roles, possibly sparing us pain and feelings of guilt. Consequently, there is very little (if any) willingness for a minimal supplementary engagement with the murders—the recognition of those who were killed as human beings and as grievable—and the individual seeks to substitute as much engagement with maintenance as possible. Such a calculation in effect entails an expropriation of grief.

Another example: After the pogrom of Rostock-Lichtenhagen, during which the main reception center for asylum seekers and a house in which mostly former Vietnamese contract workers lived were set on fire in August, 1992, amid cheers from the local population, Angela Merkel, then Federal Minister for Youth, visited neo-Nazis in a Rostock youth club. An entire neighborhood attacked the apartments of Vietnamese people and set them on fire to applause—and the Federal Minister for Youth visits neo-Nazis. This pogrom and the numerous other attacks and assaults that happened in the early 1990s were subsequently used as reasons to effectively abolish the fundamental right to asylum. Neo-Nazis celebrated (or so it seemed at least) this new law two days after the vote passed in the Bundestag by murdering two Turkish families in Solingen in an arson attack.

The phenomenon of perpetrator-victim reversal is common in the context of discrimination—the local population (and the neo-Nazis) are victims who have been overwhelmed by society changing too rapidly, and the asylum seekers are perpetrators who have invaded their peaceful lives. Nobody denies the violence against migrants. There is an implicit valuation in the way society deals with this violence, however. The violence against refugees and migrant workers is not as important as the alleged overwhelmment of the Rostock population in the face of the complexity of societal changes. In light of the life-threatening danger to which the former contract workers were exposed, their loss must have been bearable for the local population and the federal government, as compared to the confusion of the young people visited by Merkel.

When *careful consideration* takes place in relation to contempt shown towards others, pogroms and racist violence, what is up for consideration is to what extent Halit Yozgat and the Vietnamese residents of the *Sunflower House*—as the former housing complex was called because of the large sunflower on its façade—are accepted as human beings. From this perspective, this kind of consideration is more closely aligned with the perpetrators than with the victims. The victims were not killed as *individuals*, but as *specimens*—to use Adorno's terminology here—belonging to the category of *migration*, and thus de-individualized, "levelled down."[18] A process of consideration is only possible between specimens, but never between individuals, because individuals consider, and are not subjected to consideration. Any commemoration within this framework necessarily remains closer to the perpetrators than to the victims.

At the memorial ceremony in Rostock-Lichtenhagen in 2012, the Asian-German political scientist Kien Nghi Ha gave a speech in which he appealed for commemoration from a Vietnamese perspective: "It is important for myself, for us, that the processing of what happened in Rostock-Lichtenhagen is not done solely from the dominant perspective of white Germans, in order to break the silence there, but also for us to rediscover our own history and embrace that history."[19] There is a video on YouTube of the memorial ceremony, one day after Ha's speech, in which a children's choir stands on a large stage with a banner reading "Rostock for Diversity and Tolerance" and sings the traditional German children's song "If you're happy, clap your hands (clap, clap)." Beer and sausage stands are visible in front of the stage, and the German president sits inside a tent and watches the children's choir. The film team interviews two Black men who were refused entrance by the police

18 Theodor Adorno, "Meditations on Metaphysics," in Adorno, *Negative Dialektik* (Frankfurt am Main: Suhrkamp, 1966). Unpublished translation by Simon Jarvis, 2000.

19 Kien Nghi Ha, "Ich bin hier, weil ihr hier seid," http://www.youtube.com/watch?v=qMH9WLQkdqo (accessed May 14, 2013).

even though they had an invitation from the mayor—they are both members of the German-African friendship group Daraja.

The Vietnamese residents of the Sunflower House and victims of racist violence in general did not seem to be of importance at this commemoration event. It was a folk festival, without the people who had been the target of the attack. A memorial plaque was installed, but it did not mention the Vietnamese residents. Things are more obscured than remembered here. Kien Nghi Ha was all the more compelling in his grief and anger when he shouted into the microphone before an all too loud audience: "Listen to me, this is where the music is playing, I've waited twenty years for this moment, and now I want you to listen to me." There is something in this exclamation and the call to "re-discover and re-appropriate one's own history" that could constitute a commemoration from the perspective of those who were targeted. The question being asked here is not why and under what circumstances the German population in Rostock-Lichtenhagen was capable of doing such a thing, but rather: How did the Vietnamese inhabitants get there? Under what conditions did they live? How did they deal with the attack during it and afterwards? Where do they live today? What does all of this mean for other Vietnamese and Asian people, as well as for other people in Germany who are exposed to racist violence and a contemptuous economy of commemoration? Moreover, what could this mean for people whose familial and national histories were in no small way affected by racist violence connected to Germany? These questions connect Rostock and Namibia, because the commemoration of the Herero and Nama, murdered by German colonial forces, has also been carefully considered within the context of an economy of commemoration.

V Namibia: Commemoration as Violence

To date, there is still no memorial to the victims of genocide in Germany's former colony of *German Southwest Africa*, which is now Namibia. In Lüderitz, where German soldiers were stationed in 1904, timber framed houses now stand in the desert, along with a small white church and a gymnasium. Videos show the inside of the gymnasium, with an old leather pommel horse and a brown wooden piano. A young man sits down at the piano and begins to play, singing the *Südwesterlied*.[20] Lüderitz is a Namibian port town named after the merchant Adolf Lüderitz, who, by means of underhanded business deals, acquired an entire bay in southwestern Africa at the end of the nineteenth century, now known as Lüderitz Bay. Between 1904 and 1908, following the *extermination order* issued by General Lothar von Trotha, a *campaign of extermination* was waged against the Herero and Nama. The first concentration camps were located on Shark Island close to Lüderitz at the beginning of the twentieth century.

After having been scraped clean of flesh and tissue by their relatives, the skeletal remains of the victims were sent to Germany for *scientific research*. Eugen Fischer, the notorious Nazi doctor, later sought to prove the "inferiority" of the Black race on the basis of the skulls.

At the end of September 2011, a delegation of seventy-three people from Namibia travelled to Berlin to receive eleven Nama and nine Herero skulls. The magazine *freitext* published a review of the Namibian press in its spring 2012 issue. The excerpts make it clear that the delegation, and with it all of Namibia, had initially expected this to be a *great moment*, but then felt treated

20 *The Südwesterlied* is a song written by Heinz Anton Klein-Werner in 1937 for a German youth scouting organization in Namibia that became a kind of national anthem for German colonists in Namibia.

with disrespect.[21] The Namibian government had paid for the travel expenses, the delegation was not welcomed with the same level of authority, and the only government minister present—Cornelia Pieper from the German Foreign Office—did not apologize for the atrocities and left the event before Minister Kazenambo Kazenambo had finished his speech. And yet the significance of this repatriation for the Namibian side can hardly be overestimated: "October 4, 2011 was a colossal day for an independent Namibia. The country witnessed the return of twenty human skulls that had been brought to Germany from this nation-state to be studied, in order to prove that blacks are supposedly inferior to whites."[22] A chance for commemoration was squandered and on top of that turned into an act of disrespect.

In response to a question posed by the representatives of the Left Party in the German parliament, the federal government replied that the *Convention on the Prevention and Punishment of the Crime of Genocide* from December 9, 1948, was not applicable retroactively.[23] Hence, the German government did not have to recognize this genocide, but would fulfill its moral responsibility by providing *development aid*. Commemoration or not commemorating as the result of an economic calculation; a *careful consideration* happened here as well. Remembrance always has its own political economy. It is clearly not motivated by emotional necessity, because if that were the case, the Namibian delegation would have been treated with more care. Nor is it about learning from the past, because otherwise the obvious continuities in biographies (Eugen Fischer, for example) and

21 Sophie Elmenthaler, "Versöhnung – Gerechtigkeit = schlecht," *freitext*, no. 19 (2012), pp. 6-11.

22 Job Shipululo Amupanda, *New Era*, May 10, 2011, p. 21.

23 See Answer of the Federal Government to the question by representatives Niema Movassat, Wolfgang Gehrcke, Sevim Dağdelen, other members of parliament and the parliamentary group DIE LINKE. Printed matter 17/10407.

practices (concentration camps, for example) linking colonial rule and the Shoah would not be ignored.

In this case, commemoration could ultimately be a way of improving Germany's image, because development aid is associated with generosity. If the German government were to admit that the murder of the Herero and Nama was a genocide, it would also have to admit that for more than one hundred years it refused to confront the past in any way.[24] That would be disastrous for Germany's standing as a country that prides itself on its commitment to *coming to terms with the past*. The issue of standing was also an important topic in the debates surrounding Rostock-Lichtenhagen: What is Germany's standing abroad? What implications does this have on the *attractiveness* of the new federal states?

VI Grief as a Political Resource. A Directional Shift in Commemoration

As is evident in the preceding discussions, public commemorations of victims of racist violence are usually not held from the perspective of the victims. Remembrance rarely follows from an intrinsic need, but more often from a political and economic calculation, in which, for example, the economic valuation of the respective location is taken into account. Here, commemoration often reflects the effectiveness of the bureaucratic apparatus which is closely connected to the very violence whose victims are to be remembered, and which might even perpetuate this violence.

24 In 2015, the German parliament finally admitted the existence of a genocide against Herero and Nama under the German colonial power, but stressed that the use of the term genocide did not imply any legal consequences. See "Bundestagspräsident Lammert nennt Massaker an Herero Völkermord," *Zeit Online*, July 8, 2015, https://www.zeit.de/politik/deutschland/2015-07/herero-nama-voelkermord-deutschland-norbert-lammert-joachim-gauck-kolonialzeit (accessed September 5, 2022).

If the perspectives of the bereaved would be acknowledged by society, that is, by fellow citizens, as well as by policymakers and administrators, *emotional grief* could also be a political resource, because it expresses the significance of others for us. When commemorating the victims of racist violence, grief puts the human at the center. When initiated from this perspective, commemoration cannot be instrumentalized for a particular policy measure, for an immediate political demand, or for a state image campaign. And yet this radically human mode of commemoration has a powerful (and power depriving) political dimension, because it transforms *specimens* into individuals again, enabling at least partially the undoing of the dehumanization that has already happened through discourse and socialization, which made racist murder possible in the first place. Beyond *careful consideration*, remembrance motivated by grief and political anger can, in its indiscutability and non-corruptibility, to some extent counteract the reduction of those attacked to categorical specimens. In this way they can be returned—in memoriam—to their being as individuals; as human beings.

Translation: Angela Anderson

Resilience and Resistance

Stefanie Graefe

The Discreet Charm of Catastrophe

Vulnerability, Resilience, and Critique in the Era of Multiple Crises

Without a doubt, resilience and vulnerability are *en vogue*. In the media, in scientific debates—and even here in this volume. In some places, laments can be heard about a veritable epidemic of increasing sensitivity towards vulnerability.[1] In light of the general state of the world, such trends are hardly surprising: The Coronavirus pandemic, climate change, the global rise of authoritarianism, and war have heightened our awareness that we are living in a precarious present with uncertain future prospects. Against this backdrop, on the one hand there have been more and more psycho-political appeals urging us to train our resilience (that is, the ability to cope with crisis situations). On the other hand, even in the relatively secure and affluent societies of the global North, there is a deepening sense of individual and collective vulnerability. In the discursive space of social critique and sociological time diagnosis, however, there is an interesting difference between these two concepts. Whereas resilience, as a "key concept of the twenty-first century,"[2]

1 See Stephan Lessenich, "Diskurs und Corona: Verwundbar ist, wer zu uns gehört," *Süddeutsche Zeitung*, May 6, 2020, https://www.sueddeutsche.de/kultur/coronavirus-vulnerabilitaet-triage-1.4897768 (accessed June 4, 2022); and Wolfgang Krischke, "Wachsend empfindlich," *Frankfurter Allgemeine Zeitung*, August 21, 2021, https://www.faz.net/aktuell/karriere-hochschule/hoersaal/zur-karriere-des-worts-vulnerabel-17434858.html (accessed June 4, 2022).

2 Ulrich Bröckling, "Resilienz: Belastbar, flexibel, widerständig," in *Gute Hirten führen sanft: Über Menschenregierungskünste* (Berlin: Suhrkamp, 2017), pp. 113–139.

has been subjected to a wide-ranging critique (to which I myself, among others, have contributed),[3] vulnerability is regarded by many authors, in contrast, as the starting point for a radical and emancipatory reinvention of the political.[4] Stimulated above all by Judith Butler's work on the topic,[5] an important and inspiring debate has developed, and it is this debate that I will examine more closely below. Along with some preliminary considerations, I would like to explore what it means to discuss, on the basis of vulnerability, the political in general and the crisis-ridden present in particular. I am interested in what such a perspective can reveal and where it might potentially reach its limits[6]—not least in light of this volume's central question concerning the role of art and creativity in today's neoliberal society, about which I will formulate a few loose thoughts at the end.

3 Stefanie Graefe, *Resilienz im Krisenkapitalismus: Wider das Lob der Anpassungsfähigkeit* (Bielefeld: transcript, 2019); Stefanie Graefe and Karina Becker, eds., *Mit Resilienz durch die Krise? Anmerkungen zu einem gefragten Konzept* (Munich: oekom, 2021).

4 See, for example, Estelle Ferrarese, ed., *The Politics of Vulnerability* (London: Routledge, 2018); Judith Butler et al., eds., *Vulnerability in Resistance* (Durham, N.C.: Duke University Press, 2016); and Victoria Browne et al., eds., *Vulnerability and the Politics of Care: Transdisciplinary Dialogues* (Oxford: Oxford University Press, 2021).

5 See, for instance, Judith Butler, *Giving an Account of Oneself* (New York: Fordham University Press, 2005); Judith Butler, *Precarious Life: The Powers of Mourning and Violence* (London and New York: Verso, 2004); Judith Butler and Athena Athanasiou, *Dispossession: The Performative in the Political* (Cambridge: Polity Press, 2013); and Judith Butler, "Bodies That Still Matter," in Browne et al., *Vulnerability and the Politics of Care*, pp. 33–42.

6 Of course, I am not the first author to raise such (or similar) questions. See, for example, Gareth David Addidle and Joyce Liddle, "Introduction – Contested Perspectives on Vulnerability: Which Groups Are Vulnerable and Why?," in *Public Management and Vulnerability: Contextualising Change*, ed. Gareth David Addidle and Joyce Liddle (London: Routledge, 2020), pp. 1–13; Erinn Gilson, "The Problems and Potentials of Vulnerability," in Browne et al., *Vulnerability and the Politics of Care*, pp. 85–107; and Estelle Ferrarese, "The Vulnerable and the Political: On the Seeming Impossibility of Thinking Vulnerability and the Political Together and Its Consequences," in Ferrarese, *The Politics of Vulnerability*, pp. 74–89.

Resilience and Vulnerability— Two Sides of the Same (Psycho-Political) Coin

Resilience and vulnerability are concepts that have been gaining discursive significance since the 1970s—on the scientific level, on the political level, and in everyday life. Whereas resilience denotes the art of withstanding crisis, vulnerability concerns the fact that people can be hurt—by means of words, laws, relationships, structures, illnesses, violence. The two concepts refer to one another: Only those who are vulnerable need resilience; conversely, resilience is extolled in numerous articles, radio broadcasts, self-help books, and counseling services as a sort of cure for the actual or perceived vulnerability that seems to be proliferating everywhere. At first glance, resilience appears to be the more optimistic or less fatalistic concept.[7] That said, resilience has also been suspected of contributing to the "cruel optimism" of neoliberalism: You may not get everything you've ever hoped for, but with the right techniques of the self, you will somehow be able to *persevere* more effectively.[8] Vulnerability, in contrast, has been treated as a critical and emancipatory alternative to resilience. Sarah Bracke, for example, has argued that vulnerability represents an "ethical condition of human life" that contains "transformative power" and refuses to be tamed by neoliberal concepts of resilience.[9] However, vulnerability and resilience are logically complementary. Whenever there is

7 See Brad Evans and Julian Reid, *Resilient Life: The Art of Living Dangerously* (Cambridge: Polity Press, 2014).

8 See Lauren Berlant, *Cruel Optimism* (Durham, N.C.: Duke University Press, 2011). In Berlant's words, "optimistic attachment is cruel when the object/scene of desire is itself an obstacle to fulfilling the very wants that bring people to it," p. 227. Consider, for example, the widely shared neoliberal desire to be as successful as possible professionally, to be as fulfilled as possible personally, to be as physically attractive and socially successful as possible, even though what is realistically attainable by most people looks quite different.

9 Sarah Bracke, "Bouncing Back: Vulnerability and Resistance in Times of Resilience," in Butler et al., *Vulnerability in Resistance*, pp. 52–75.

talk of vulnerability, it can be inferred that there is a lack of resilience; conversely, resilience is only necessary when there is or might be a risk of being harmed.

To most people, resilience and vulnerability are familiar as psychological concepts.[10] This is no surprise, given that their association with the psychological concept of trauma is obvious. However, the semantic horizon of the two concepts extends far beyond the terrain of psychology. As concepts, vulnerability and resilience alike have long been incorporated into global governmental programs. From communal social work to the United Nations, strategies have been developed for strengthening the resilience of especially vulnerable populations.[11] Not only people, however, but also financial markets, river landscapes, and democracies are considered potentially vulnerable; with the help of resilience, it is thought that they can be made fit to survive in times of crisis. To this end, the catalogue of measures that can be taken ranges from psychological training and unemployment programs to military armament. Also, that which is understood as the cause of vulnerability and as a resilient counter-strategy varies from one context to the next. Women, especially, are often said to be particularly vulnerable, on the one hand, while they are also, on the other hand, assigned responsibility for the resilience of individuals and communities.[12] In the realm of international humanitarian aid, too, resources and support can be allocated or denied in the name of

10 See José Brunner, *Die Politik des Traumas: Gewalterfahrungen und psychisches Leid in den USA, in Deutschland und im Israel/Palästina-Konflikt* (Berlin: Suhrkamp, 2014); and Markus Brunner, "Trigger-Warnungen: Zur Politisierung eines traumatheoretischen Konzeptes," in *TRIGGER-WARNUNG: Identitätspolitik zwischen Abwehr, Abschottung und Allianzen*, ed. Eva Berendsen et al. (Berlin: Verbrecher-Verlag, 2019), pp. 21–35.

11 See Graefe, *Resilienz im Krisenkapitalismus*, pp. 167–176.

12 See Sybille Bauriedl and Christa Wichterich, Ökonomisierung von Natur, Raum, Körper: Feministische Perspektiven auf sozial-ökologische Transformationen (Berlin: Rosa Luxemburg Stiftung, 2014).

vulnerability as well as that of resilience.[13] Finally, both concepts can easily be deployed on behalf of the individualizing imperative of neoliberal marketization, the motto here being: Take your individual vulnerabilities as the starting point for working on your resilience.

From Ontological Excess to the Naturalization of Violence

We can see that with regard to their governmental co-optability and contrary to Bracke's claims, the two concepts, vulnerability and resilience, in fact hardly differ. This raises the question of what, exactly, constitutes the specific critical content of vulnerability. Following Judith Butler,[14] one could say that this is a matter of recognizing the basic contingency of human life and the fact that people can only survive in structures of social relationships. It is thus essential not to think of vulnerability in a socio-technocratic manner, that is, as an empirically determinable feature of specific groups or situations. The issue, according to Butler, is rather to acknowledge that vulnerability concerns all people equally: "[T]here are no exceptions."[15]

According to this understanding, examining vulnerability thus reveals important insights into the true nature of human existence, among them the insight "that I am the kind of being whose persistence is already from the start dependent on a social form for its existence, and that means that my life is a social organic life, and depending on that social form, my life will be more or less livable."[16] From this basic assumption of the onto-

13 See Usche Merk, "Wachstum durch Anpassung an globale Krisen? Resilienzdiskurse in der Entwicklungszusammenarbeit und humanitären Hilfe," in Graefe and Becker, *Mit Resilienz durch die Krise?*, pp. 87–110.
14 Butler, "Bodies That Still Matter."
15 Ibid., p. 37.
16 Ibid.

logical vulnerability of humanity as a whole, the first-person plural is often used in the critical debates about the topic: *we* are vulnerable, *we* are dependent on others, *we* have bodies that can only survive under certain conditions, and finally *we*—as Butler remarks, citing the example of protesting refugees—oppose the destruction of our living conditions.[17] Accordingly, the concept of vulnerability is associated with a strong anthropological assumption: What "the human" is, in and of itself, can be defined by one central concept—vulnerability. Implicit in this are additional and equally strong social-theoretical assumptions: Vulnerability, according to Butler, refers to the environment of humankind, to a "social organic life" that, depending on the circumstances, can flourish and thrive but can also fail and be violent. How this social form is produced and whether—and, if so, how—it could be changed or even overcome remains completely abstract.

It is in the sense of this social vitalism, if you will, that critical concepts of vulnerability almost unanimously emphasize the all-encompassing importance of care, intersubjectivity, affectivity, dependence, and being exposed. Implicitly or explicitly, the overarching negative foil to this perspective is the old European conception of a person (usually marked as male, white, European, etc.) as a self-identical, sovereign, rational subject who understands the world around him as a separate externality that can and must be dissected, managed, and dominated. Indeed, according to this conception, which is still widely influential today, certain fundamental facts of human existence such as mortality, vulnerability, and dependence on others somehow represent regrettable exceptional circumstances that can ideally be overcome with the assistance of the bourgeois-capitalist social order. With reference to vulnerability, this persistently powerful idea is currently being flipped upside

17 Ibid., p. 41.

down, so to speak. However, the discrediting of the old European rational subject, which is long overdue, is justified less on historical or political grounds than it is on ontological grounds. At the same time, vulnerability is understood not as *one* but as *the* decisive characteristic of human existence to which all other human features and capabilities remain logically subordinate. In other words, what reason or rationality was to the pioneering thinkers of "Western" modernity, vulnerability is to the debate outlined here: a universalizing category that can be used to explain and classify practically every human and social experience.

As a result, some authors regard all forms of culture, from cave painting to parenting, as no more than attempts to cope with the fundamental vulnerability of human existence. The meaning of cultural and social practices seems to be entirely confined to the idea of arming oneself against potentially existentially threatening "adversities in the world"[18] such as "wars, human cruelty, natural disasters, injustice, or illnesses."[19] Furthermore, as vulnerability is claimed to be the general *conditio humana*, the differences between human-made conditions of violence, on the one hand, and unavoidable facts of life and natural catastrophes, on the other, disappear. At the same time, experiences of violence, helplessness, privation, or fear are considered a driving social force with strong ethical implications: "Acts of exposure," according to Christine Hentschel and Susanne Krasmann,[20] can enable an "ethics of being-in-common" and "create new sites of contestation, belonging, identification, and struggle"—regardless of whether they have been "created by a natural disaster or a con-

18 Daniel Burghardt et al., *Vulnerabilität: Pädagogische Herausforderungen* (Stuttgart: Verlag W. Kohlhammer, 2017), p. 56.

19 Ibid., p. 61.

20 Christine Hentschel and Susanne Krasmann: "Acts of Exposure and Their Affective Publics," in *"Exposure": Verletzlichkeit und das Politische in Zeiten radikaler Ungewissheit*, ed. Christine Hentschel and Susanne Krasmann (Bielefeld: transcript, 2020), pp. 15–34.

glomerate of chaotic human agencies."[21] In short, the notion of vulnerability seems to imply an ontological excess that leads to the conceptual naturalization of socially produced violence. Differences between the general fact of mortality and the psychophysical vulnerability of life on the one hand, and discriminatory or exploitative social structures on the other, are implicitly erased. The general vulnerability of all of us is regarded as an essential feature of the *conditio humana* and as the basis of culture, sociality, and creativity.

Of course, it cannot be denied that mortality and vulnerability are a part of human or even biological existence. However, whether our existence is determined by these phenomena in every possible respect, as some authors suggest, seems at least worthy of discussion. Not least, when vulnerability is taken to be an all-inclusive horizon of sociality, the question of why, exactly, some people are clearly harmed more than others fades into the background. Furthermore, within the context of the debate outlined here, one encounters surprisingly few references to such things as concrete political processes and constellations of power, e.g. to wealth inequality, power hierarchies, or processes of exploitation. Instead, attention is directed toward the multiple forms and manifestations of vulnerability.

The Transformative Power of Catastrophe

Despite the absence of a substantive power analysis, the critical vulnerability discourse, as I have already mentioned, is strictly opposed to a specific powerful concept: the old European idea of the self-identical, autonomous, and sovereign subject. From the perspective of vulnerability, this notion of the subject seems reductive—it obscures central dimensions of humanity—and is also

21 Ibid., p. 22–23.

regarded as the cause of violence, domination, and the general crisis-ridden nature of our contemporary world.[22] From this perspective, the many forms of discrimination, endangerment, and oppression, and the hierarchization of forms of life in the globalized present have a clear but also highly generalized cause: a form of supremacism that established the (post-)colonial, racist, and sexist success story of Western modernity and perpetuates it to the present day. Politics, therefore, should be reconceived on a level that is just as general; a false way of thinking should be replaced by one that is completely different. Following Estelle Ferrarese's critique of the socio-philosophical vulnerability concept discussed here, politics is *replaced* by ethics. Politics, the point of which is "to publicly express [...] universality, to give a materiality to the fact that I, precisely, am not just this specific individual exposed to a set of specific injustices,"[23] is exchanged for the demand to *perceive* and *recognize* vulnerability, which, in the same breath, is attributed quite a remarkable degree of transformative power.

According to the approaches under discussion here, transformations that arise from vulnerability are essentially non-deliberative; that is, they are not plannable or negotiable. They simply happen—or not. As an ethical and transformative concept, vulnerability is accordingly associated in many texts, implicitly or explicitly, with the category of the *event*. This is neither a new nor an implausible line of thinking.[24] No one will deny that the political (like historical processes in general) cannot be fully predicted and planned; it often unfolds in unforeseen and disruptive ways. What is new in this regard, however, is that transformative and even emancipatory potential is being attributed to existential threats and excessive acts of violence, e.g. the right-

22 See Butler, *Precarious Life*.
23 Ferrarese, "The Vulnerable and the Political."
24 See Lasma Pirktina, *Das Ereignis: Martin Heidegger, Emmanuel Levinas, Jean-Luc Marion* (Freiburg: Verlag Karl Alber, 2019).

wing terrorist attack in Christchurch, New Zealand in 2019, which took the lives of fifty-one people. According to the argumentation of Christine Hentschel and Susanne Krasmann, as mentioned above, such events seem to have a considerable amount of transformative potential: On the one hand, they "may create new sites of contestation, belonging, identification, and struggle."[25] On the other hand, situations of existential "exposure" allegedly strengthen—and my impression here is that the authors consider this to be a positive thing—feelings of identification with one's own nation and government.[26]

In arguments such as Hentschel and Krasmann's, however, the apparently unproblematic connection between terrorism and community is not the only disturbing matter. The idea of the miraculous social power of violence and catastrophes also draws a connection between vulnerability and the neoliberal psychology of resilience, which likewise sees, in the experience of existential trauma, considerable potential for change, growth, and personal maturation.[27] In both cases, however, it remains unclear how such desirable transformative effects of vulnerability can be distinguished from those effects that no one but the perpetrators themselves could wish for. Furthermore, the assumption that vulnerability is a general phenomenon that in times of social change and crisis only becomes more visible complicates the critique of politically questionable vulnerability claims, e.g. in the context of migration debates or scandalizations of so-called "white vulnerability."[28] One might therefore ask: Is it enough for anybody to *feel* vulnerable in order to make claims for recognition, attention, and care? Who decides which claims are justifiable, which experiences of vulnerability are credible, and which are

25 Hentschel and Krasmann, "Acts of Exposure," pp. 22–23.
26 Ibid., p. 31.
27 See Graefe, *Resilienz im Krisenkapitalismus*, pp. 129–139.
28 See Gilson, "The Problems and Potentials of Vulnerability."

not? Furthermore, which forms of violence can be understood as "transformative" in an emancipatory sense (if this is possible at all), and which forms instead reinforce the ways in which society excludes people, creates hierarchies, and renders certain groups invisible? The latter question gains even more significance if we take into account forms of unseen structural violence. Typically, these are often not even experienced by those affected as violence or discrimination at all, but rather as no more than their individual fate, as, for example, in the case of radically unequal life expectancies caused by socio-economic factors.[29] Just as a subjective feeling of being harmed might not necessarily reflect the actual degree of the harm in question, the reverse may also be true as well: The absence of subjectively experienced vulnerability might not necessarily indicate the absence of power or violence. Unfortunately, such questions have received too little attention in the debate at hand.

Vulnerability and the Imperial Way of Life in Times of Global Warming

I would now like to take this point even a little further. As noted above, critical conceptions of vulnerability distance themselves from the modern Western construction of the autonomous rational subject. At the same time, they share a remarkable common feature with the latter, namely a strong ontological basis from which to make statements about what is human, and about trans-temporal and ethically desirable forms of living. What seems desirable in critical vulnerability accounts is precisely what the artistic figure of the autonomous subject radically negates: dependency, vulnerability, exposure. In

29 See Thomas Lampert et al., "Soziale Ungleichheit der Lebenserwartung," *Aus Politik und Zeitgeschichte* 42 (2007), https://www.bpb.de/shop/zeitschriften/apuz/30179/soziale-ungleichheit-der-lebenserwartung-in-deutschland/ (accessed June 4, 2022).

fact, critically intended conceptions of vulnerability are based on a number of binary constructions: individuality vs. relationality, sovereignty vs. vulnerability, autonomy vs. dependence, production vs. reproduction, etc., and in each of these binaries, the second pole seems to be ontologically and ethically more relevant than the first. In this way, what was formerly excluded is now declared to be more "real" and more desirable.[30] The radical emphasis on intersubjective relations, affects, care and suffering subordinates any claim that social, political and economic conditions can be rationally and collectively *configured* in favor of *perceiving* and *recognizing* their allegedly general ontological dimensions. Ultimately, this line of argumentation amounts to replacing the self-assured voluntarism of the masculine autonomous subject of Western modernity by idealizing the inescapable (and perhaps implicitly female-coded) vulnerability of "all of us" to unpredictable conditions of violence.

On the basis of this juxtaposition, critical vulnerability debates are interested in how people organize their lives or their survival in light of the explicit or structural violence that they face.[31] From this perspective, the everyday lifeworld seems, on the one hand, like a sphere in which vulnerability can be countered and processed with the practices of care and solidarity,[32] while on the other hand it also seems like a starting point for opposing discrimination, exclusion, and violence.[33] What this

30 See, for instance, Sandra Laugier, "Politics of Vulnerability and Responsibility for Ordinary Others," in Ferrarese, *The Politics of Vulnerability*, pp. 57–73.

31 See, for example, Butler and Athanasiou, *Dispossession: The Performative in the Political*; and Victoria Browne et al., "Vulnerability and the Politics of Care: Transdisciplinary Dialogues," in Browne et al., *Vulnerability and the Politics of Care*, pp. 1–29.

32 According to Laugier in "Politics of Vulnerability," this is a matter of shifting from "the 'just' to the 'important'" (p. 58) and thus about making vulnerability, instead of rights, the basis for citizenship (p. 68).

33 See, for example, Leticia Sabsay, "Permeable Bodies: Vulnerability, Affective Powers, Hegemony," in Butler et al., *Vulnerability in Resistance*, pp. 278–302.

perspective easily loses sight of, however, is that quotidian behavioral routines are not only a sort of utopian counter-world to the prevailing (neo)liberal world order but are also deeply embedded in this order themselves. As has been shown in various ways, the "imperial way of life" in the global North,[34] which, on an individual level, is fundamentally based on unlimited consumption and the quest for comfort and personal self-actualization, contributes significantly to deepening and perpetuating the social, economic and ecological vulnerabilities of other human and non-human beings around the globe (now and into the future). It does so, for instance, by accelerating global warming and exposing people to temperatures above the 45°C threshold, as is currently the case in India, where many are dying prematurely of heat exposure. On the basis of the assumption that "all of us" are more less equally vulnerable, however, it is not necessarily obvious that one should question, in a systematic way, one's own way of life with respect to its "vulnerantiality" (*Vulnerantialität*), that is, its "potential for causing harm, damage, discrimination, etc."[35] The big *we* of vulnerability is not terribly interested in paradoxes, such as the fact that "we" are vulnerable and yet can simultaneously harm others, sometimes even without wanting to or knowing about it. Of course, everyone is affected in some way by global warming, and some members of politically, economically, and climatically more moderate zones of the world already find the impending climate apocalypse downright traumatizing. Such feelings, in fact, have already given rise to a new genre of art.[36] However, to repeat, it is possible

34 Regarding this way of life, see Ulrich Brand and Markus Wissen, *Imperiale Lebensweise: Zur Ausbeutung von Mensch und Natur im globalen Kapitalismus* (Munich: oekom, 2017).

35 Burghardt et al., *Vulnerabilität*, p. 12.

36 In literature and film, E. Ann Kaplan has examined the rise of a futuristic-apocalyptic genre in the wake of 9/11 and has argued that the emergence of this genre should be understood as a sort of "pretraumatic" way of processing future catastrophes. See E. Ann Kaplan,

to be vulnerable oneself *and nevertheless* also harm others, and this is probably even often the case in our complex, capitalist, and globalized society. Yet in the literature on critical vulnerability, one gains the impression that "vulnerantiality" has something to do with rather diffuse powers or obvious cruelty but has hardly anything to do with customs, routines, supposedly self-evident claims, or comforts. This, of course, significantly complicates any (self-)critique of the imperial way of life that really wants to make a difference. One reason for this lacuna might be that interrogating one's own privileged way of life requires, among other things, insight into complex and abstract interrelations—and thus an ability that, according to the logic used in the discourse on critical vulnerability, is associated with the problematic phenomenon of Western rationalism. But the fact that deaths by heat exposure in India are related to the car traffic outside my front door is not something that can be sensually or intersubjectively experienced; this is something that needs to be explained to me with numbers, data, and scientific insights. A true transformation of imperial ways of life would require, moreover, that I am prepared to implement relatively abstract universal moral principles in my daily life—possibly even against my own needs and those of others in my immediate social environment. This scenario, too, becomes all the more difficult to envision when everyday life, affectivity, and sociality are conceived of as an innocent lifeworld in which the main concern is "just about living life"[37] and in which we focus on our "enduring dependency on social and economic forms"[38] while ignoring our consumption of resources and the extent to which we more or less constantly benefit from exploitative conditions elsewhere in the world. At any rate, it is ironic

Climate Trauma: Foreseeing the Future in Dystopian Film and Fiction (New Brunswick, N.J.: Rutgers University Press, 2016).

37 Laugier, "Politics of Vulnerability," p. 58.

38 Butler, "Bodies That Still Matter," p. 37.

to declare that an ontology of vulnerability, affectivity, situatedness, and sociality should serve as the starting point of a new form of political ethics when what is needed, more so than ever before, is the insight that the lives of current and future generations are in fact threatened above all, and perhaps catastrophically, by more or less abstract social, economic and political interrelations and power interests on the one hand, and everyday routines and intersubjective shared values on the other. In this case, again, "we" are not at all equally vulnerable. On the contrary, the reality of the climate catastrophe shows that, in the most radically conceivable way, "some are more vulnerable than others."[39]

Contra Dystopian Realism

In closing, as announced above, I would like to formulate a thought that came to me while engaging with the literature under discussion here—a thought that is absolutely preliminary and speculative. In short, I wonder to what extent concepts such as vulnerability can really help us to understand the current shift in neoliberal governmentality. Or whether they might not, though unintentionally and indirectly, even contribute in a certain way to this shift, which has been referred to as disaster capitalism[40] or zombie neoliberalism[41]—if only by not taking note of it at all. Various recent analyses of neoliberalism have attempted to demonstrate that we are dealing with a transformation of the neoliberal ideology, over the course of which the central neoliberal figure of

39 Alyson Cole, "All of Us are Vulnerable, But Some Are More Vulnerable than Others: The Political Ambiguity of Vulnerability Studies, an Ambivalent Critique," in Ferrarese, *The Politics of Vulnerability*, pp. 110–128. See also Burghardt et al., *Vulnerabilität*.

40 Naomi Klein, *The Shock Doctrine: The Rise of Disaster Capitalism* (New York: Metropolitan Books/Henry Holt, 2007).

41 Mitchell Dean, "Rethinking Neoliberalism," *Journal of Sociology* 50, no. 2 (2014), pp. 150–163, here p. 159.

the entrepreneurial self has become fragile. The entrepreneurial self, one could say, has become increasingly vulnerable, given that such a person is living in a rather opaque and utterly complex world in which one crisis follows another and in which the future seems radically uncertain. Within the framework of neoliberalism's so-called "complexity turn,"[42] there is apparently more at stake than simply preserving and protecting the system of supposedly free enterprise. Now, the plan is to profit as much as possible from the crises that have already occurred and from those expected to occur—and to prepare everyone to accept the idea that any sort of plannability and security will soon be a thing of the past.[43] Given the unpredictable nature of the world and the markets, moreover, any attempts to regulate and tame the accumulation of capital can simply be dismissed. According to these analyses, in short, new justifications for capitalism refer less to growth and competition as ends in themselves than they refer to what is "necessary"—that is, to what must be done in the name of survival and in light of mounting crises and catastrophes.

At this point, finally, *art* comes into play. In order to understand this connection, a brief retrospective is necessary. Art has played a central role in the recent history of sociologically informed social critique and in the "strange non-death of neoliberalism,"[44] and it has done so in three respects:[45] First, as Luc Boltanski and

42 Jeremy Walker and Melinda Cooper, "Genealogies of Resilience: From Systems Ecology to the Political Economy of Crisis Adaptation," *Security Dialogue* 42, no. 2 (2011), pp. 143–160.

43 See Felix Syrovatka, "Resilienz als Fortschreibung neoliberaler Krisenbearbeitung: Das Resilienzkonzept in der europäischen Arbeitsmarktpolitik," *PROKLA: Zeitschrift für kritische Sozialwissenschaft* 197, no. 4, pp. 597–615.

44 Colin Crouch, *The Strange Non-Death of Neoliberalism* (Cambridge: Polity Press, 2011).

45 For further discussion of this topic, see Thorsten Schneider's contribution in this volume.

Ève Chiapello have shown,[46] the demands for autonomy, individuality, and authenticity that were so vehemently expressed by the New Social Movements of the 1970s—the so-called "artist critique"—contributed significantly to the rise of neoliberalism. Second, under neoliberal conditions, art is *itself* organized in the mode of marketization and global competition.[47] Third and finally, as Michael Makropoulos has analyzed,[48] neoliberal governmentality *itself* follows the model of art. According to Makropoulos, the neoliberal introduction of competition into practically all spheres of society radically reorganized the relationship between *reality* and *possibility* in favor of the latter, and this has taken place according to a logic that was previously reserved for the sphere of art: the logic of possibility, or the logic of removing boundaries. It is at this very point where art and the neoliberal dynamics of competition meet and reinforce one another:

> The basis for generalizing competition is [...] a fictionalization of society's horizon of possibility, the general model of which is the counter-reality of autonomous art, because this is the social sphere that is constitutively concerned with transgressing the boundary between what is real and what is possible.[49]

Accordingly, neoliberalism can also be interpreted as a sort of perverted generalization of the artistic principle: That which was previously inconceivable is made conceivable; natural, social, and personal boundaries are

46 Luc Boltanski and Ève Chiapello, *The New Spirit of Capitalism*, trans. Gregory Elliott (London: Verso, 2005).

47 Sofia Bempeza's article in this volume discusses this very phenomenon.

48 Michael Makropoulos, "Kunstautonomie und Wettbewerbsgesellschaft: Nachtrag zur 'Ökonomisierung des Sozialen'," in *Kreation und Depression: Freiheit im gegenwärtigen Kapitalismus*, ed. Christoph Menke and Juliane Rebentisch (Berlin: Kadmos, 2010) pp. 208–225.

49 Ibid., pp. 214–215.

transgressed again and again, though not in the sense of artistic vision but rather in the name of radicalized marketization.

So much for the analyses of neoliberalism as it developed from the 1980s to the beginning of the new century. As already mentioned, neoliberalism is not timeless and unchanging; it is permanently transforming. And if we are indeed currently undergoing a shift toward catastrophe realism, then the popularity of concepts such as resilience and vulnerability may not be a coincidence but rather a *symptom* of this shift. We are still dealing with neoliberalism, but no longer exclusively with efforts to promote and perpetuate growth and deregulation. Above all, we are faced with accepting the fact that we live in an utterly catastrophic present that, in the name of the (market) system's *survival*, is demanding that we adapt in new (and possibly drastic) ways.[50]

Within the framework of this new dystopian realism, the first casualty might in fact be creativity itself. As a counter-movement against the older logic of neoliberalism described by Makropoulos, art and fiction devoted to representing ongoing catastrophe might potentially come under suspicion of deceiving us about reality, that is, about the perilous and unpredictable nature of the present. Against this background, it is perhaps no coincidence that our often catastrophic reality has long been an important point of reference in the world of art. Here, too, there has been discussion about a new form of realism,[51] which is concerned less with the search for

50 Under the radically unpredictable conditions of the present day, moreover, it is most likely democracy itself that will be suspected of standing in the way of making necessary structural adjustments. See Thomas Biebricher, *Die politische Theorie des Neoliberalismus* (Berlin: Suhrkamp, 2021); and Stefanie Graefe, "Systemrelevanzen: Zur Biopolitik der Resilienz in Coronazeiten," in Graefe and Becker, *Mit Resilienz durch die Krise?*, pp. 111–139.

51 See Birgitta Kumrey et al., eds., *Realitätseffekte in der deutschsprachigen Gegenwartsliteratur: Schreibweisen nach der Postmoderne?* (Heidelberg: Universitätsverlag Winter, 2014).

radical perspectives beyond the existing world than it is with the problematic nature of documenting what actually exists—and also with increasing the visibility and recognition of vulnerabilities. In terms of perspective, the horizon of possibility in the field of art is perhaps not expanding further and further, as Makropoulos suggests and as is always thought to be the case; instead, our (catastrophic) reality might simply be catching up with it.[52]

Interestingly, a similar trend can be seen in the work of Judith Butler. Whereas her earlier works are primarily concerned with the unpredictable, creative, and potentially even harmful power of language,[53] her more recent work has focused on the inescapable vulnerability of human beings, a condition in which the creative element has almost completely disappeared. In Estelle Ferrarese's words, Butler's "new vulnerability is synonymous with destructibility."[54] Of course, this is not to say that "realistic," i.e. documentary (or partially documentary) art is uninteresting or politically less desirable, but only that we are perhaps dealing with a shift or trend toward regarding creative, fictional, and utopian representations of the world as unrealistic or superfluous. Conversely, this might also mean that creativity, fictionality, and art have an entirely new critical objective in today's crisis capitalism, namely the task of ensuring that the collective imagination, in Cornelius Castoriadis's terms,[55] is not exhausted by perceiving, documenting, and scandalizing our catastrophic reality.

52 This is not to say, of course, that the processes of competition, marketization, and precarization described in this volume are not taking place in the art world. After all, dystopian and capitalist realism are not mutually exclusive; see Mark Fisher, *Capitalist Realism: Is There No Alternative?* (Winchester: Zer0 Books, 2009).

53 See, especially, Judith Butler, *Excitable Speech: A Politics of the Performative* (New York: Routledge, 1996).

54 Ferrarese, "The Vulnerable and the Political," p. 76.

55 Cornelius Castoriadis, *The Imaginary Institution of Society*, trans. Kathleen Blamey (Cambridge: Polity Press, 1987).

And who knows? Perhaps such a revitalization of the utopian imaginary might also help to revive the "artist critique" that Ève Chiapello had called for more than a decade ago.[56]

Of course, in light of the actual state of the world in the early summer of 2022, when this text was written, there is little reason to make an argument against dystopian realism, especially not in the realm of art. As scientists, artists, citizens, and everyday people, we have no choice but to engage with the world as it currently is and thus with its uncertainties, fears, and vulnerabilities. The question, however, is this: Do concepts such as resilience and vulnerability make it easier for us to deal with this situation in a better way? Presumably they do, in their own way. But do they also help us to imagine a world beyond catastrophe and mobilize our willingness to act collectively in the ways necessary to prevent such catastrophes? As Sarah Bracke has rightly argued, resilience, as a guiding normative concept, contributes to the "dispossession of underdeveloping the skills and capacities of imagining other possible worlds, as well as the agential modalities to pursue those imaginations."[57] But what about vulnerability? Does it, as a concept, also free our imaginations and encourage us to act toward a different and better future? I still have my doubts.

Translation: Valentine A. Pakis

56 Ève Chiapello, "Evolution and Co-optation: The 'Artist Critique' of Management and Capitalism," *Third Text* 18 (2004), pp. 585–594.
57 Bracke, "Bouncing Back," pp. 63–64.

Thorsten Schneider

Artists in Resilience, or: How to Organize Yourself?

"Never let a good crisis go to waste"
Winston Churchill

The critique that artists are compelled to serve as an "exemplary instrument for modelling cultural work in the mold of entrepreneurship, self-enterprise, and start-up energy"[1] has perhaps nowhere been discussed with the same intensity as in the discourse of cultural workers themselves. Since Luc Boltanski and Ève Chiapello's *The New Spirit of Capitalism*[2] retraced the appropriation and simultaneous hollowing-out of "artist critique" in the rhetoric of neoliberal management literature, art discourse has been haunted by the suspicion that artists, rather than meeting capitalism with the resistance due to it as per their own self-image, have actually persisted in collaborating in its renewal. This has repeatedly led to new diagnoses of crisis, proclaiming either the "misery of critique"[3] in general or a more specific—and hopeless—dependence of all art upon the culture industry.

1 Gerald Raunig, "17 Tendenzen der Modulation der Kreativität," in Gerald Raunig, *Industrien der Kreativität. Streifen und Glätten 2* (Zurich: Diaphanes, 2012), pp. 31–36, here p. 31.

2 Luc Boltanski and Ève Chiapello, *The New Spirit of Capitalism* (London and New York: Verso, 2005).

3 Bruno Latour's "Why Has Critique Run out of Steam? From Matters of Fact to Matters of Concern," in *Critical Inquiry* 30, no. 2 (Winter 2004), pp. 225–248, appeared German with a title translatable into English as "the misery of critique": Bruno Latour, *Das Elend der Kritik. Vom Krieg um Fakten zu den Dingen von Belang* (Berlin: Diaphanes, 2021).

During the "decade of creativity,"[4] the demand to "be creative"[5] became an almost unavoidable social imperative.[6] Richard Florida's *The Rise of the Creative Class*[7] was even then able to illustrate the blithe manner in which art and culture were appropriated for neoliberal investment plans. Adorno's conviction that "It is self-evident that nothing concerning art is self-evident anymore"[8] does not stand entirely in contradiction to observations of a wide-ranging—and no less self-evident seeming—appropriation of art to serve economic interests: "The forfeiture of what could be done spontaneously or unproblematically has not been compensated for the open infinitude of new possibilities that reflection confronts."[9] While art has the capacity to act as a medium for or object of critique, it can equally present merely as a unique selling point; as a commodity.

Such rhetorics—for which the concept of "artist critique" is of only limited usefulness—are accompanied by the (self-)precarization of cultural producers,[10] whose social capital is profitably siphoned off by various stakeholders. At the art schools and various other places of education for artists and cultural producers, neoliberalization has intensified via multitudinous evaluations, rankings, and a "catering regime"[11]—as Pascal Gielen and Paul De

4 Angela McRobbie, "Re-Thinking Creative Economy as Radical Social Enterprise," *Variant* 24, no. 41 (2011), pp. 32–33.

5 Angela McRobbie, *Be Creative* (Cambridge: Polity Press, 2020).

6 See Andreas Reckwitz, *Die Erfindung der Kreativität. Zum Prozess gesellschaftlicher Ästhetisierung*, 2nd ed. (Berlin: Suhrkamp, 2012).

7 Richard Florida, *The Rise of the Creative Class: And How It's Transforming Work, Leisure, Community, and Everyday Life* (New York: Basic Books, 2005).

8 Theodor W. Adorno, *Aesthetic Theory* (London and New York: Continuum, 1997), p. 1.

9 Ibid.

10 See Isabell Lorey, "Vom immanenten Widerspruch zur hegemonialen Funktion. Biopolitische Gouvernementalität und Selbst-Prekarisierung von KulturproduzentInnen," in Gerald Raunig and Ulf Wuggenig, eds., *Kritik der Kreativität* (Vienna, Linz, Berlin, London and Zurich: transversal texts, 2016), pp. 257–282.

11 See Pascal Gielen and Paul De Bruyne, "Introduction: The Catering Regime," in Pascal Gielen and Paul De Bruyne, eds., *Teaching Art in*

Bruyne have described it, with no little irony—alongside various programs offering to increase each student's employability. Simultaneously, and perhaps even for this very reason, there was an increase in the number of artists and cultural producers—Gregory Sholette coined for them the descriptor "dark matter"—compelled to adjust to living precariously below the radar of cultural recognition.[12] (We could in a broader sense also speak of a "dark matter" of academia, where the problems are quite different but nevertheless comparable.[13])

To keep a long story short: the promises of good fortune made to the "creative class" have been accompanied with an ongoing crisis. But within a "risk society,"[14] the attraction of playing the art card seems to have proven its staying power. But what happens when the climate shifts and social diagnoses of the present move away from an "enterprise culture"—with almost infinite promises of growth—and towards a crisis or disaster capitalism[15] in which the logic of "preparedness"[16] is reckoning at all times with the worst-case scenario? Would it not be absurd to here uphold commitment to the idea of a "culture of creativity" that, entirely unmoved, continues to regard art and culture as refuges of unlimited possibility? When resilience becomes the key term of a contemporary governmentality[17] that makes political

the Neoliberal Realm: Realism versus Cynicism, 2nd ed. (Amsterdam: Valiz Antennae, 2010), pp. 1–14.

12 Gregory Sholette, *Dark Matter: Art and Politics in the Age of Enterprise Culture* (London: Pluto Press, 2011).

13 See Amrei Bahr, Kristin Eichhorn and Sebastian Kubon, eds., *#IchBinHanna: Prekäre Wissenschaft in Deutschland* (Berlin: Suhrkamp, 2022).

14 Ulrich Beck, *Risik Society: Towards a New Modernity* (London: Sage Publishing, 1992).

15 See Naomi Klein, *The Shock Doctrine: The Rise of Disaster Capitalism* (New York: Metropolitan Books/Henry Holt, 2007), and Stefanie Graefe, *Resilienz im Krisenkapitalismus. Wider das Lob der Anpassungsfähigkeit* (Bielefeld: transcript, 2019).

16 See Pat O'Malley, "Resilient Subjects: Uncertainty, Warfare and Liberalism," *Economy and Society* 39, no. 4 (2010), pp. 488–509.

17 See Sarah Bracke, "Bouncing Back: Vulnerability and Resistance in Times of Resilience," in *Vulnerability in Resistance*, ed. Judith Butler

and economic capital from a state of permanent threat, art and culture can hardly remain unscathed.

My aim in the following is to sketch out a number of the corollaries that emerge when transposing recent critiques of resilience into the discourse on art and culture. Sarah Bracke has previously discussed the remarkable topicality of resilience in pop cultural discourses: "The way in which resilience permeates popular culture is truly striking, finding a notable expression in the popularization of psychological theories that revolve around the notion of the 'resilient self.'"[18] Elsewhere Angela McRobbie has remained true to her self-doubts, having professed to abandoning her teaching of cultural studies for several years in light of the fact that the knowledge she sought to convey in her seminars—one aimed at emancipation—"could too easily be translated into a snazzy pitch."[19] In a manner as sharp as it is nuanced, she concludes from this experience that "it also suggests that creative professionals are de-politicized and concerned only with their own self-advancement. The awkward reality is that the political leaning and affiliations of those working in the creative and cultural sector are so diverse as to make it difficult to draw any generalizations."[20] Preferable to an all-too-simple animosity between "artist critique" and "social critique" would be an interrogation of the practices, ideas, and forms of subjectification that cultural workers deploy in order to assert themselves within the culture industry.

Following Diedrich Diederichsen, the key issue here is not the actual surplus value that cultural workers generate as part of the gross domestic product, but rather

et al. (Durham, N.C. and London: Duke University Press, 2016), pp. 52–75. See also Ulrich Bröckling, "Resilienz: Belastbar, flexibel, widerständig," in Ulrich Bröckling, *Gute Hirten führen sanft: Über Menschenregierungskünste*, 3rd ed. (Frankfurt am Main: Suhrkamp, 2019), pp. 113–139.

18 Bracke, "Bouncing Back," p. 53.

19 McRobbie, *Be Creative*, p. 8.

20 Ibid.

their "identified production."[21] He distinguishes three stages and forms of identifying with paid employment: (1) unskilled workers experience their labor as enforced suffering or necessary evil. The proletariat of industrial production is engaged in alienated or de-identified labor relations and, as such, is potentially revolutionary. (2) The "Fordist compromise" of post-war production led to a relative increase in the number of skilled workers. They remained wage-dependent but identified more strongly with their labor, as they were better able to deploy their skills and felt a greater sense of security—and thus better able to find another job should they lose their current one. In this model, personnel planning and labor-market policy aimed to create balance between identifying with one's role and skilled workers' identification with their skills as a tradeable commodity within the labor market. (3) Artists and cultural workers become role models only at the moment in which specialist knowledge and high-quality education start being viewed more skeptically and lose value. Simultaneously, production steps and personnel organization are subject to increased outsourcing, resulting in more businesses becoming platforms in which production and the skimming of excess profit flow alongside one other—without operational costs and risks appearing on the balance books. Artists and cultural workers are working more than ever at their own expense—meaning that they also bear the burden of self-organization. Diederichsen concludes from this that the appeal of creative work is in fact that

> Life knowledge is in demand as creative-cognitive knowledge (and concomitant techniques) still oriented around classical models of skills and abilities. Culture and creativity have here served not only as models for

21 Diedrich Diederichsen, "Kreative Arbeit und Selbstverwirklichung," in *Kreation und Depression: Freiheit im gegenwärtigen Kapitalismus*, ed. Christoph Menke and Juliane Rebentisch (Berlin: Kadmos Verlag, 2012), pp. 118–128, here p. 119ff.

culturalization and personalization (to the point of psychologization) of job performance in other industries; they have also succeeded as novel industries in their own right and developed new forms of labor that may then, in turn, serve as models of a further radicalization in the general reconstruction of the world of work.[22]

Described here is a process in which profit maximization is redistributed via the outsourcing of risk and cost.

The "entrepreneurial self"[23] outlined here is subject to the increased pressure of permanent adaptability to a labor market which demands maximum identification with the product of your own "corporate identity." Sabeth Buchmann and Kai von Eikels have distilled this permanent challenge down into a succinct word of advice: "you should always have a product that's not you."[24] (In their art, Andrea Fraser, Renzo Martens, and Santiago Sierra have each depicted the polar extremes of external exploitation and artistic self-exploitation.)

If the focus was switched away from the numerous, speculative promises of happiness made to the creative class and instead toward the enormous pressure to adapt, then the issue becomes one of resilience. In her foundational critique of contemporary discourses of resilience, Stefanie Graefe recognizes a systematic reconfiguration of autonomy that is also enlightening in the narrower context of art labor and cultural labor:

While the pertinent sociological diagnoses of the times largely focus on autonomy as *self-actualization* and *self-determination*, under conditions of "doubly doubled" subjectification (comprising both aspirations and requirements, and representing both a threat and a won-

22 Diederichsen, *Kreative Arbeit und Selbstverwirklichung*, p. 122.

23 See Ulrich Bröckling, *Das unternehmerische Selbst: Soziologie einer Subjektivierungsform*, 7th ed. (Frankfurt am Main: Suhrkamp, 2019).

24 Sabeth Buchmann and Kai von Eickels, "Im Körper von Kuratieren: 'You should always have a product that's not you'," in *Art Works: Ästhetik des Postfordismus*, ed. Netzwerk Kunst & Arbeit (Berlin: b_books, 2015).

derful promise), it is requirements made on subjects' ability to self-organize that increase most clearly. Autonomy as *self-organization* follows a significantly different logic to that of self-actualization or self-determination, however, [as the latter] address both companies and employees as (sub-)systems whose "survival" depends on their entrepreneurial self-organization abilities and thus their skills of "agile adaptation" to mutable, incalculable, and radically uncertain environmental conditions; a constellation that subjects must ascertain and deal with in terms of their own identity.[25]

There are particularly high expectations on art and culture's abilities, as fields of activity, to intensify *self-actualization* and *self-determination*. The costs and pressures of *self-organization* are here easily overlooked—or priced in as a necessary evil of the market. The latter arrives, however, hand in hand with something "self-evident"—"that nothing concerning art is self-evident anymore"[26] and that it is precisely here that the fundamental reasons for art's (relative) autonomy are to be sought. Many cultural producers have thus long since ceased to be drawn solely to the neoliberal promise of success that Thomas Hoving, former director of New York's Metropolitan Museum of Art, brought together into a cynical slogan: "Art is money-sexy! Art is money-sexy-social-climbing-fantastic!"[27] Artists and cultural producers are instead frequently seeking to do no more than find a "self-determined" place of retreat, so as to avoid being determined entirely by the market of capitalism. It is in keeping with this that the artist Caroline Woolard describes the situations of many artists, in the starkest conceivable contrast to the capital market: "I've never sold any art. I don't know many artists who have ever sold anything. Most art will never sell

25 Graefe, *Resilienz im Krisenkapitalismus*, p. 163f.
26 Adorno, *Aesthetic Theory*, p. 9.
27 Quoted from Gregory Sholette, *Dark Matter*, p. 36.

and most artists won't make money from their art."[28] Put more simply, it has long since been established that "dishwashing" as a part-time way of earning your keep is almost irreconcilable with work as an artist. The greatest challenge is often in (self-)organizing the precarious balance between jobs that ensure (economic) livelihood in the moment while not standing in the way of self-determined, self-actualizing art production—irrespective of whether the latter is now speculating on a successful future or merely seeking somehow to establish a sustainable place of retreat.[29]

Fittingly, Isabelle Graw suggests replacing the (relative) autonomy of art with a "model of 'relative heteronomy'" in which art is relegated to its market: "Where the artistic product's remoteness from the market is invoked, this remoteness is also the driving force behind its commercial exploitation. I attribute the art market's internal contradictions to this unique constitution of art as a commodity. Analogously to other commodities, I conceptualize the commodity of art as one split into a symbolic value and a market value,"[30] writes Graw. The ability to generate a "knowledge of life" with one's own art—in keeping with Diederichsen—thus depends

28 Quoted from Leigh Claire La Berge, *Wages Against Artwork: Decommodified Labor and the Claims of Socially Engaged Art* (Durham, N.C. and London: Duke University Press, 2019), p. 1.

29 See also Hans-Jürgen Hafner and Thorsten Schneider, "Mach mal: Oder Produktion ist anderswo," in *Involvierte Autonomie. Künstlerische Praxis zwischen Engagement und Eigenlogik*, ed. Birgit Eusterschulte and Christian Krüger (Bielefeld: transcript, 2022), pp. 111–133.

30 "Wird die Marktferne des künstlerischen Produkts beschworen, dann ist dies auch Triebfeder seiner Vermarktung. Es ist die besondere Verfasstheit der Ware Kunst, auf die ich die inneren Widersprüche des Kunstmarktes zurückführe. Analog zu anderen Waren wird die Ware Kunst von mir als sich in einem Symbol- und einen Marktwert aufspaltend konzipiert"; Isabelle Graw, *Der große Preis: Kunst zwischen Markt und Celebrity Kultur* (Cologne: Dumont, 2008), p. 9f. This book has been translated into English as *High Price: Art Between the Market and Celebrity Culture* (Berlin: Sternberg Press, 2009) with a partially rewritten foreword, for which reason the published English translation is not directly quoted here.

on placing these two values in favorable relation with one another. Should this not work out, the sustenance labor should at least leave requisite time and space for artistic work—or at least the potential for its future realization. If such a model also became key to making a qualitative distinction between pros and amateurs, a great deal more artists and cultural workers would come to be regarded as amateurs than is currently the case, either in their self-perception or in the eyes of others. It emerges here with remarkable clarity how strongly market relations affect all areas of life in capitalist societies, even if some sections—art production and reception, for instance—are still declared to be (relatively) autonomous. Graw thus proposes the metaphor of the "net" and analyzes its constitutive "holes."[31] But to the degree that this metaphor has the desired effect, it can also easily become a trap for those excluded within it or trapped outside it. The possibilities for escape are none. Gerald Raunig's critique of Graw's idea has focused on this very inescapability.[32]

The shift in artistic labor's value as delineated above also changes the relationship between the kind of discussion of creative labor as conducted in art discourse and the discourse on resilience within crisis capitalism. Contemporary art is—in its more advanced forms, at least—too attentive to social discourses and its production conditions too interwoven with those of capitalism for resilience not to have long since established itself as a concept. It is nonetheless possible to discern an asymmetry between thematic engagement in the symbolic form of artworks and the discourse on the increasingly precarious labor and living conditions of artists themselves. Even where socially engaged art problem-

31 "Netz" and "Löcher"; Graw, *Der große Preis*, p. 9.

32 See Gerald Raunig, "Anti-Kanonisierung: Das differenzielle Wissen der Institutionskritik," in Stefan Nowotny and Gerald Raunig, *Instituierende Praxen* (Vienna, Linz, Berlin, London and Zurich: transversal texts, 2016), pp. 25–38.

atizes the precarious living conditions of specific individuals or groups within a socio-political context and attempts, from this position, to develop agency, the conditions under which said art is produced are often omitted. The symbolic capital of art—and its associated economic capital—is often perceived as such an enormous privilege that its problematization is identified as unique in relation to other forms of injustice, exploitation, and adversity. Supplementing this with reflection on the conditions under which this critique is produced could easily be understood as a hubristic levelling-off of the enormous differences between the various forms of injustice. Rather than being seen as a multi-perspective problematization from which connecting perspectives might emerge, basic comparability is—as a mode of differentiated observation—often met with skepticism.

Nevertheless, protests emanating recently from social movements—and which have also shown their effects within the art world—have made it very clear that racism, classism, discriminatory treatment of women and non-binary people are, alongside the exploitative accumulation of capital, much more than merely symbolic disputes that take place both within the art world and elsewhere. Ana Teixeira Pinto and Kerstin Stakemeier have pointed to the strong media presence of "struggles over the politics of representation—with the involvement of groups like W.A.G.E. or Decolonize this Place," similarly noting trenchantly that "parallel attempts to organize artists and other art workers, though no less crucial, remain restricted to a less publicized horizon."[33] Attributing this only to increased willingness to show affect or indignation within a contemporary society of the spectacle would, however, be too narrow a reading. What actually becomes apparent here is how much promise would be held within a bringing-together of

33 Anna Teixeira Pinto and Kerstin Stakemeier, "A Brief Glossary of Social Sadism," *Texte zur Kunst* 116 (2019), pp. 82–115.

activism and art—especially where this could create a field for discussing social conflicts. The kind of strict distinction between "artist critique" and "social critique" made by Boltanski and Chiapello—and previously present in the accusation that critical theory is merely "cultural critique"—is essentially untenable. More instructive here would be to once again interrogate all those notions of "art's autonomy," especially where such notions rip the symbolic values of art from their existing market relations—thus also excluding them from social power relations—while, at the same time, ensuring that artistic forms of critique are too easily understood as cultural critique and thus attributed to those self-same power relations. But where critical art is too explicit in taking sides in favor of a "cause" that seems to lie beyond art's (relative) autonomy, it may be too quickly classified as social criticism and denied its character as art. Oliver Marchart attributes this to an art criticism that makes arbitrariness or "enigmaticalness"—to speak in Adorno's terms[34]—its sole decision-making criterion, thus allowing it to attribute to activism an apparent unambiguity as propaganda.[35] Conflictual aesthetics, as disseminated by Marchart himself, challenge this definition of autonomous art and call instead for the discussion of art to be understood as a permanent negotiation process that, rather than being conducted either inside or outside art discourse, chooses to localize that very discourse within a public sphere. In place of absolute insistence on (relative) autonomy or, inversely, on the emphatic liquidation of art into life practice, it would instead be a question of constantly trialing new differentiations:

> [I]t would be a mistake to think that a political event can only be sparked from within the terrain of conventional

34 Adorno, *Aesthetic Theory*, p. 118ff.
35 See Oliver Marchart, *Conflictual Aesthetics: Artistic Activism and the Public Sphere* (Berlin: Sternberg Press, 2019).

> politics. It may be tested out everywhere. Even the art field may potentially contribute to this collective experiment—and many artists have been contributing to it for a long time with their activist practices. Insofar as art proves to be responsive to the triple exigency of agitating, propagating, and organizing, it may easily turn into politics—more easily and more frequently, in any case, than the functionaires of the art field will admit.[36]

Where experiments are an established and expected part of the art context, that which Marchart here describes often brings with it a certain ressentiment in regard to politics, due to the association with risk, destabilization, or danger—or even with anarchy. If we were instead to understand the normative ideal of democracy as the institutional interplay of highly varied stakeholders "in the name of whom it seeks to expand the zone of civil participation,"[37] as suggested by Étienne Balibar in his discussion on free speech, it would be easier to regard this "as belonging to the *commons*, which must be generalized and expanded to the greatest degree possible."[38] Balibar emphasizes the foundational democratic idea, following which it must be possible "to switch sides in the relationship of the govering to the governed."[39] Following this democratic principle, why should it be impossible to be both an artist and a political activist? Could we not also imagine bringing Graw's proposed model of relative heteronomy to bear within the relationship of art to politics? Doing so would admittedly require major efforts, as the relationship of individuals to "politics" or "art" is not locked into fixed identities and must, on the contrary, always be open to scrutiny or change. Democracies are, following this (self-)conception, always in the process of change and reconsti-

36 Ibid., p. 41.
37 Étienne Balibar, *Freie Rede* (Zurich: Diaphanes, 2019), p. 11.
38 Ibid., p. 9.
39 Ibid., p. 36.

tution. Or, to put it more succinctly: in crisis. This has historically proven itself time and again as the quality required to adapt to changing demands under changing conditions. Similar qualities are attributed to art—for, as Adorno knew long ago, nothing about art seems to be self-evident anymore.

By no means, however, does this solve all problems. On the contrary: if the crisis mode were now to be declared *ultima ratio* and used in the constellation described above to justify a constitutive (free) play of forces between art, politics, and the market, a conflict would emerge in which it would not be the possibilities for participation as part of the commons that are strengthened, but the right of each person who manages to assert themselves. The short-circuits among "crisis capitalism," "crisis democracy," and "crisis art" would in practice lead to disaster. The tension described by Graefe—between autonomy (in the form of self-actualization), self-determination, and the demand for subjects' ability to self-organize. Were artists' and cultural workers' efforts to organize their own political autonomy likewise left only to their abilities to *self*-organize, their "survival" would be to an even greater extent dependent on their abilities vis-à-vis "'agile adaptation' to mutable, incalculable, and radically uncertain environmental conditions; a constellation that subjects must ascertain and deal with in terms of their own identity."[40] Key is to establish a

> new politics-in-becoming, in a process within which the meaning of political actions is not decided following their conformity with established institutional forms [or the anticipation of their future characteristics – T.S.], but rather following their ability to lend social experiences and challenges a new political meaning, and to lend this new meaning persistence.[41]

40 Graefe, *Resilienz im Krisenkapitalismus*, p. 163f.
41 Nowotny and Raunig, *Instituierende Praxen*, p. 11.

Stefan Nowotny and Gerald Raunig thus insist "that a future can only be had as a common one."[42] They too take aim at what Graefe describes as the "doubly doubled" subjectivization that makes all organization—economic, political, and cultural—the (personal) responsibility of individuals. "Given that precarization and enforced, self-entrepreneurial subjectivizations increasingly precipitate into illnesses of isolation (anxiety, depression, etc.) instrumental relationship forms that harm the actual ability to reconstruct sociality,"[43] the first priority is to defend or re-create the preconditions under which (relative) autonomy and non-all-encompassing relations of dependency can prevail at all. "Workfare strategies constantly in refinement increasingly dominate the time, space, and energy that would otherwise be open for trialing other possible modes of action; and these strategies are supported in their effectiveness by precarization's subjective effects of uncertainty and social atomization."[44] But if these possible modes of action are the very ones that are key to democratic participation and political economy, they cannot under any circumstances be relinquished. Art is merely a possible space for collectively trialing democratic capacities for participation and cannot assert any special status for itself.

Sofia Bempeza has highlighted that even in an art strike following a period of refusal, a "temporary adeneia" as a delaying moment of reflection and experimentation with "new politics-in-becoming" as sociality must be unfurled if demands are to be made persistent in the long term. What emerges here however, once again, is the question of which organizational form is required to lend strikers' demands that long-term persistence. This must be given particular emphasis, for the strike

42 Ibid., p. 15.
43 Ibid., p. 14.
44 Ibid., p. 16.

demands self-organization abilities from subjects in an intensified form and must be endured before new time, space, and energy can be unleashed.[45]

These challenges must all contend with the established assertion of (relative) autonomy in the art context. As Marina Vishmidt has accurately pointed out, this is as much an intractable as it is a

> neuralgic point—with a highly contested history—within the system of material and conceptual denials that holds together the all-encompassing cosmology of art in its current version. Art's autonomy, in the Adornian and still corrosive sense for me, is the scar of what it can't get rid of, namely its roots in the division of labor and class society; the magnetic repulsion between art and labor, art and money, art and all the parameters of capitalist reality, which provide it with life and toys.[46]

In Adorno's own work, this repulsion that cannot be gotten rid of is even named as an open contradiction. Correspondingly, he at one point asserts that "a contradiction of all autonomous art is the concealment of the labour that went into it."[47]

Where art production is then generalized as a model for organizing work in an increasingly deregulated and flexibilized way, this contradiction widens. In critiques of entrepreneurship, self-enterprise, and start-up energy—which, following their self-image as "creative labor," increasingly seek (or are supposed) to be understood as "artistic"—the concealment of labor as labor has already been the subject of wide-ranging discussion.

45 See Sofia Bempeza, *Geschichte(n) des Kunststreiks* (Vienna, Linz, Berlin, London, Malaga and Zurich: transversal texts, 2019).

46 Kerstin Stakemeier and Marina Vishmidt, "The Value of Autonomy—a Conversation between Marina Vishmidt and Kerstin Stakemeier about the Reproduction of Art," *Texte zur Kunst* 88 (December 2012), pp. 102–117.

47 Theodor Adorno, *In Search of Wagner* (London and New York: Verso, 2005), p. 72.

However, these workfare strategies are not limited to a clearly defined field of work: they rather extend to all areas of life. The spheres of activity in which it still even remains possible to conceive of art's autonomy will be put under radical pressure by an overarching expansion of work. Graefe's criticism that autonomy in the form of *self-organization* merely rewards the capacity to make far-reaching adaptations would thus, in the final analysis, have long since eroded—and proven the absurdity of—any autonomy of art. The scope for "artistic experiments" still capable of trialing forms of democratic sociality would be virtually illusory under such conditions.

Vishmidt concludes that a "critique of political economy that would be adequate to our current context should be interested in the place of art in the attenuated conditions of the post-crisis quotidian."[48] The challenge would be in also seeking to establish the "magnetic repulsion between art and labor"—to use Vishmidt's own words—beyond the narrower context of art (which can in any case no longer be enclosed within clear perimeters) in all other social spheres. "It is precisely through tracing those relations that both the typicality and singularity of art and labour, respectively, can be understood in a determinate way, as the all-too proximate poles of speculation as a mode of production."[49] However, this cannot mean understanding speculation as an invisible hand that, as a self-valorizing value, turns everything it touches into gold and from which there is no escape. It must rather be a case, in the face of the appropriation of art as captured in *The New Spirit of Capitalism*, of working toward an autonomy of art that is not only beautiful and expensive, but which is also

48 Marina Vishmidt, *Speculation as a Mode of Production: Forms of Value Subjectivity in Art and Capital* (Chicago: Haymarket Books, 2018), p. 26. Vishmidt also refers here to Laurent Berlant, *Cruel Optimism* (Durham, N.C. and London: Duke University Press, 2011).

49 Vishmidt, *Speculation as a Mode of Production*, p. 23.

hard work—as Karl Valentin has previously noted in a *bon mot*:

> While it is crucial to distinguish the unpaid intern in a cultural centre from the artist producing commodities, in either case the valorisation of creativity is a mode of producing subjectivity that aligns the interests of workers with the speculative nature of capital, a way of installing speculation at the most intimate levels of subjective existence (whereas the "ordinary" instance of the wage-relation sees the interests of labour and capital aligned through the wage, which is separable from the person). This calls for a delineation of the current determinate forms of speculation as they both exceed the politics of labour and the forms of class belonging they presupposed, and prefigure other ones.[50]

In the face of the "doubly doubled" subjectification of artists and cultural workers caught between the threats and grand promises of art and labor, it is imperative to find spheres of activity in which these contradictions can somehow be made bearable. If this bare-minimum livelihood is not guaranteed, all else becomes superfluous. The idea that it is in permanent crisis that art would unfurl its greatest creativity has always been false.

Translation: Matthew James Scown

50 Ibid., p. 26f.

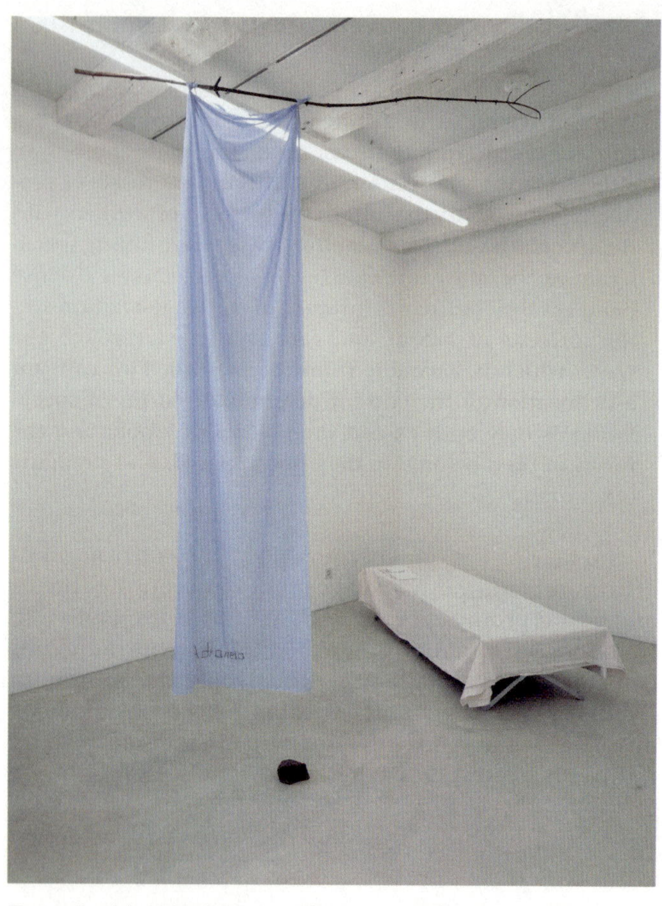

Temporäre Adraneia, 2021, Ausstellungsraum Klingental, Basel.

Sofia Bempeza

The Desire of the Exhausted

Notes on Resilience, Resistance, and Adraneia

> The exhausted have a desire: to no longer be exhausted. The exhausted can have this one desire, to no longer be exhausted, as the pre-requisite for the possibility of again having many desires, to no longer be exhausted so that they can want something other, to want what they really want, which is to no longer be exhausted, so that their bodies can offer the possibility again of love or art or pleasure, of thinking without regretting, of achievement, too, or something beyond failed and sorrowful trying at the barely.[1]
>
> Anne Boyer

Beginning the text with the word desire opens a horizon of various possibilities to pursue, including accounts of my own desires: imaginative thinking, speculative feeling, and swimming in the open sea. When being exhausted though, to get your limbs into the water, to plant tomatoes in the garden, to work creatively and engage in critical analysis and community action can be hard to achieve. Not all forms of exhaustion, inertia and negativity are the same, but their somatic and mental presence makes me think of the binary distinctions between positive and negative affects—i. e. hyper-

1 Anne Boyer, *The Undying: Pain, Vulnerability, Mortality, Medicine, Art, Time, Dreams, Data, Exhaustion, Cancer, and Care* (UK: Penguin edition 2019), p. 291.

activity, depression, (not)belonging—the different kinds of attachments to (our) environment and social geography, as well as the engagement and, disengagement with precarious work and the so-called professional life in the cultural field.

The second key word is exhaustion. Being drained is both a physical condition and a burdensome state of mind, in which care as a core social value and collective responsibility cannot be ignored. In her Pulitzer Prize-winning book, *The Undying: Pain, vulnerability, mortality, medicine, art, time, dreams, data, exhaustion, cancer, and care*, poet and essayist Anne Boyer follows the chronicle of her own illness and medical treatment. In her forties, she is a single mother, diagnosed with highly aggressive triple negative breast cancer, working for a living as an art teacher in Kansas City. Boyer tells the story of a sick woman in the first person, as a historian of her own body, while observing other women writers who suffered from breast cancer. She writes her experience of vulnerability from the perspective of a precarious, feminist writer while building her story on the legacies of Susan Sontag, Audre Lorde, Eve Sedgewick, Kathy Acker, and Charlotte Perkins Gilman, whose writings about their disease shaped the literary canon of so-called cancer literature. Her personal traces interweave with a social critique of (un)healthy bodies and a sharp political critique of the breast cancer hospitalization industry. While avoiding common sentimentalities on the disease Boyer speaks firmly of (non)-pleasurable moments, care politics and medical history. If we think that most of the hospital workers (nurses, receptionists, paraprofessionals) are women "who transmute bodies into data" for doctors to interpret them, to write on one's own malady brings into light both gender hierarchies and the division of (care) labor.

In this text I am weaving my own threads in a different story from the perspective of a queer-feminist writer, visual artist, and cultural producer. This can be a story of *non-resilience* in a post-burnout condition and yet a story of refusal, that connects the dots of art histories and collective actions. This is as well a fluid endeavor to approach resilience, resistance and adraneia (inertia) as mingled conditions in precarious times. This text is dealing with different temporalities: It slightly touches upon regimes of discipline and autonomous self-making that constitute the modern independent self, it contains thoughts on the notion of (creative) labor and the symptomatology of our neoliberal (time) regime, it goes back further to memoir dissident art practices of previous decades, and it sketches out thoughts on resilient art and cultural producers in the ongoing Covid-19 pandemic.

Pandemic Without Resilience

As I write these lines, it's more than one year that we are living in the Covid-19 pandemic. Time passes as we unfold our thoughts within art and academia, drawing on life practices with different resources, privileges and contingencies depending on where we are located (geographically, economically, socially). I cannot promote a sense of euphoria, nor do I wish to delve into dialectical negativity and the problems of the either/or dualism. Neither do I wish to speak of a coming time *beyond* the pandemic, in which we will supposedly have proven our resilience as the latest neoliberal model of competent living in multiple crises. Rather I am speaking of a feasible present within the contingent pandemic period.

Resilience, to put it briefly, is the capacity to recover from a collective crisis or to bounce back after a trauma. I am following here Sarah Bracke's critique of the neoliberal notion of *resilience*,[2] which imposes on us the

2 Sarah Bracke, "Bouncing Back: Vulnerability and Resistance in Times of Resilience," in *Vulnerability in Resistance*, ed. Judith Butler et al. (Durham, N.C. and London: Duke University Press, 2016).

exercise of social and ethical skills such as adaptability, self-regulation and persistence, in order to be able to respond to all the different crises that became predominant in the twenty-first century: neoliberal governmentality, ecological damage and neo-extractivism, pandemics, wars, post-democracy, new authoritarianisms and identitarianisms coupled with racism, ethnonationalism, and the anti-gender offensive which attacks women and LGBTQI+ people. The neoliberal concept of resilience, as a contemporary technology of subjectification, is indifferent to the causality of all crises. "Neoliberal citizenship is nothing if not a training in resilience as the new technology of the self: a training to withstand whatever crisis capital undergoes and whatever political measures the state carries out to save it," noted Mark Neocleous in his pre-emptive strike against the resilience agenda.[3] Therefore, resilience as a sociologically relevant concept of crisis management prevents the ability to imagine anything other than the adaptability of the subject in times of crisis. Practicing resilience as the latest self-technique can block any transformative attempts that reject the neoliberal mantra of economic growth, trade liberalization and blooming financial markets. The training of a resilient self also avoids analyzing systemic accounts of power and violence, focusing instead on individual survival techniques or the paternalist protection of so-called vulnerable groups under the latest capitalist ethos.[4]

As a matter of fact, living in capitalism creates certain obstacles to physical and mental flourishing. Yet flour-

3 Mark Neocleous cited in Bracke, "Bouncing Back," p. 62. Original source Mark Neocleous, "Resisting Resilience," *Radical Philosophy* 178 (2013), pp. 2–7, https://www.radicalphilosophy.com/commentary/resisting-resilience (accessed December 9, 2022).

4 Stefanie Graefe proposes to rethink the concept of vulnerability in a critical way—particularly for analyzing the antithesis between resilience and increased vulnerability in less dualistic terms. See Stefanie Graefe, *Resilienz im Krisenkapitalismus: Wider das Lob der Anpassungsfähigkeit* (Bielefeld: transcript, 2019), pp. 161–185.

ishing sounds too harmless, if we consider how perniciously it is built on constitutive social inequalities and labor divisions, racialized accumulation and the overexploitation of human and natural resources. But still, as Lauren Berlant notes, in contemporary societies of control with respect to security and capital (primarily in the global North), people hold tightly to fantasies of upward mobility, success, recognition, job security, liberal values, and positive affectivity, even though there is enduring evidence that these fantasies are unattainable for the vast majority, and despite the awareness that the normative political system appears as shrunken and broken. Berlant describes *cruel optimism* as the subject's relationship to an object/scene of desire that is, in fact, an obstacle to living.[5] Bracke's analysis of Berlant's work offers an understanding of resilience as a symptom of the neoliberal economy of desire, in as much as cruelty is one of the political terms for the impossible condition of "a good life" in capitalism.

When located in Europe's southeastern Mediterranean periphery (in the Greek context for the author), the call upon people to fortify *resilience* can pick up a specific tone. One can hear it directly or indirectly: as individuals we should enhance resilience to survive another crisis—in other words, we should practice damage control and train our well-being according to the actual motto "crisis management is self-responsibility." There are different types of resilience expected: Refugees should survive death camps and illegal pushbacks in the Aegean Sea, migrants based in Greece should exercise adaptability and employability, low- and middle-class populations should prove their capacity to pay higher prices for energy, housing, nutrition, and medicine.

Now, more specifically, I wish to turn my perspective to her* in order to understand the complexity of the

5 Lauren Berlant, *Cruel Optimism* (Durham, N.C. and London: Duke University Press, 2011), p. 227.

resilient subject within the social relations of gender in the art field. Recalling Bracke's subject of (post-)feminist resilience, I need to contextualize my perspective within the western gendered politics that shape the figure of resilient *postfeminist femininity*, namely "the female subject who continues to survive patriarchy, is increasingly exposed to the neoliberal labor conditions of flexicurity and is considered individually responsible for her survival."[6] I don't wish to foster the postfeminist exception narrative of "Look, I Overcame,"[7] but rather to underline the different figures of resilient subjects, considering vulnerability, agency, and resistance as related to social conditions, material dependencies and fragile relationships. So, I am writing with a gendered voice from a situated perspective of her* who doesn't wish to exercise resilience for stabilizing or renewing dominant modes of re/production, neither in the pandemic nor in crisis capitalism. I am located in theory, art and cultural production, and I am particularly interested in historical and contemporary practices of withdrawal, namely art strikes and transversal organizing, that oppose(d) the trained institutional credo of *business as usual.*

Strike My Tongue

The notion of labor, at least in highly capitalized control and service societies, is determined by free market principles (i. e. flexibilization of working time and place, digitalization of work, competitive individualism, labor exploitation), following the economic demands of financial capital, global trade and neo-extractivism.

6 Sarah Bracke, "Bouncing Back," p. 65.

7 This narrative and its "particular ethos of resilience is marked by these same positionalities and stands in contrast to the post-feminist 'bad girls,' who continue to suffer from fragility, fail to turn their damage into opportunity, or are in need of rescue or protection." See ibid., pp. 52–75.

Most notably, the perception of work (and waged labor) in neoliberal societies is crucial: work turns into the main ontological horizon of (social) life and working, under more or less precarious conditions, has become the only legitimate "way of life." In addition, the neoliberal working doctrine of "do what you love," not only underlies the fact that some forms of work (e.g. highly-skilled employment, socially attractive professions in the creative sector) are considered more worthy than others (e.g. low-wage or unpaid care work, tech or textile factory work), but also devalues the work of all those who need to work for wages.[8] Nonetheless, this neoliberal rationality uses the ritual of work (paid employment) and its manufactured scarcity (unemployment) to maintain the late capitalist class order.[9]

In addition, the economic transformation which has happened under the late capitalist order and the restructuring of power relations in biopolitical terms come into prominence in the discussion on social value production and the feminization of labor. As Nanne Buurman notes, it is precisely those characteristics of reproductive and affective labor,[10] to be found within unsalaried female domestic work (multitasking, caring, affective communication), that play a decisive role in the labor market of service societies and the new economies of symbolic production. An illustration of this, for example, is the expectation to identify emotionally with one's own working tasks in a company or an institution out of passion and love. The late capitalist myth of "work-as-love" persuades people in specific branches (media, culture, academia, fashion, and the arts), to work for cheap or free in the name of "love," no matter the levels

8 Miya Tokumitsu, *Do What You Love: And Other Lies About Success and Happiness* (New York: Regan Arts, 2015), pp. 42–44.
9 Peter Fleming, *The Mythology of Work: How Capitalism Persists Despite Itself* (London: Pluto Press, 2015), pp. 19–23.
10 Nanne Buurman, "From Prison Guard to Healer: Curatorial Authorships in the Context of Gendered Economies," *On Curating* 52 (2021), pp. 21–34.

of work exploitation in post-industrial societies. This understanding of labor as a supposedly autonomous,[11] self-determined, passionate activity, is almost identical to the notion (or interpretation) of work in the creative field: Working in the arts is considered to be a technique or a multitalented activity for crafting our subjectivity and professional persona within the attention economy of the art field.

> Art labor juggles between a conditional autonomy, vis-à-vis capitalist functionalization, and heteronomy yet considering art labor as commodity, service, social activity and a form of unproductive labor and its relation to reproductive labor. At the same time, to claim art's autonomization becomes itself part of the formation of its autonomy within commodity and service capitalist societies. In this respect, this autonomous claim cannot simply abolish the contradictions of the capitalist division between productive and unproductive labor. (...) Thus art production in neoliberalism is, on the one hand, consistently subject to political as well as economic imperatives that prevent its supposed autonomy. On the other, critical institutional positions addressing working conditions within the art field as well as the intertwining of criticality and systemic appropriation are present in the art/cultural institutions.[12]

Artists and cultural producers work in interconnected, sensitive, reflexive, and possibly critical or subversive ways, from different positions and perspectives. Work is work—for some as an intellectual necessity, for others as

11 See the conversation on the arts' autonomy between Kerstin Stakemeier and Marina Vishmidt, "Der Wert der Autonomie – ein Gespräch zwischen Kerstin Stakemeier und Marina Vishmidt über Reproduktion in der Kunst", *Texte zur Kunst*, February 26, 2018 (online), https://www.textezurkunst.de/articles/der-wert-der-autonomie-ein-gesprach-zwischen-kerstin-stakemeier-und-marina-vishmidt-uber-reproduktion-der-kunst (accessed December 9, 2022).

12 Sofia Bempeza, *Geschichte(n) des Kunststreiks* (Vienna, Linz, Berlin, London, Malaga and Zurich: transversal texts, 2019), p. 39.

lifelong self-realization, for many as self-conception and self-optimization within the neoliberal mode of existence and subjectification. Whether in the name of the social, gender-specific and racialized distinctions in the art field or in the name of a precarious artistic bohemia, contemporary artists and cultural workers are expected to adapt to the neoliberal common sense (which is, to use the late capitalist jargon, the "entrepreneurial spirit" of the creative industries), but also to critically shape and perform an alternative common sense in inspirational ways.

What happens with the figure of artist/cultural worker per se? The longer we remain, or can afford to remain, active in the art field, the more we are confronted with a certain neoliberal rationality that sets individual competition and opportunism as a prevailing behavior and normalizes the entrepreneurial model of professionality. In other words, as artists and cultural producers, we must make sure that we stay fit, productive, mobile, and flexible;[13] we are supposed to generate social, economic, and symbolic capital while positioning ourselves in cultural institutions and/or the art market. Thus, for some or many of us, there is a feeling of constant loss of places of retreat, mutual care, and solidarity. Precarious art labor and a project-based life without back-ups and hidden capital has its price: it often leads to hyperactivity, exhaustion, and depression.

A strike in the art field? For many years, I have been concerned with forms of refusal and the possibilities of pause in the arts, focusing on the engagement and disengagement of artists, the notion of *adraneia* (inactivity), and the art strike as forms of non-adaptation within the capitalist framing of art production. Strike not only

13 Isabell Lorey, "Vom immanenten Widerspruch zur hegemonialen Funktion. Biopolitische Gouvernementalität und Selbst-Prekarisierung von KulturproduzentInnen," in *Kritik der Kreativität*, ed. Gerald Raunig and Ulf Wuggenig (Vienna: transversal texts, 2016).

implies the disruption of (wage) labor and the genealogy of political organizing and radical withdrawal, but it also refers to the micro-practices of refusal and the making visible of relations of production within a capitalist art system. It may sound paradoxical to strike from one's own creativity, yet art strikes have a distinct history in the cultural field. In my book I highlight three contemporary dimensions of the art strike, *Refusal, Temporary adraneia* and *Organization,* which occupy time and space in different ways. We can imagine the art strike concept and its three dimensions illustrated as a triangle.

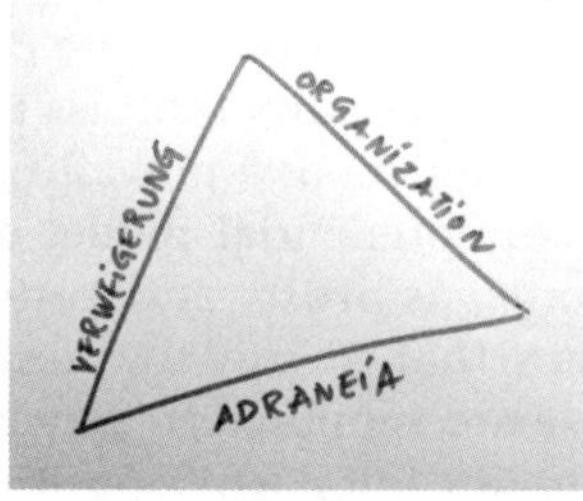

These dimensions are not hierarchically determined but rather contingent and complementary to each other as they involve collective and individual practices.

Refusal is neither a total withdrawal nor a radical walkout, illusionary exodus, and escapism. In fact, refusal is a minimal political action, a form of killjoy. It is an attempt to cross habitual borders (i. e. social status in the arts) and raise awareness of being able to say "No." The art strike is a gesture of refusal, a *negation placed in space and time,* but not a non-action. It is both an interruption of art production and a manifestation of arts' social and material dependencies, its distribution, and representation modes under capitalism.

Temporary adraneia is the second dimension of the art strike concept. Adraneia, in Greek, means no action, inactivity or inertia. I argue that a time of temporary adraneia is required for deepening ways and concepts of working modalities in the arts, which are not primarily shaped by the canonization of neoliberal cultural policies and by art market economies.[14] Adraneia is the state of sensing one's own position, yet suspending the permanent visibility, productivity and mobility demanded by the attention economy in the arts. Temporary adraneia is to persist in a temporal state: on the one hand, in order to arrive at a point of disarticulation that breaks with certain modes of art production and creative ethics; on the other, in order to find a political re-articulation with fellow artists and cultural producers through synergy and collaboration. However, temporary adraneia is not a technique of self-regeneration or "detoxing" from social media and professional networks. Adraneia is a state of reflection on one's own perspective and *situatedness*[15] within the field we act in individually or collectively.

The third art strike dimension is organization, as it refers to social struggles within the cultural field and beyond. It derives from the genealogy of political intervention and concrete action for contesting cemented structures of social, gender and class hierarchies in the art world. To get organized collectively (grass roots initiatives, associations, union formation) embraces the nexus of political and aesthetic practices that turn against (labor) precarization as the norm. Organization as a collective process must be polyphonic and polyvalent in order to bring together emancipative practices (antiracism, gender equality, social justice) that seek a critical dissent in the arts and beyond.

14 On the redistribution of capital and its influence on the art market, see Andrea Fraser, "L'1%, C'est Moi," in *Texte zur Kunst* 83 (2011).

15 Donna Haraway, *Staying with the Trouble: Making Kin in the Chthulucene* (Durham, N.C. and London: Duke University Press, 2016).

Art Strike Examples

The Art Workers' Coalition, formed at the end of the 1960s, put pressure on New York museums to cease gender and racial discrimination in exhibitions and collections. In 1969, the group wrote a public letter to MoMA director Eates Lowry with thirteen demands addressing "The Museum's Relationship to Artists and Society" as well as the exhibition arrangements and working ethics between artists and institutions. AWC asked the museums to open up for female and black artists, and further for black, Hispanic and other communities —in other words for non-white, non-bourgeois publics—and made proposals for improving institutional policies. AWC's cultural policy agenda, formed through weekly plenary discussions (open hearings), was informed by the cause of the US feminist and people of color movements and influenced by the anti-war movement. AWC struggled for better working conditions and fair deals between artists and museums, yet the cultural diversity among the group members and its various political interests and priorities is remarkable. AWC split into smaller groups such as the Guerilla Art Action Group, the Woman Artists Revolution (WAR) and the New York Ad Hoc Women Artists' Committee; all three were closer to political activism.[16] The New York Ad Hoc Women Artists' Committee consisted of members of the groups Women Artists in Revolution and Women Students and Artists for Black Art Liberation (founded by Faith Ringgold and Michele Wallace) and single members of the broader Art Workers' Coalition, which was rather male-dominated.

In the following decades, many artists experimented with the art strike as conceptual refusal or symbolic

16 The cultural and political diversity of the AWC members is also one of the reasons that eventually led to the dissolution of the group in 1971. See Julia Brian Wilson, *Art Workers: Radical Practice in the Vietnam Era* (Berkeley and London: University of California Press, 2009), pp. 154–155.

intervention. Gustav Metzger launched the strike call "Years Without Art 1977–1980," attempting to convince his colleagues to strike from art for three years, to stop exhibiting and producing. He proposed instead to intensify artists' engagement with the critical potential of art. Metzger's art strike also inspired Goran Djordjević, who called for an International Artists' Strike in Belgrade (1979) in order to abolish the bourgeois concept of art. In the 1990s Stewart Home and the Neoists launched an art strike as a means of encouraging a critical debate on the concept of art—their propositions, called the "Art Strike Papers," were published in YAWN magazine. Last but not least, the artist collective Claire Fontaine updated the concept of the *human strike,* as coined by Italian feminism in the 1970s, for striking out the relation between affect, art and reproductive labor in the art world. The human strike in the present focuses on the libidinous economy and the structures of desire disregarded by political economy.[17]

Cut in time. After the world financial crisis in 2008 and parallel to the Occupy[18] and anti-austerity movements in 2011–2012, artists and cultural producers formed organizations and initiatives to address institutional economic policies, cultural censorship, and the precarization of so-called creative (human) capital. Groups like Working Artists and the Greater Economy (W.A.G.E.) and Gulf Labor Coalition in New York, the Precarious Workers Brigades in the UK, the initiative Haben und Brauchen in Berlin, the Civic Forum of Contemporary Art (OFSW) in Poland, the platform ArtLeaks and the Alytus Biennale in Lithuania, and most recently—due to the pandemic—the groups Wages for Wages Against in Switzerland and Support Art Workers in Greece. The

17 Claire Fontaine, *Human Strike Has Already Begun and Other Writings* (Lueneburg: Mute & PML Books/ Leuphana University, 2013).

18 Yates McKee, *Strike Art: Contemporary Art and the Post-Occupy Condition* (London and New York: Verso, 2016).

various organizations and initiatives seek to change the standard neoliberal working conditions in museums and art spaces (such as minimal expenditure and no-payment practices) while proposing guidelines on institutional policymaking and tools for surviving in the art system. These initiatives draw on the long history of activism focusing on art as labor: From symbolic concepts of dissidence, critical negation, and aesthetic resistance to organized cultural interventions regarding institutional policies, all the contemporary examples mentioned question the concept of the artist-as-worker. In that sense, they reveal the production, distribution, and marketing of art as well as its status as productive and unproductive "work" within capitalist economies.

Most recently, the art strike concept gained a postcolonial perspective, as it became linked to decolonization struggles in the museums and cultural institutions of the global North. Initiatives such as Strike MoMa and Decolonize This Place (Brooklyn Museum), as well as European queer/feminist and antiracist social movements, are based on voicing, caring and solidarity practices, in order to target cultural degradation and political exclusion.

As discussed so far, the concept of the art strike, conceived as refusal and negation of the capitalist and patriarchal working-time regime, addresses social distinctions and class divisions in the field of culture. Regarding an actualization of the art strike today, I wish to emphasize its connection to current feminist strike movements. From an intersectional feminist perspective, we think of strike as a process rather than an event. Verónica Gago talks about the feminist dimension of work, which is different from the masculinist self-understanding of wage labor.

> The strike appropriated by the women's movement is literally overflowed: it must account for multiple labor realities that escape the borders of waged and unionized work, that

> question the limits between productive and reproductive labor, formal and informal labor, remunerated and free tasks, between migrant and national labor, between the employed and the unemployed.[19]

To this extent, we should face the different labor realities within the art and cultural field (free and waged work, productive and reproductive routines, social and symbolic capital) and deconstruct social hierarchies and gender asymmetries. Or even more, we must speak of the elephant in the room, which is that *class* (and social background) matters—in particular, if we wish to approach concepts of resilience in the pandemic and beyond.

Open End

The current transformative crisis of capitalism due to the pandemic endangers people and ecosystems alike. Yet the call to train our resilience capacity faced with the social, ecological, and (geo-)political crisis is based on wrong premises. How can we, as artists, cultural workers activists and intellectuals acknowledge our own political agency but also our systematic failures in a way that can be enabling?

There is no lack of analytical tools. Thanks to Berlant, Butler, Cvetkovich, Foucault, Lorde and many critical thinkers, we can recognize, for instance, that the failure of our own body system means a systemic failure, insofar as the subject's autonomy, conceived as self-realization and self-optimization, is being appropriated within a capitalist context. So, I am turning back to Boyer's words in order to highlight exhaustion through capital-

19 Verónica Gago, "The Feminist International: Appropriating and Overflowing the Strike," *Viewpoint*, March 7, 2018, https://viewpointmag.com/2018/03/07/feminist-international-appropriating-overflowing-strike/ (accessed April 20, 2022).

ism that turns to be both, the lack of desire and a state of failure.

> Our wanting is not our wanting, exactly, when it is exposed like this through being too tired to want anything. What the exhausted once believed was a desire from inside them showed itself to be a desire from what was outside, what had been there before them and what was ordered by whatever wasn't them. But it's not that abstract, energy and lack of it; and not that abstract, being too worn out to want anything but to not be worn out anymore; and not that abstract, the hyperfocused forever of not having enough of any life to do with it what one could. The exhausted are exhausted because they sell the hours of their lives to survive their lives, then they use the hours they haven't sold to get their lives ready for selling, and the hours after that to do the same for the other lives they love.[20]

However, an actual challenge for engaged art and cultural producers seems to be the counterbalance between (art) practice and theory, critique and involvement, positionality and appropriation of criticality, between the use of political statements along with certain forms of doing, thinking, working, caring etc. In other words, to face the desire of institutional, queer-feminist, and post-colonial critique not just as cognitive training or competitive advantage, but as an urgency for expanding language, infrastructures, and time for (new) possible ways of instituting far-reaching structural changes.

During the pandemic and the numerous lockdowns, we noticed that many art peers suffered from the fact that art as a social activity has been abruptly stopped or reduced, since the usual business (art events, openings, parties etc.) hardly existed. Therefore, in small talk, it was common to encounter the plausible desire to return to the non-covid "euphoric" situation as quickly as pos-

20 Boyer, *The Undying*, p. 292.

sible. Nevertheless, there has also been this rapid institutional response to develop resilience concepts asap for remaining creative, innovative, and productive within the pandemic—at least, this was the case in museums and well-situated art institutions. Well, how (and above all why) are we supposed to become highly adaptive or resilient in this new situation?

In my view, reclaiming *adraneia* (inactivity) in the pandemic is a way of reprogramming our mind set. Instead of adapting our activities to the newest institutional standards or smoothly joining the reframing of capitalist creative (metaverse) economies in the pandemic condition and beyond, I propose to insist on the temporary time of adraneia and to continue to put our efforts into a thinking-feeling process for deepening and expanding practices of concern, feminist care and accountability. Why should we be conditioned to overcome all crises of the capitalist system? And how do we see the glass—half empty or half full? Or can we get rid of this logic of evaluation and quantification of our efforts?

To answer this, I am thinking of Ann Cvetkovich's concept of political depression. She faces the question of engaging in critical analysis and direct action that does not necessarily change the world or make us feel better.

> Our meetings, whether public or among ourselves, are as likely to start with a mood as an idea; at one of our national gatherings, for example, many of us admitted to feeling exhausted and overwhelmed by our professional obligations, and we considered what kinds of projects might emerge out of those conditions and how to produce scholarship not timed to the rhythms and genres of conferences, edited collections, and books.[21]

21 Ann Cvetkovich, *Depression: A Public Feeling* (Durham, N.C. and London: Duke University Press, 2012), p. 1.

At the same time, to give enough space and attention to the discussion of negative affects is a form of caring, it's the core of queer-feminist politics. Where to locate this discussion is a matter of (my) concern. It seems that art and cultural institutions, with few exceptions, can possibly host the discourse on practices of commoning, collective care and diversity, but often they cannot afford the killjoy subjects in their yard. In many cases, art and cultural institutions, likewise higher education institutions, fail to create spaces for working against social distinctions, discrimination, and harassment. Sara Ahmed writes about the implications of institutional complaining: "A complaint seems to amplify what makes you not fit, picking up what you are not. A complainer becomes a stranger, a trespasser, a foreigner, not from here, not really from here, not."[22]

Finally, to face the problem of liberal western-type institutions with a macro perspective, I am following Berlant's critique when they talk of the breaking-down moment of collective life as such and the massive institutional failure that led to collapse of "economies, health systems, practices and fantasies of intimacy and ideas of what equality can look like."[23] In recognizing the poetics of infrastructure and the modes of counter-organization Berlant juxtaposes institutions to the collective work that can be done within infrastructures:

> Institutions enclose and congeal power, resources, and interest, and represent their legitimacy as something solid and enduring, a predictability on which the social relies.

22 In her latest book *Complaint!* (Durham, N.C. and London: Duke University Press, 2021) Ahmed explicates complaint as a queer method and a counter-institutional work, focusing on the feminist killjoy as the figure of the "complainer" in the institution (university/higher education). See Sara Ahmed, "After Complaint," *Feminist Killjoys*, March 13, 2022, https://feministkilljoys.com/2022/03/13/after-complaint/ (accessed December 9, 2022).

23 Lauren Berlant, *On the Inconvenience of Other People* (Durham, N.C.: Duke University Press, 2022), p. 96.

> Institutions norm reciprocity. What constitutes infrastructure in contrast are the patterns, habits, norms, and scenes of assemblage and use. Collective affect gets attached to it too, to the sense of its inventiveness and horizon of dynamic reciprocity it entails. This is what it means to invent alter-life from within life, what I called in the introduction the heterotopian impulse. (...) What remains for the pedagogy of unlearning we derive from the aspirational commons, then, is to build affective infrastructures that admit the work of desire and the work of ambivalence as the tactics of commoning.[24]

In this sense we can think of social and cultural practices, as well as art practices, that seek to hold on to collective forms in a dissensual way as they attempt to share (or reclaim) common infrastructures.

In conclusion, social transformation, understood as a just redistribution of material and immaterial resources, calls for (art) strikes no less than for other forms of resistance against neoliberalism, financial capitalism and neo-extractivism. Going against the formation of the newest resilient art subject and the business-as-usual consensus means to be confronted once again with the embodied patriarchal conformism and the post-colonial conditioning in the art field and beyond. To resist those hierarchical modes of thinking and doing calls for a different time regime, one that refuses the late capitalist principle of high performance and resilience as self-techniques of optimization. Not least—to speak of my own desire—it calls for situatedness and transversal practices of commoning and a habitus that grounds in dissent.

24 Ibid., pp. 95–96.

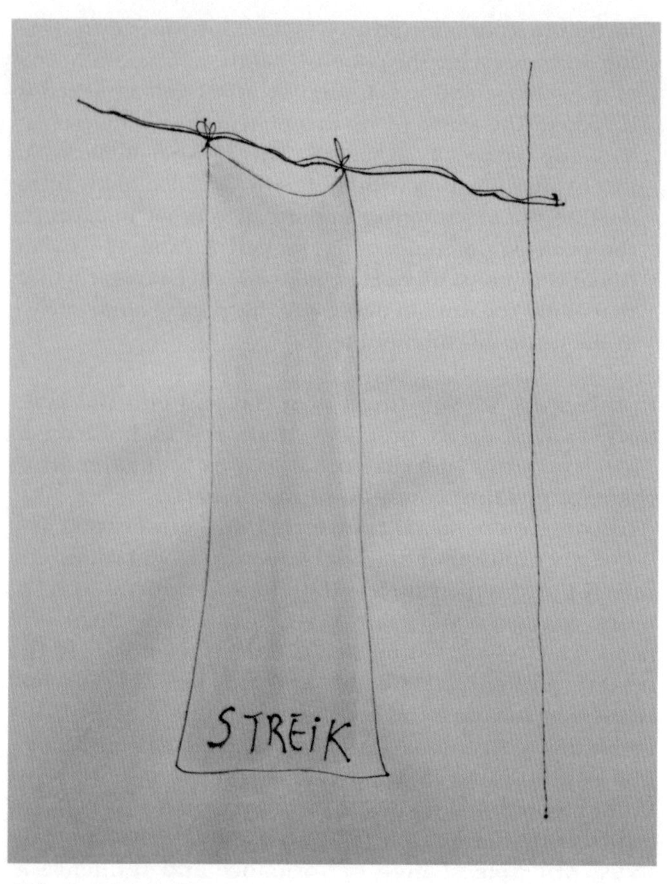
STREIK

Nele Wulff

"Let us be a gear in the machinery and at the same time the obstacle of its operation"

Some Thoughts on House of Tupamaras' Manifesto *El fracaso es mi estilo*

> "We" is an orientation, an attitude. It is a name for critical queer of color and punk negativity that turns getting negated into acts and attitudes that move the future around.[1]

Formulations founded on the pronoun "We" have, quite rightly, been getting a bad press. The years which brought both the Covid-19 pandemic and protests against police violence towards Black people and people of color highlighted yet again why a hasty rhetorical embrace can turn out problematic. Instead of demonstrating solidarity, it tends to flag up an invisible privilege rather than to seriously address social wrongs or different but intricately related categories of discrimination. That said, in their text "Democracy—The Commons: Infrastructures for Troubling Times," Lauren Berlant put forward a We that does have the potential to play an important role in forging another kind

1 Lauren Berlant, "Democracy—The Commons: Infrastructures for Troubling Times," in *On the Inconvenience of Other People* (Durham, N.C.: Duke University Press, 2022), p. 85.

of sociality and intimacy.[2] Drawing on José Esteban Muñoz, they call upon a utopian, queer We that derives from the experience of exclusion and develops within the negation of public norms. The idea that another life is possible is built into the foundations of this community, which is not the culmination of a long, teleological process, but is always embedded within a contingent, relational fabric. Berlant talks of conceiving structure as something that is in a constant state of mutation.[3]

The online project *100 Ways of Saying We* initiated by the Theater Neumarkt in Zurich together with the Goethe Institute might be read as operating a concept similar to Berlant's. It features videos by artists, activists, and theorists who, each in their own way, explore "a pre-enactment of multiple future visions, a speculative-utopian take on the possibilities of the concept of 'We'."[4] In their statement, the organizers also address the conflict inherent in these various notions of We, where a tension is articulated between pitfalls on the one hand and a necessity on the other.

The online platform also hosts the video manifesto *El fracaso es mi estilo* (Failure is My Style) from House of Tupamaras, a queer performance and voguing collective from Bogotá in Colombia. As the name and stylistic aspects of the manifesto suggest, they identify with the ballroom culture born in New York within the Black and Latinx LGBTIQ+ community. In Bogotá they run a dance school, organize balls, take their (voguing) performances out onto the streets of Colombia, and in recent

2 "Berlant thought that queer forms of sociability and intimacy unstructured by the state provided an experimental venue for developing the commons in which we would all like to live. Such trajectories were not straight lines, but deviating and converging pathways." Judith Butler, "Ways of Hoping," *The Nation*, July 8, 2021, https://www.thenation.com/article/culture/lauren-berlant-obituary/ (accessed June 10, 2022).

3 Berlant, "Democracy—The Commons," p. 82.

4 Hayat Erdoğan, Nikolai E. Prawdzic and Florian Malzacher, "100 Ways to Say We: An Archive of the Future—About," https://100ways.space/about.html (accessed June 10, 2022).

years have been involved in projects in Berlin[5] and other German-speaking regions, not least Zurich.

The group first caught my attention at an event during the SoS (Soft Solidarity) program put on by Galerie Wedding, which I was following online. They were taking part in the SoS Assembly, which lasted for three days in November 2020 and where the audience could only join online due to the pandemic.[6] There was an interview with the three members of House of Tupamaras present, Honey Vergony, Pvssy Divx, and Jona Tamara, and afterwards they put on a voguing performance. In other words, the broad context in which I came across the group was that of a European art discourse. If I am writing about them here, it is a sign that this discourse is beginning to take note of them. The art context provides a travel opportunity for struggles and critique like those narrated by House of Tupamaras and expressed in their practice. But it is important to bear in mind that the vehicle is primarily discursive and that in the context of Bogotá and Colombia the impact and significance of their practice may be very different.

Coming from a European discursive space, I want to draw on the manifesto *El fracaso es mi estilo* in this essay to think about resistance in the practice of the performance collective. In this section, which repeatedly takes issue with resilience as a neoliberal strategy for adapting to a general proclivity for crisis, the manifesto by House of Tupamaras is interesting in that it illustrates an atti-

5 In 2020, for example, they ran a series of workshops at Feldfünf (https://feldfuenf.berlin/house-of-tupamaras/) and were involved in a project by artist Anna Ehrenstein entitled "Technophallus Tupamaras" at a number of venues including KOW (https://kow-berlin.com/artists/anna-ehrenstein/tupamaras-technophallus-2020). They also took part in the SoS (Soft Solidarity) Assembly at Galerie Wedding with a performance and a conversation (http://galeriewedding.de/sos-assembly/) (accessed December 6, 2022).

6 The video can still be seen on YouTube under the title "SoS (Soft Solidarity) Assembly: In Conversation with House of Tupamaras": https://www.youtube.com/watch?v=2S4Fs088Rwg (accessed June 10, 2022).

tude to failure that is neither resigned nor adaptive. Failure, in its various forms, is posited instead as the basis for a shared counter-hegemonial political practice. So in this essay I intend to collect some thoughts about House of Tupamaras that are devoted to the function of failure in constructing a queer "transformational infrastructure."[7]

Which Community?

The video manifesto *El fracaso es mi estilo* begins to the accompaniment of spherical sound that gradually transforms over time into a melodic techno beat, underscoring the various sequences and sceneries with a rising and falling volume. The video was shot in an empty building in Bogotá. In the first sequence, which shows a spacious, empty interior, the place and time fade in as text in the bottom right-hand corner. We find ourselves in the future in "Bogotá – Colombia, Anõ – 2122." Night and day alternate in the ensuing scenes. By day the big spaces, sprayed in places with graffiti, seem desolate. Wide windows look out onto multi-lane highways with passing vehicles and tall tower blocks. Inside we sometimes see a single performer moving around the space, sometimes several performers engaging together or separately in movements and poses familiar from voguing. Sometimes they wear striking make-up and body- or catsuits. In another sequence, individual performers pose one at a time on a big black amplifier that stands there like a plinth in an otherwise empty space. Crouching or arching their backs, the bodies present as sculptures; a museum aesthetic blends here with an aesthetic of ballroom culture. The nocturnal scenes seem to be taking place in the same building, but now the interiors are bathed in red light. People from the LGBTIQ+ community are crowded together, relaxed as they party

7 Berlant, "Democracy—The Commons," p. 86.

and dance. The image and sound are overlaid with a voiceover in Spanish, backed by English subtitles, which continues with interruptions throughout the video:

FAILURE IS MY STYLE

Sometimes I'd like to know what it feels like to be okay
I just want to learn to fly
'Cause I've never been able to reach those kinds of heights
I question everything
But...what would happen if I didn't?

Failure is something that people do...
And something that we have always done very well.
We are a cluster of flesh and tissues,
We are built out of incompatibilities
Materials that don't belong together.

If so,
What does success offer us?
Success is just statism,
An impossible state;
order discards,
chaos encompasses.
Chaos must be the movement
And failure is the ability to move within it.
The future is failure
Not as disappointment
But as a strength
ENERGY
Finding ourselves extremely humans,
Within ideological contradictions.
I self-sabotage more and more consciously,
I am stubborn with myself
It's a form of putting me against the wall
I have learned to harden my skin
Now I know how to fail with precision
Let's love ourselves as failures of the same great impostures.

Let's love each other
chaos that interposes immobility.
Let's keep loving each other in this swamp of contradictions.
Failure is my style,
I already use it as a coat
However heavy it is,
I don't yet know if it is my friend or
my enemy.
I need to check my interior,
Where the only thing I perceive from the world...
is its bad smell.
How cold.
The failure is my style
I already use it as a coat
Love is like the soul:
A substance that nobody sees
But that we know exists, because they tell us so
Because although we deny it,
Sometimes we savor its illusion.
Love could not be possible
Would penetrate you...
my anxiety.
Is it a failure for dissidence to cry for love?
I insist to resist
And I want others to feel it too.
I had dedicated myself to masturbating for fear of facing life
in the flesh.
Failure as a kind of mask,
A kind of game.
We take one step and a thousand steps at a time.
Let's kiss
let's cuddle
let's share,
let's flourish.
Our beautiful monstrosity.
A passionate storm of feelings, more than living.
An intensity of loving exchanges.
Let's be one,

Let's be the solution
Let's be the mistake
Let's be the problem, let's be nothing, let's be all...
or nothing.
Let us be a gear in the machinery
and at the same time the obstacle of its operation.

House of Tupamaras tell of a (future) community that does not define itself through success but adopts failure as its style instead. Whereas the hegemonial neoliberal system subscribes to personal responsibility and in particular to the individualization of defeat and failure, this collective urges us to grasp failure as something everyone does. House of Tupamaras argue that being marked by failure enables us to love ourselves and others differently, to achieve closeness in another way. Success is static, but acknowledging failure creates a space of opportunity where people can move about freely and try things out as if in play. It follows that in a setting of chaos as movement, any path and any expression can be accepted as equally legitimate. Failure is translated by House of Tupamaras into what Jack Halberstam describes in *The Queer Art of Failure* as "refusal of mastery, a critique of the intuitive connections within capitalism between success and profit, and as a counterhegemonic discourse of losing."[8] In the White meritocracy success and straightness are revered, not only in a career trajectory but in any person who wants to be taken seriously. A range of pathological conditions (depression, burnout), all on the increase today, indicate that this ethos puts people under pressure, leads to stress, and generates a fear of failure and, ultimately, failure too.[9] The resistance in the community blueprint

8 Jack Halberstam, *The Queer Art of Failure* (Durham, N.C.: Duke University Press, 2011) p. 11.
9 See, for example, Alain Ehrenberg, *Das erschöpfte Selbst. Depression und Gesellschaft in der Gegenwart* (Frankfurt am Main: Suhrkamp, 2008).

sketched here by the group derives from turning these values and notions of reality upside down. When House of Tupamaras say "Let's love ourselves as failures of the same great impostures," that is a call to love oneself—within a loving community—and to turn the doubts not against oneself but against a deceitful system that fosters contempt for people's ability to take strain. Evidently, then, the systemic critique in the manifesto has its origins in a counterculture (a "punk negativity," as Berlant would say) that rejects adapting to notions of normality in the neoliberal meritocracy as an objective. Nevertheless, the powerful, urgent desire to resist is seen initially as being in conflict with a great simultaneous need for love, or at least for giving way to the illusion: "Is it a failure for dissidence to cry for love?" they ask. The answer is immediate: "I insist to resist and I want others to feel it too." What this articulates is a negotiation of the possibility for resistance that defines itself not through an explicit opposition to something but at least as much through a different way of being together or feeling affection, and in particular through powerful affective attachments (like love). Physical expression ("Let's kiss, let's cuddle") is one side of the coin, emotional connection ("let's share, let's flourish") is the other. While the question still hints at uncertainty about the "right" form of dissidence, what follows is an affirmation of contradictions within the resistance. The voiceover concludes with the plea "Let us be a gear in the machinery and at the same time the obstacle of its operation" and with this a call to acknowledge one's position within ideological entanglements (or "ideological contradictions," as they put it), a position from which it is by all means feasible to expose ideologies while preventing them from doing their work.

At a visual level, as I began to describe earlier, an impression is conveyed of this resistant community and the real forms in which it currently exists. The building where the video was shot can be seen as a microcosm that allows encounters and expression outside cis- and heteronormativity. The party and ball scenes that unfold in slow motion, bathed in red light, are especially sensuous; they also reveal a sense of tension, suggesting that there are nights when everything is open and possible. This contrasts with the daytime scenes, which seem rather to illustrate the constraints in this queer microcosm. Even if the outside world is visible through the wide windows, the glass panes are nevertheless an insurmountable boundary. That is especially clear in a sequence where one performer braces their muscles against a window as if they were trying to smash it. This is one scene of several where mucking around or meaninglessness is mixed with despair, and where the boundaries this inevitably runs up against, the hurdles that must be surmounted if a person does not correspond to a range of social norms, acquire literal form. In another scene, a performer keeps throwing themself at a sofa standing against the wall, and in the next a performer clambers awkwardly over a row of identical bicycles stacked close together. In yet another sequence, a performer tries in vain to squeeze into the compartment of a sideboard. These unsuccessful or at least very arduous attempts to fit in, to adjust to the mold, and to overcome recurrent impediments, stands as a metaphor for the lives of most LGBTIQ+ people. If the acoustic and visual levels are taken together, they convey that urgent need, highly specific to context, for shared imaginings about another way of living. They show that the community portrayed by the group in their manifesto is not a universal or generalizable We, but one based on very specific struggles that must be recognized.

The Need to Imagine, Becoming Otherwise

In *Undoing Gender* Judith Butler writes: "The thought of a possible life is only an indulgence for those who already

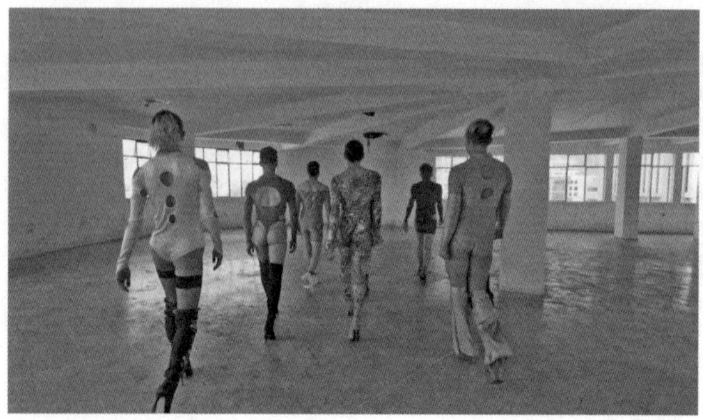

Fig. 1: House of Tupamaras, EL FRACASO ES MI ESTILO. Un manifesto de H.o.T., 2021, 12:38 min, film still. © House of Tupamaras.

know themselves to be possible. For those who are still looking to be possible, possibility is a necessity."[10] Butler is talking about the (existential) need to think the possible; for those who are not yet possible (but who are negated, as Berlant puts it), there is no alternative. The manifesto, and the whole practice of House of Tupamaras, can be read with this message in mind. Although, in broader terms, Colombia has one of the most robust legal frameworks in Latin America for the defense of LGBTIQ+ rights, this framework is hardly implemented in practice.[11] People who do not correspond to the cis or/and hetero norm face danger everywhere from police violence, paramilitaries, and civilian assault.[12] The life

10 Judith Butler, *Undoing Gender* (London and New York: Routledge, 2004), p. 31.

11 Matthew Bocanumenth, "LGBT+ Rights and Peace in Colombia: The Paradox Between Law and Practice," *WOLA: Advocacy for Human Rights in the Americas*, July 3, 2020, https://www.wola.org/analysis/lgbt-rights-and-peace-in-colombia-the-paradox-between-law-and-practice/ (accessed June 10, 2022).

12 Lisa Logan, "The transgender community's push for progress," *The Bogotá Post*, March 6, 2018, https://thebogotapost.com/the-transgender-communitys-push-for-progress/27458/ (accessed June 10, 2022).

expectancy of trans people in Latin America is around thirty-five years.[13] The suicide rate for LGBTIQ+ people in Colombia is ten times as high as the national average.[14] These facts are the context for the practice of the collective. In the light of these realities, all the things they do in the Colombian public space, whether as activists, organizers of a dance studio, or performers, are gestures of resistance. Not that a particular sexual orientation or gender identification is automatically resistance in itself. But expressing them and making them visible where lifestyles that depart from the binary norm still encounter aggression, especially from the state apparatus, does mean resistance, and above all it means declaring vulnerability.[15] The manifesto only hints at the dangers and limitations of this lifestyle, but its significance is lost if these details are not understood.

Exclusion and marginalization are implicit in the concept of failure formulated in the manifesto by House of Tupamaras as a principle of their community and an expression of counterculture. They regard failure as a constituent element and it lies at the roots of their self-definition. Because the Black and Latinx ballroom culture in the United States with which they identify evolved from precisely that, the experience of being denied suc-

13 IACHR—Inter-American Commission on Human Rights, "Violence against Lesbian, Gay, Bisexual, Trans and Intersex Persons in the Americas," November 2015, p. 15. Pdf available online at: http://www.oas.org/en/iachr/reports/pdfs/ViolenceLGBTIPersons.pdf (accessed June 23, 2022).

14 This is the conclusion of a report published in July 2021 by the Williams Institute at UCLA School of Law titled "Sexual Orientation and Gender Identity Change Efforts and Suicide Morbidity Among Sexual and Gender Minority Adults in Colombia": https://williamsinstitute.law.ucla.edu/publications/conversion-therapy-colombia/ (accessed June 21, 2022).

15 The fact that visibility must be seen as a highly ambivalent strategy, depending on context, and certainly not as a contribution to a more inclusive society, has to be borne in mind. On this see Terre Thaemlitz, "'Ich habe eigentlich keine andere Identität als die innerhalb eines Kontexts'. Im Gespräch mit Terre Thaemlitz," in *Fragile Identitäten*, ed. Kerstin Stakemeier and Susanne Witzgall (Zurich and Berlin: Diaphanes, 2015), pp. 69–84, here p. 71.

cess and frequently excluded and discriminated against in both the White fashion world and the White drag ball scene.[16] For this subculture, exclusion and rejection were and are the experience through which they forged a new We and to which House of Tupamaras can relate from their own perspective. Moreover, the very name of the collective references mainstream culture in Colombia. In the ballroom milieu, houses often take their names from well-known fashion designers or fashion hubs (House of Gucci, for example), but "House of Tupamaras" contains a pointer to Colombia's own pop culture, governed by machismo. Los Tupamaros are a Colombian merengue band of international acclaim. Their lyrics and videos perform the heteronormative ideal of romantic love. In this way, by appropriating and signaling their difference from a whole range of influences, House of Tupamaras have created a community of people excluded from the mainstream while also demonstrating how to turn the exclusion into its reverse.

If, in Butler's spirit, we read the manifesto as reflecting the need to think the possible, then I do not feel it is enough to describe it under the heading of artistic practice. I see it more as an expression of the radical imagination that Max Haiven has in mind in *Crisis of Imagination, Crisis of Power*:

> It [radical imagination—author's note] is what provides the idea that things could be different, and that we could live life otherwise. The radical imagination both feeds and is fed by common spheres of our life where other values (anti-capitalist values like love, solidarity and equality) are in the ascendant. As such, I argue that the "radical imagination" is not just a personal act of "thinking differ-

16 Michael Cunningham, "The Slap of Love," *Open City*, no. 6 (1996). Available online at: https://opencity.org/archive/issue-6/the-slap-of-love (accessed June 22, 2022).

> ently" [...]. The radical imagination is a matter of acting otherwise, together.[17]

Radical imagination needs community. The essence of the radical imagination described here is that it evolves between people, that it establishes different ways of acting, and that in this manner it translates into values unlike those pursued in hegemonial behavior. What follows disrupts the reproduction of norms. House of Tupamaras need each other as a collective where they can express themselves, and they need the community so that each of them can exist as an individual subject. The manifesto is part of an "acting otherwise, together," and other aspects of this practice are also indicated in the video. Voguing performances, illustrated by the video but also featured at the balls, are part of the ballroom culture with which House of Tupamaras identify, and so is their rehearsal of alternative family relations. For members of the community, the House is a replacement for home, something conventionally provided by a biological family and yet often a hostile environment for queer people, offering neither a retreat nor intimacy.[18] Citing the writer D. Soyini Madison, Marlon M. Bailey calls ballroom houses "practices of possibility," signaling that there is nothing inevitable about the hegemonial concept of family and that it harbors potential for reformulations.[19] House of Tupamaras inscribe themselves, the way they see themselves and their lives, within the history of this subculture but from a Colombian perspective, subverting the reproduction of a family ideal shaped by religion, class, and hetero- or cisnormativity. Although they do not specifically address

17 Max Haiven, *Crises of Imagination, Crises of Power: Capitalism, Creativity and the Commons* (London and New York: Zed Books, 2014), p. 211.

18 Marlon M. Bailey, "Engendering space: Ballroom culture and the spatial practice of possibility in Detroit," *Gender, Place and Culture* 21, no. 4 (2014), pp. 489–507, here p. 496.

19 Ibid., p. 497.

family as a hegemonial institution in their manifesto, they do talk about love as an institution of intimacy. The rhetorical question quoted above, "Is it a failure of dissidence to cry for love?," also leaves room for an idea of love that can be reconciled with resistance. The form of love that House of Tupamaras seek to deconstruct is a hetero-cisnormative institution of romantic love coded in monogamous terms. In their essay "'There's the Problem': On Love's Role in Feminist, Lesbian, and Queer Arts Organizing," Robin Alex McDonald discusses the significance of love as a foundation for radical "practices of commoning."[20] As the title indicates, they are referring here to Michel Foucault's comment: "I think that's what makes homosexuality 'disturbing': the homosexual mode of life, much more than the sexual act itself. To imagine a sexual act that doesn't conform to law or nature is not what disturbs people. But that individuals are beginning to love one another—there's the problem."[21] Echoing Foucault, then, the question posed by House of Tupamaras can be answered straight away with a resounding No. A way of loving perceived by the mainstream as unnatural can by all means be dissident in the community lifestyles and relationships to which it gives rise.

In their manifesto, the collective goes on to describe their own notion of attachment and community as "Our beautiful monstrosity. A passionate storm of feelings, more than living. An intensity of loving exchanges." In embracing "monstrosity," they are professing their "disturbing" lifestyle. As in the case of "failure," a negativity is affirmed and presented as a space where potential can play out. This space, symbolized by the empty building where the video was filmed, defies the fixed norms,

20 Robin Alex McDonald, "'There's the Problem': On Love's Role in Feminist, Lesbian, and Queer Arts Organizing," *n.paradoxa* 39 (2017), pp. 65–70, here p. 65.

21 Robin Alex McDonald is quoting here from Michel Foucault, "Friendship as a Way of Life," in Michel Foucault, *Essential Works: Ethics, Subjectivity and Truth, Vol. 1*, ed. Paul Rabinow (New York: The New Press, 1997), pp. 136–137.

determinations, and rituals of a conception and performance of love recognized by society. Invoking passionate feelings and intensity implies acknowledging uncontrollable and indeterminable affects. The last sequence of the manifesto adopts a very literal approach to illustrating what society sees as monstrous or abject by presenting a symbolic place of male homosexuality. The performers, dressed solely in bodysuits, pile across each other in fours. The camera shows them from behind, revealing two heaps of arse. Where does your own being end and the next person's begin? This joint resolution is heralded by the voiceover with the invitation "Let's be one." Understood not as a heterosexual idyll of coupledom but rather as the imagining of one great togetherness, it is simultaneously a plea to question the specific patterns of ownership that have always played a part in structuring relationships.

Both the self-definition and the artistic idiom of House of Tupamaras reveal the articulation of a sharedness, a We, which is crucial to asserting existence in the face of constraining institutions such as the state, family, or love. The radical imagination expressed by House of Tupamaras is a lifestyle that seeps into artistic practice. Their queer bodies are places of resistance which they use in different ways. In an interview they describe how they treat their bodies as a manifesto. This can be seen in *El fracaso es mi estilo* not only in the heaps of arse but equally when they display themselves by posing on loudspeaker boxes resembling plinths. Apart from in the manifesto and their various (often voguing) performances, it is reflected in their organization of balls and the dance school in Bogotá. Both the balls and the dance school can be seen as places for connection and expression and for the representation of bodies, and as opportunities for identification enabling the community to expand, which is important in the spirit of the togetherness painted in the manifesto. In their interview for the Soft Solidarity (SoS) Assembly, Honey Vergony, Pvssy

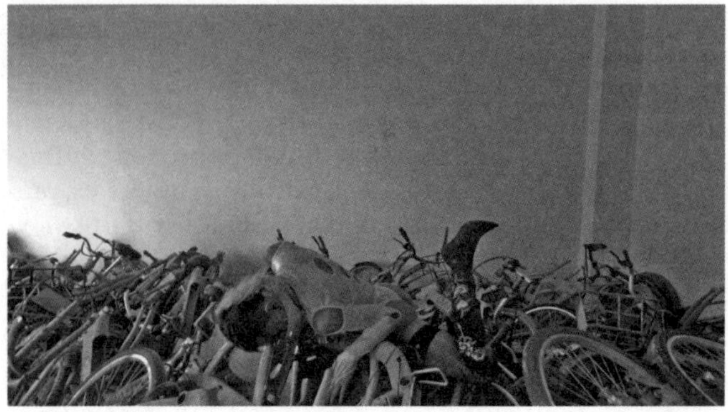

Fig. 2: House of Tupamaras, EL FRACASO ES MI ESTILO. Un manifesto de H.o.T., 2021, 12:38 min, film still. © House of Tupamaras.

Divx, and Jona Tamara also talked about their experiences of Berlin.[22] Because of Covid-19, they found themselves stuck in the city in 2020. Communicating through dance and their bodies offered them both a way to make themselves understood to others and a kind of participation that they would otherwise not have enjoyed because they did not know the language. In Berlin they also earned money as sex workers for the first time, partly out of financial necessity but partly, too, as a way of exploring bodies. They describe partying, dancing, and sex under the influence of drugs as experiences that interested them not least from an aesthetic angle, which feeds into their artistic (body) work.[23] As the manifesto describes, their everyday life and their work permits a search and a desire for the chance to be bodies, perceptions, intensities, rather than being predetermined by certain forms of knowledge, attributions of significance, and (physical) boundaries.[24]

22 YouTube video "SoS (Soft Solidarity) Assembly: In Conversation with House of Tupamaras."

23 Ibid.

24 Without wishing to ignore the different context, the body research undertaken by House of Tupamaras is reminiscent of Lauren Berlant's

Insist to Resist

"Let us be a gear in the machinery and at the same time the obstacle of its operation" is the last of the calls from the voiceover in the manifesto. It is accompanied by the video sequence in which one of the performers is polishing a metal rod clasped between their legs with a Flex. Sparks fly. The sexual connotation is unmistakable. There is an exaggerated male potency here, reinforced by the imagery of gear and machinery. The virility is attenuated by the performer's outfit—a shiny orange bodysuit with round cut-outs and white shoes with platform heels. This scene expresses the interpretation of resistance that the group sees as constituent of community: a gear failing to perform.

This form of resistance as a malfunctioning cogwheel fits well, perhaps, with Legacy Russell's proposal for an approach to institutional critique that she sets out in *Glitch Feminism*. Rather than demolishing the institutions, she talks of "mutiny in the form of strategic occupation."[25] Like House of Tupamaras, Russell advocates entering the institutions and working on the inside to prevent them from functioning. This is the gear that can only be activated inside the machinery, where it cuts out unpredictably. The machinery might be translated as an institution such as family, romantic love, the police, or religion—or, indeed, as Russell also points out, the normed body.[26] All of these feature fixed structures, performances, and hierarchies. In "The Commons" Berlant contrasts their definition of institu-

description of affective knowledge: "Seeing subjects as fundamentally permeable rather than fundamentally possessive of what they apprehend is a way of talking about affective knowledge: Marx calls this turning the senses into theorists." Berlant, "Democracy—The Commons," p. 91.

25 Legacy Russell, *Glitch Feminism: A Manifesto* (London and New York: Verso, 2020), p. 25.

26 Ibid.

tions with their concept of infrastructure, highlighting the constraints imposed by the former. Berlant writes:

> Institutions enclose and congeal power, resources, and interest, and represent their legitimacy as something solid and enduring, a predictability on which the social relies. Institutions normalize reciprocity. What constitutes infrastructure, in contrast, are the patterns, habits, norms, and scenes of assemblage and use. Collective affect gets attached to it, too, to the sense of its inventiveness and the horizon of dynamic reciprocity it entails.[27]

In a period marked by uncertainties and instability due to wars, natural disasters, or similar crises, institutions with their familiar structures can offer people security and something to lean on. However, this only applies to a small group of people—those who already know themselves to be possible (as Butler puts it), or in other words, those who have not been excluded a priori. Everyone else will, to differing degrees and in different ways, be marginalized or excluded by these various institutions or will run up against their constraints. Glitched bodies, as Russell calls them, or failures, to use the term chosen by House of Tupamaras, pose a threat to the institutions of White cis-heteronormativity because they do not allow themselves to be programmed or fixed[28] but choose instead to withdraw, or "fail." They draw attention to the indeterminability of life, which calls not for patient tolerance in the face of ever new disasters, but for agency. This is what Lauren Berlant is talking about when they refer to "affective infrastructures that admit the work of desire and the work of ambivalence as the tactics of commoning."[29] To quote the House of Tupamaras manifesto, the infrastructures that

27 Berlant, "Democracy—The Commons," p. 95.
28 Russell, *Glitch Feminism*, p. 25.
29 Berlant, "Democracy—The Commons," p. 116.

Berlant has in mind are constantly in a state of flux and embracing chaos ("chaos encompasses"), whereas institutions, as rigid, ready-established orders, have the effect of excluding people ("order discards"). The infrastructures posited by Berlant are always in transition and constantly undergoing practical negotiation. That is also the reason why, in this idea, resistance cannot be boxed into a form. The quality of resisting lies rather, as House of Tupamaras formulate it, in the attitude "insist to resist." Being resistant implies being able to fail and to carry on in spite of it, or perhaps even because of it. Perhaps the practice of House of Tupamaras can be read as taking ownership of various institutions, such as family or the normed body, in order to create a queer transformational infrastructure of sharing. These infrastructures might be balls, parties, or maybe a dance studio. They are not intended to last, but the communities they engender always represent opportunities for (common) expression, including a place for withdrawal and intimacy, for sharing experience and for shared values. As Lauren Berlant says in a talk: Just because these infrastructures can fail, that does not necessarily mean that they are a bad idea.[30] Maybe this is the spirit in which to read the year indicated at the beginning of the manifesto *El fracaso es mi estilo*—it is 2122. As described earlier, these are the imaginings of a futurity. But at the same time there is a personal and reciprocal assurance within and for this Here and Now that infrastructures can fail and that new ones can be conceived, but that the community will still be there in a hundred years. Today this is especially relevant. The manifesto was written during a national strike in Colombia in 2021. On April 28, protests broke out against a controversial tax reform that the Colombian government, led by the

30 Online lecture and discussion with Lauren Berlant, available on YouTube under the title: "Lauren Berlant—Cruel Optimism (Online Lecture @ Skopje Pride Weekend 2020)": https://www.youtube.com/watch?v=xR7Iuf_jJIU&t=2531s (accessed June 10, 2022).

right-wing conservative president Ivan Duque, wanted to introduce in the wake of an economic crisis severely exacerbated by the Covid-19 pandemic. The protests quickly spread around the country. Most people took to the streets peaceably, not only to protest against the tax reform, but with numerous other demands related, among other things, to widespread economic inequality, massive police violence, and the lack of protection for particularly vulnerable groups in the country.[31] The police responded with their customary brutality. Human rights organizations expressed concern over violations of human rights, especially gender-specific violence towards women* and LGBTIQ+ persons.[32] Right at the start of the protests, a video went viral that showed three vogue dancers from the trans community in Bogotá performing, surrounded by ESMAD units,[33] on the steps of the Capitol.[34] Demonstrators had gathered on Plaza de Bolivar, the central square in the Colombian capital, and police units were guarding the Congress building where the Colombian parliament meets, when the three dancers Piisciiss, Nova, and Axid climbed up to the level where the police officers were standing and began voguing between them. In the video, it looks as though the police are out of their depth for a moment and do not quite know how to respond to the three dancers. It takes a few minutes before they finally push them away, and during those minutes the dancers, who have wrapped

31 Human Right Watch, "Colombia: Events of 2021," https://www.hrw.org/world-report/2022/country-chapters/colombia (accessed June 10, 2022).

32 OAS, Inter-American Commission on Human Rights, "Observations and Recommendations: Working Visit to Colombia (June 2021)," p. 14. Pdf available online at: http://www.oas.org/en/iachr/reports/pdfs/ObservacionesVisita_CIDH_Colombia_ENG.pdf (accessed June 13, 2022).

33 Esucadrón Móvil Antidisturbios (Mobile Anti-Disturbances Squadron), a riot control squad. The government has been called upon numerous times to reform the unit because of its brutal treatment of civilians.

34 The video is available on YouTube under the title "RESISTENCIA": https://www.youtube.com/watch?v=V2NyG7AdW-Y&t=40s (accessed June 10, 2022).

yellow barrier tape with the word *peligro*—danger—around their chests, move among and around the officers, swinging the Colombian flag as they dance to the cheers of the protesting crowd. They take ownership of the "danger" label, leaving the police briefly bewildered and disoriented, and preventing the machinery from functioning. By taking up their place on the steps of the seat of Colombian government, at the same height as the police, they are signaling gaps in the system and the lethargy of the institution, which initially has no idea how to counter this spontaneous occupation by voguing. After a few minutes, the dancers are forced away, but their intervention can be seen as a sign of the existence of resistance by oppositional infrastructures that will not be stifled by the persistent rejection and hostility leveled at them. This demonstrates that resistance is possible.

Without formulating them in detail, this essay has picked up several aspects of failure that are relevant for House of Tupamaras. Failure as a real consequence, as a risk to which persons in the LGBTIQ+ community are exposed in an oppressive, marginalizing system; failure as a political practice that exercises criticism of a neoliberalism focused on achievement and success and of the binary system of hetero-cisnormativity; and, as the culmination of all these, failure as an empowering and shared self-conception.

The statement in the title, "Failure is My Style," emphasizes an attitude—in the spirit of a punk negativity—that resists adaptation to the system in its many forms. Moreover, calling failure a style expresses the performativity that failure signifies for the group. Like fashion, it can be altered, it is temporary. Reading failure as a style, then, also means adopting a certain detachment from one's own position or situation. Like an item of clothing ("I already use it as a coat," as the manifesto says) it can be taken off, worn, and/or paraded. It can make circumstances more bearable. It means both taking ownership and self-empowerment.

One way the body can fail is to fall. In voguing (especially vogue fem), the dip—a controlled fall synchronized with the music—is a particularly effective element. It features both in the video manifesto by House of Tupamaras and in the protest dance by Piisciiss, Nova, and Axid. With an arching back, the dancer falls to the ground over a bent knee as the other leg stretches into the air. It can be read as a physical reflection on coping with failure that does not capture the fall so much as embraces it, transforming the dancer's relationship with it.

I am particularly grateful to Catalina González González for the important insights and conversations about the Colombian context.

Translation: Katherine Vanovitch

Judith Sieber

Refusal of Form

The Critical Potential of W.E.B. Du Bois's[1] Charts for the Paris World's Fair, 1900

In 1900—over one hundred years ago—US sociologist W.E.B. Du Bois and students from Atlanta University began work on a commission from Du Bois's former study colleague Thomas Calloway[2] to prepare sixty-three informational charts for the African American section of the World's Fair in Paris. The resulting works can be seen as a critique—even a rejection—of the still-new form of graphical statistics. In the context of the exhibition, the charts' rejection of conventions and visual expectations can be understood as an early attempt at a still-ongoing decolonial critique of charts in their conventional forms, not least due to the recent rediscovery of the Du Bois charts. Born in 1868 in Massachusetts, Du Bois studied at Harvard—where he was the first African American to gain a doctorate—and later at Berlin's Humboldt University. His dissertation focused on the transatlantic slave trade and living conditions among the African American population during the Jim Crow era;[3] upon graduation, he became a professor of history, sociology, and economics at Atlanta University.

1 In the following, any reference made to Du Bois is also a reference to his team. No clear analysis has yet been made of which share he took on himself and which share was taken on by his students. All previous publications on the exhibition have focused on Du Bois.

2 He had previously worked with Calloway—the lawyer who issued the invitation on behalf of the World's Fair—at Tennessee's Fisk University, an African American university.

3 The Jim Crow era involved a legislative wave that followed the legal abolition of slavery in 1865, remained in force until the Civil Rights

The charts were integrated into *Exposition des Nègres d'Amérique*, the Du Bois-curated section of the World's Fair; collating and describing the circumstances and the lives of the Black population in the US for a largely White, European audience, they were resolute in challenging racist cliché. Du Bois's aim was to use the charts—alongside photographs, artefacts, and legal texts—to convey factual knowledge to the public, while at the same time sketching out new images of Black identity and ways of life, both as a "visual anti-racism and [a] counter-archive."[4] Key alongside this visual material was the display of books by Black authors and a three-volume, handwritten work by Du Bois that catalogued the texts of Georgia's Black Codes—the racist laws in force in the state prior and subsequent to the abolition of slavery.[5] The charts had been preceded by sociological studies at Atlanta University on the African American populace in Georgia, a former slave state that then had the largest, most diverse, and fastest-growing Black population of any US state.[6] A second set of graphs with a more national and global focus aimed to place the Georgia study into a broader context.[7] The charts themselves—either hung flat against the wall in wooden frames or mounted vertically onto hinges, thus allowing visitors to leaf through them—were central to the exhibition and were its most heavily

Act in the 1960s, and provided a framework for the systematic oppression and exploitation of Black Americans.

4 "Visueller Antirassismus" and "Gegen-Archiv"; see Iris Därmann, *Undienlichkeit. Gewaltgeschichte und politische Philosophie* (Berlin: Matthes und Seitz, 2021), pp. 199–201.

5 See Whitney Battle-Baptiste and Britt Rusert, "Introduction," in *W.E.B. Du Bois's Data Portraits: Visualizing Black America*, ed. Whitney Battle-Baptiste and Britt Rusert (New York: Princeton Architectural Press, 2018), p. 19.

6 Ibid., p. 11.

7 Each of the two parts has a distinct title: "The Georgia Negro: A Social Study" and "A Series of Statistical Charts Illustrating the Condition of the Descendants of Former African Slaves Now in Residence in the United States of America." See ibid.

visited part.[8] Beyond the exhibition winning one of the World's Fair grand prizes, Du Bois also received a gold medal as curator of the charts. Despite this success and following a number of exhibitions in the US,[9] the charts disappeared into the Library of Congress in Washington D.C. in 1909; it was not until 2018 that they were rediscovered by Whitney Battle-Baptiste and Britt Rusert, both professors at the W.E.B. Du Bois Center at the University of Massachusetts Amherst, and gathered together for publication.

The rediscovery forces the question as to why there has been no decolonial critique of informational graphics—no questioning of conventions or highlighting of the power structures present in the production and transmission of knowledge that takes place in this regard. Of Du Bois's charts I will focus on three examples, highlighting their critical and oppositional potential by drawing on the contexts in which they were created—a history that stretches back into the eighteenth century.

City and Rural Population, the eleventh chart in the series *The Georgia Negro*, shows the 1890 figures for African Americans resident in cities (differentiated by size) relative to those in rural areas. A green line commencing beneath the title in the upper area of the image announces a bar chart, breaks in the center of the page into three downward-pointing diagonals, then curls into a large red spiral, creating a dynamic that opposes the linear bar in the upper area. The initial chaining-together of the bars inaugurates a break both formal and

8 Lynda C. Olman uses a report from the era to describe visitors' engagement with the exhibition: they spent most of their time with the charts, then with the photographs, and showed little interest in the book; they "tended rather to consume the exhibit as spectacle." Lynda C. Olman, "Decolonizing the Color-Line: A Topological Analysis of W.E.B. Du Bois's Infographics for the 1900 Paris Exposition," in *Journal of Business and Technical Communication* 36, no. 2 (2022), p. 143.

9 See Battle-Baptiste and Rusert, "Introduction," p. 22.

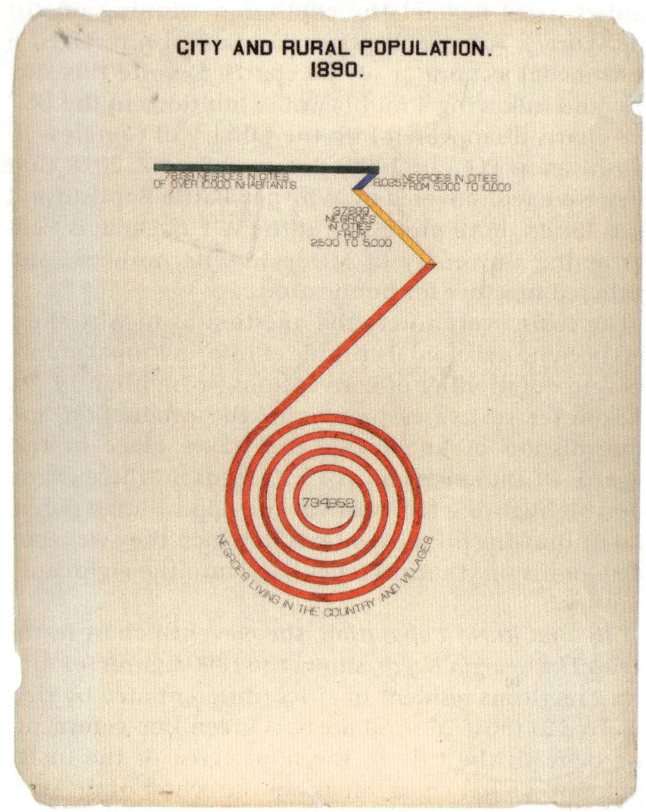

Fig. 1: W.E.B. Du Bois, *The Georgia Negro: City and Rural Population. 1890.* Ink and watercolor, 710 x 560 mm. Library of Congress: https://www.loc.gov/.

aesthetic with the conventions of bar charts—comparability between the differently colored sections is thus lost. Without consulting the accompanying numbers, any attempt to visually gauge the lines or to estimate the titular relationship between the city and rural populations is led literally into the void. Beyond the difficulty in comparing the length of a straight line and

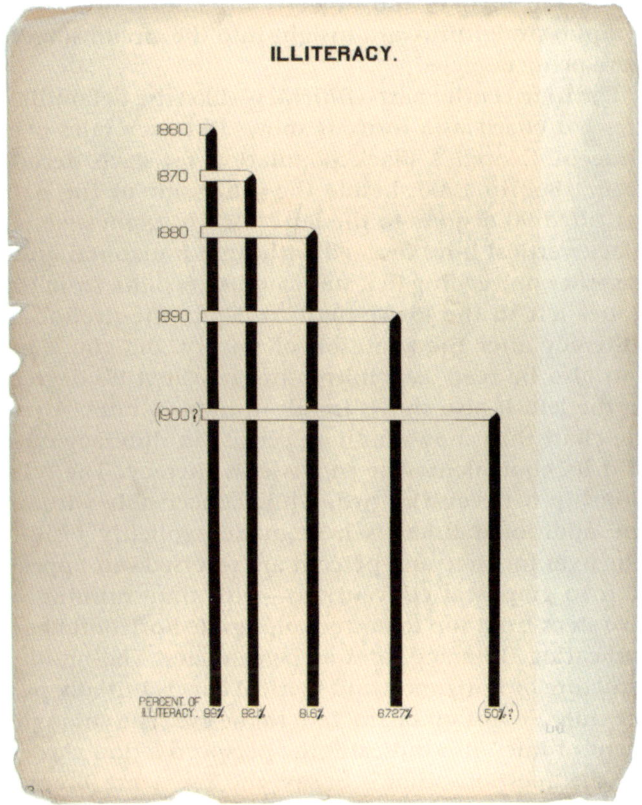

Fig. 2: W.E.B. Du Bois, *The Georgia Negro: Illiteracy*. Ink and watercolor, 710 x 560 mm. Library of Congress: https://www.loc.gov/.

a spiral—other than stating that the spiral is longer, indicating that the rural population is substantially larger—the end of the spiral's line also tapers toward the center of the circle, suggesting openness and incompleteness. The open spiral corrupts the mathematical approach expressed in the initial ratio's straight line and the clear separations between the sections. The chart thus invokes and subverts any notion of gaining a rapid, straightforward insight into the circumstances here being depicted.

The fourteenth chart—*Illiteracy*—likewise defamiliarizes bar charts as a form. It shows illiteracy rates over time in Georgia's Black population for each decade from 1860 to 1900, beside the other side of the data set tilted 90 degrees to the left.[10] At first glance we see black vertical lines meshed with light horizontal ones, together proceeding in a staircase-like fashion from the upper left to the lower right to depict the decline in illiteracy after the abolition of slavery. But the chart can also be read as a mirror image; tilted 90 degrees to the left, it also shows trends in literacy rates. A single chart thus shows both a decrease in illiteracy rates and its equivalent—the increase in literacy. The relationship between the two, while conceivable without the additional lines, is here made explicitly visible. The axes for time and percent are reversed—in opposition to graphical conventions—with time running in five steps from top to bottom alongside horizontal bars indicating illiteracy rates as percentages. The braided structure of horizontal and vertical bars is initially perplexing, a constant distraction to the eye. The entanglement of lines also indicates the perspectivation chosen for the question—that is to say, the key word (literacy or illiteracy) and connotation under which the data is collected and presented. Another chart shows Georgia's illiteracy rates compared with those of Russia and Hungary, revealing Georgia's rate to be identical to Hungary's and better than Russia's.[11]

Both charts refuse to be easily, quickly comprehensible, choosing instead to undermine conventions of representation in ways that remain unusual today. Con-

10 The entries for 1900 are accompanied with a question mark.
11 See Aldon Morris, "American Negro at Paris, 1900," in *W.E.B. Du Bois's Data Portraits*, ed. Battle-Baptiste and Rusert, p. 35.

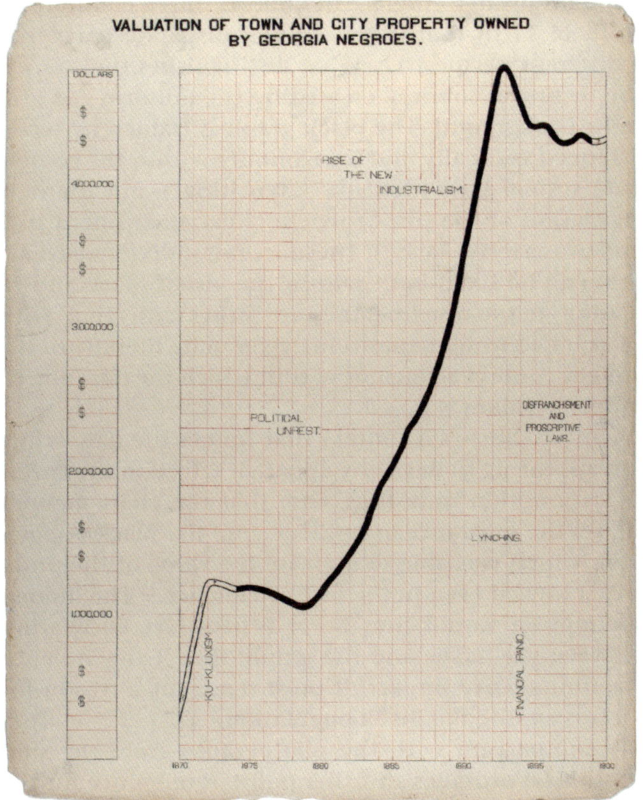

Fig. 3: W.E.B. Du Bois, *The Georgia Negro: Valuation of Town and City Property Owned by Georgia Negroes*. Ink and colored ink, 710 x 560 mm. Library of Congress: https://www.loc.gov/.

trasting these, however, there are charts such as the twenty-first plate, *Valuation of Town and City Property Owned by Georgia Negroes*, that do show a clear form and whose critical qualities are more difficult to ascertain.

A rising and mostly black line shows the strong growth from 1870 to 1900 in the value of property owned among the urban and rural African American populations in Georgia. The chart is thus a counterpart to Plate 11 in that it reassembles disparate parts into a different perspective. What distinguishes the chart is the technical sobriety created by the uniform red grid of its background. The black graph is framed by terms arranged vertically and horizontally within the coordinate system ("Ku-Kluxism," "lynching") and the new legislation of the Jim Crow era ("disfranchisment [sic] and proscriptive laws"). These are not individual events that can be fixed both within the visual space and in relation to the timeline: they are rather terms that, with their indeterminate positions, refer quite literally to the violent context against or within which the question of property values is posed.

This establishes a context that frames the data while not appearing to have any apparent effect on the curve; an assumption may thus arise that the chart demonstrates the resistance or resilience[12] of the Black population, which was able to increase the value of the property it owned even in the face of violence.[13] The hidden assumption would thus be of a necessary correlation between the labels and the graph; that if the violence has no negative impact, it must represent a reason for success among the Black population.

A comparison with the photographs from the sub-exhibition provides a further point of reference for the use of the still little-studied charts. These photographs are artful, individual portraits whose titles—such as *Young African American Man, Half-Length Portrait,*

12 The concept of resilience describes individual, community, or material toughness or resistance to crisis. It is a term whose use has been increasing for a number of years; marginalized and oppressed groups in particular have been ascribed a capacity for resilience and thereby pushed into the position of role models for White, neoliberal subjects. For a critique of the concept, see Stefanie Graefe's text in this volume.

13 See Hua Hsu, "What W. E. B. Du Bois Conveyed in His Captivating Infographics," *The New Yorker*, November 26, 2019, https://www.newyorker.com/books/page-turner/what-web-du-bois-conveyed-in-his-captivating-infographics (accessed April 20, 2022).

Facing Right—also evoke stereotypical anthropological representations.[14] The portraits are complemented with views of businesses or images of the grand interiors of properties owned by the African American population of Georgia. Styled in keeping with the sublime, the portraits combine with the documentation of Black success to destabilize the stereotypical notions held by White, European audiences,[15] not least because the remainder of the World's Fair was dominated by a colonial and racist imagery.[16] Iris Därmann has described how the photos—created by the Black photographer Thomas E. Askew using the codes of the educated, White bourgeoise—thus contradict racist imputations. She describes in following how Du Bois was "not least interested in the visual rejection of slave servitude and forced labor in the name of a new, bourgeois respectability and non-servitude,"[17] thus emphasizing the political aspect of the exhibition. Ultimately, Du Bois had recognized the sociopolitical power of prestige conventions, which he subverted and inverted in the name of a demand for equality.[18] In keeping with Därmann, the photographs can be understood as instruments for a visual politics

14 In total, 363 photos were exhibited in albums collected under the title *Types of American Negroes*. See Library of Congress, "African American Photographs Assembled for 1900 Paris Exposition," https://www.loc.gov/pictures/collection/anedub/dubois.html (accessed April 20, 2022).

15 Olman confirms that the audience was largely White and European—and the remainder of the Fair racist. See Olman, "Decolonizing the Color-Line."

16 The exhibition was replete with ethnographic display stands, including a replica of a Dahomey village presented in contrast with a depiction of the White progress typified by steam engines and similar. See ibid., pp. 140–145.

17 Därmann, *Undienlichkeit*, pp. 196–197.

18 Saidiya Hartman describes Askew's photographs in sharp contrast to the Du Bois photos of Black life in Philadelphia that form the basis of her narrative in her book *Wayward Lives*—"on the one hand, the morgue, prison and the workhouse; on the other, the privatized household and the sovereignty of the husband and father." Saidiya Hartman, *Wayward Lives: Beautiful Experiments* (Durham, N.C. and London: Duke University Press, 2018), p. 19.

of the same anti-racism Du Bois later pursued with the activist journal *The Crisis.*[19]

The charts differ from the photographs, however, in that they show no individuals, instead—and entirely in contrast—showing abstract relations of time and quantity. The photographs involve a shift on the representational level (with Black people assuming the codes and poses of a White, middle-class bourgeoise); the charts likewise question their own form. What, however, is problematic in the form of the chart or the graph?

While also addressing the problem of charts and their formal conventions, Lynda Olman has described how Du Bois's charts can be understood as a first attempt to decolonialize informational graphics. Her approach is guided by a keenness to examine the interlocking of the various, alternately synoptic and analytical levels of charts and graphs. Keying into Foucault, she describes the graphical conventions of graphs and charts, and expectations for them to provide clarity, as "panopticism": as a reduction of a situation to a synoptic, at-a-glance[20] intelligibility.[21] The problem with these synoptic conventions is to be found, following Olman, in their hidden political

19 Katherine Fusco and Lynda C. Olman describe the continuation of this photographic project, focusing on Du Bois launching and, from 1910, editing the journal *The Crisis*, the official publication of the National Association for the Advancement of Colored People. See Katherine Fusco and Lynda C. Olman, "Techniques of Justice: W.E.B. Du Bois's Data Portraits and the Problem of Visualizing the Race," in *MELUS: The Society for the Study of the Multi-Ethnic Literature of the United States* 46, no. 3 (2021), pp. 20–24.

20 In its ideal form, the synopsis allows everything to be grasped at a glance, thus standing in opposition to the seeing of individual elements such as numbers. The synopsis thus represented an ideal for many of the Early Modern attempts at optimization undertaken by books offering surveys on a particular theme.

21 Olman here refers to B. Barton and M. Barton's important 1993 essay "Modes of Power in Technical and Professional Visuals," which applies Foucault's theory on the disciplinary technique of the panopticon to the knowledge form and rhetoric of charts and graphs. See Olman, "Decolonizing the Color-Line," p. 128, and B. Barton and M. Barton, "Modes of Power in Technical and Professional Visuals," in *Journal of Business and Technical Communication* 7, no. 1 (1993), pp. 138–162.

agendas, as "panopticism as a rule reinforces the dominant political hegemony."[22] Panopticism—like many charts and graphs—is thus always hegemonial and never critical. Olman also offers the critique that our view of infographics comes hand-in-hand with a belief in their neutrality, thus obscuring their immanent power structures.[23] She describes how Du Bois's charts undermine these visual expectations and thus resist at-a-glance seeing and gathering of information. This, she claims, is done to emphasize causal connections *between* the charts and the variety of information and perspectives they offer, but also to create frustration among the audience and counter expectations of the living conditions of African Americans being reduced to consumable form. Olman's description of this frustration strategy focuses on the eleventh chart and its central red spiral, to which she attributes the capacity to disorient the gaze.[24] Her point—that connections are made between the charts—is echoed in the examples enumerated above, which describe correlations between the proportionally large rural population, rising literacy rates, and rising property values. Du Bois's focus on connections and contexts was, in the 1900s, a scholarly counterargument to the then-widespread racial difference theory of Social Darwinism used to legitimate White supremacy.[25] Following this theory, which Du Bois encountered on all sides even as a student,[26] the Black population's poor living conditions were grounded not in external factors but in

22 See Olman, "Decolonizing the Color-Line," p. 128.

23 Olman sees abstraction as the reason for a lack of critical attention: "This makes infographics seem politically neutral in a way that renders them a less obvious target for decolonial approaches than photographs of African American astronauts, for instance. Nevertheless, decolonizing infographics remains an urgent task because they are a primary genre for communicating stereotypes and generalizations about marginalized populations." Ibid., pp. 130–131.

24 See ibid., p. 147, and Fusco and Olman, "Techniques of Justice," p. 14.

25 See Olman, "Decolonizing the Color-Line," pp. 143, 151; and Battle-Baptiste and Rusert, "Introduction," pp. 18–19.

26 See Battle-Baptiste and Rusert, "Introduction," p. 35.

Black people having different dispositions. Illustrations of difficult lives were understood as confirmation of this interpretation, such that prejudices became entrenched by way of visual customs; a short circuit that can also operate in the form of charts. In keeping with this, Katherine Fusco and Lynda Olman identify in Du Bois a strategy of disrupting expectations; a tactic of "making information about black Americans less easy to view, identify, and file away."[27]

Alongside this resistance to the presentation of information in easily and rapidly consumable forms, however, there is also the role played by the historical emergence of charts and diagrams; I intend to illustrate this here in order to shed light on the critical potential of Du Bois's graphs. The historical developments and circumstances in which they emerge have however been little studied; one hundred years ago, even scholars such as Du Bois and his team had no access to any critical studies on charts and graphs. Theirs were, on the contrary, created at a time when the conventions had not long existed and were only just beginning to solidify.[28] Du Bois's charts must thus be understood as an intervention into then-formalizing diagrammatic conventions—but also as a proposal for *different* such conventions.

The Historical Origins of Informational Graphics

Even today, infographics are viewed with expectations of a faultless functionality; which is to say, that they will convey information as efficiently as possible. This also means that a critical, historicizing discourse at times

27 Fusco and Olman, "Techniques of Justice," p. 14.

28 While something of an infographic tradition has existed since the late eighteenth century, with isolated heydays during the nineteenth, the informational graphics we are familiar with today did not become more widely disseminated until the 1930s.

takes a back seat to a more practice-oriented approach.[29] The design researcher Edward Tufte likewise accords to charts the same universality—and thus the same problematic neutrality—as mathematics, as he notes in the opening section of his survey: "The design of statistical graphics is a universal matter—like mathematics—and is not tied to the unique features of a particular language."[30] U.S. scholar Li Li has recently articulated the problem of uncritical use of research in support of a pragmatic focus on efficiency: "In discussions of the perceptual-cognitive effectiveness of data graphics, many scholars leave out the consideration of social and contextual factors on the periphery (...)."[31] She, in contrast, calls for critical contextualization. In an article on Francis A. Walker's nineteenth-century statistical atlas using survey data from the first censuses held in the US, Li focuses on an atlas that was, as for Fusco and Olman, a key model for the Du Bois charts.[32] In the Walker atlas, Li identifies a racist visual rhetoric that seeks to highlight and stigmatize Chinese immigration. In regard to the context in which the atlas emerged, she

29 Historical surveys—such as statistician Edward Tufte's work on the early days of data visualization, historians Anthony Grafton and Daniel Rosenberg's work on timeline-based charts, or Howard Wainer's work on statistics—provide proof of this while also offering important foundations for further efforts. These surveys, however, mostly remain at a surface level, thus allowing them to present a wealth of material; or, as with Tufte, they are underpinned by positive associations with and reference to historical examples of infographics. See Edward R. Tufte, *The Visual Display of Quantitative Information* (Cheshire, Conn.: Graphics Press, 2007 [1983]); Anthony Grafton and Daniel Rosenberg, *Cartographies of Time* (Princeton and New York: Princeton University Press, 2010), and Howard Wainer, *Graphic Discovery: A Trout in the Milk and Other Visual Adventures* (Princeton and New York: Princeton University Press, 2005).

30 Tufte, "Introduction," *The Visual Display of Quantitative Information*, np.; Tufte refers here to William Playfair.

31 Li Li, "Visualizing Chinese Immigrants in the U.S. Statistical Atlases: A Case Study in Charting and Mapping the Other(s)," in *Technical Communication Quarterly* 29, no. 1 (2020), pp. 1–17, here p. 3.

32 Olman and Fusco also highlight the *Statistical Atlas of the United States* by Francis A. Walker, which visualized the 1870 US census—the country's first—in 1874. See Olman, "Decolonizing the Color-Line," p. 138, and Fusco and Olman, "Techniques of Justice," p. 9.

emphasizes that Walker was not only a key figure in statistics: he was also a part of the Immigration Restriction League, in support of whose cause he wrote numerous articles and books. His atlas was thus not a neutral survey; it was rather a contribution to the political propaganda that eventually led to the Chinese Exclusion Act of 1882.[33]

What Li, Battle-Baptiste and Rusert, Olman and Fusco all point toward is that informational graphics had their beginnings in the late eighteenth century, one hundred years prior to the Walker atlas. They also cite the Scottish engineer, journalist, and economist William Playfair's (1759–1823) *Commercial and Political Atlas* of 1786 as a precursor to Du Bois's charts. This atlas, up until now more familiar to scholars of design history and in the history of statistics, is a chart-based pamphlet covering the import/export balances of England and the national budget of Great Britain as a whole.[34] As something of a journalist, Playfair focused in this title and other publications on economic issues of the era such as rising national debt and fluctuating wheat prices. In presenting these statistical trends, he used graphs in coordinate systems rather than, as previously, data in tabulated form. Playfair—as would later Walker—titles his work as an *Atlas*, thus linking it with Early Modern geographical atlases and their vivid overviews of the globe.[35] He also commissioned well-known cartographers to provide copperplate engravings that he later recolored by hand.[36] In borrowing from the linguistics and visuals of

33 See Li, "Visualizing Chinese Immigrants in the U.S. Statistical Atlases," p. 2.

34 Of these, forty-three graphs and one bar chart are included in the first edition of the atlas.

35 A first example of this is provided by Gerardus Mercator with *Atlas, sive Cosmographicae Meditationes de Fabrica Mundi et fabricati figura* (1595). Prior to this, Mercator had published maps that project the globe in its entirety onto a square grid.

36 These were John Ainslie (1745–1828) and Samuel John Neele (1758–1824). For more information on the recoloring and production processes, see Ian Spence and Howard Wainer, "Introduction," in

cartography, the aim was to establish verisimilitude for his still-unfamiliar mode of representation, but also to provide simplicity and vividness, as Playfair aimed to attract a wide new audience for his publications.[37] In creating this link with cartography, concepts of synoptic overview and quantifiability were also carried over to the new charts. Furthermore, adoption of the coordinate system ultimately suggested scientific objectivity. [38] As with geographical maps, Playfair sought with his charts in the *Commercial and Political Atlas* to create a visual overview of global economic relations. This overview was one that also brought with it control and comparability: "As the knowledge increases amongst mankind, and transactions multiply, it becomes more and more desirable to abbreviate and facilitate the modes of conveying information from one person to another, and from one individual to the many."[39] That this overview

The Commercial and Political Atlas and Statistical Breviary, ed. Ian Spence and Howard Wainer (Cambridge and New York: Cambridge University Press, 2005), pp. 1–35.

37 "Figures and letters may express with accuracy, but they never can *represent* either number or space. A map of the river Thames, or of a large town, expressed in figures, would give but a very imperfect notion of either, though they might be perfectly exact in every dimension; most men would prefer *representations*." William Playfair, *The Commercial and Political Atlas: Representing, by means of Stained Copper-Plate Charts, the Exports, Imports, and General Trade of England* (London: J. Debrett, 1786), p. 3. Emphasis in the original.

38 Cartography's neutrality was produced in particular by the mathematical coordinate system that Playfair adopted for its charts. The historian Alfred W. Crosby has described within the coordinate system a violent neutralization that "treat[s] the earth's surface as neutral space by slapping a gridwork on it"; Alfred W. Crosby, *The Measure of Reality: Quantification and Western Society, 1250–1600* (Cambridge: Cambridge University Press, 1997), p. 98. Bernhard Klein has criticized the fact that qualitative knowledge—on matters such as the properties of soil—was suppressed in favor of quantification. See Bernhard Klein, *Maps and the Writing of Space in Early Modern England and Ireland, London* (Basingstoke and London: Palgrave Macmillan, 2001).

39 William Playfair, *The Commercial and Political Atlas: Representing, by Means of Stained Copper-Plate Charts, the Progress of the Commerce, Revenues, Expenditure, and Debts of England, during the Whole of the Eighteenth Century, 3rd ed.* (London: T. Burton, 1801), p. vii.

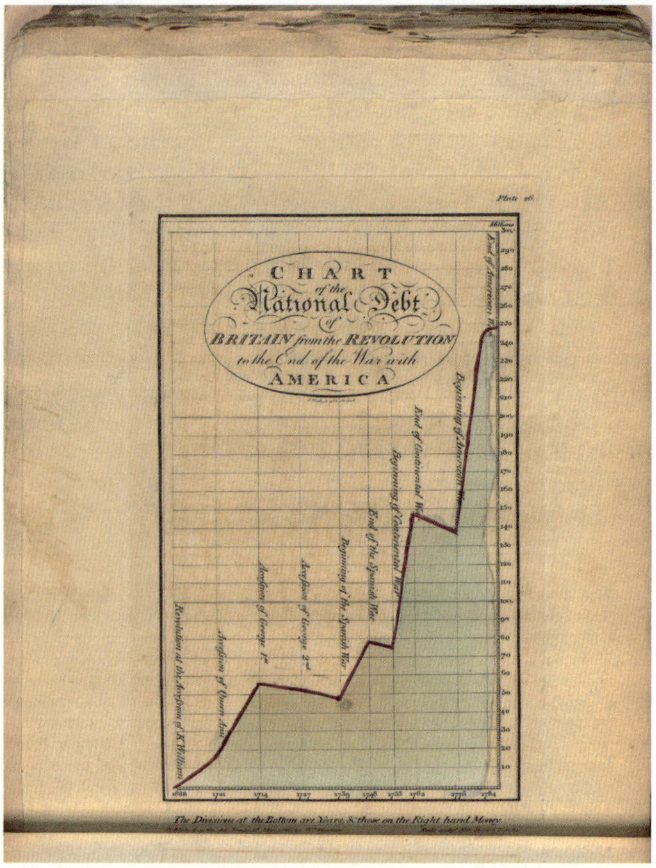

Fig. 4: William Playfair, *Chart of the National Debt of Britain from the Revolution to the End of the War with America*, in: *The Commercial and Political Atlas* (plate 26), 1786. Copyright: Staats- und Universitätsbibliothek Hamburg, C/9050, of which Plate 26 (CC BY-SA 4.0).

was created from within Britain's position of power, and that the comparability delivered by the standardized charts concealed relations of violence, remains largely hidden in the charts—just as it does in cartography. The explanations that accompany the charts in Playfair's atlas provide an insight into the foundational racist assumptions and the violence present in global commerce[40]—without questioning Britain's claims to supremacy. Playfair criticized the government of his day for its accumulation of debt, but not for the English claim to global dominance. The entire first section of his atlas visualizes this English supremacy in the form of trade relations.[41] Conflicting with today's notions of objectivity, the charts formed part of a political pamphlet in which Playfair even called for overthrow of the government.[42] One of the graphs central to the politics of the *Commercial and Political Atlas* and used by Playfair in all three of its editions was the *Chart of National Debt*, showing the overall debt burden arising from the actions of the British government.

The *Chart of National Debt* shows the increase in debt over a period of nearly one hundred years up until 1786. It bears at first glance a resemblance to Du Bois's chart demonstrating increases to property values. Playfair shows the national debt as a rising line highlighted in

40 In his remarks on English commerce in Africa, Playfair contradicts himself when the matter of trade fairness arises, in that he ultimately describes a fraud involving inferior goods. This is a fraud that he seeks to justify by way of a racist logic in which trade—like humans—is not equal, and in which "with these Barbarians (…) no honour, humanity, or equity, were at all necessary." Playfair, *The Commercial and Political Atlas*, 1st ed., p. 90.

41 The curve charts in the first part of the *Atlas* visualize trade balances: within the coordinate systems there appear two curves, one representing imports and the other exports. The distance between the two indicates the positive or negative trade balance. The charts are intended to show which trade relations were good for England, and which not.

42 "The Government must end, a temporary anarchy ensue, and a new Government, *of different identity*, and that is not responsible for former engagements, will take its place." Playfair, *The Commercial and Political Atlas*, 1st ed, p. 116 (emphasis in original).

red, atop a coordinate system with time on the horizontal X-axis and the sum of debt on the vertical Y-axis. At ten points above the line (which ascends in a jagged manner from the lower left to the upper right) and mostly above its high and low points, vertical lines of text within the visual space indicate the beginnings and ends of wars and changes of government. These lines of text can be traced back along the lines of the time axis on which the dates of the events are noted. In the context of the graph, the ten lines of text in the background of the image clearly act as indicators of the statistical trend. This results in correlation: in a causal link between the curve and the events, showing that debt increases with the onset of war.[43] Linking the visual parameters thus indicates the political perspectivization of the data, providing a narrative that can be easily understood by those viewing the chart.[44]

Looking at Du Bois's depiction of property values among Georgia's African American population, a key difference from Playfair's narrative form becomes clear—one to be found in the relation of the graphs to the visual background and the terms marked upon it. With *Chart of Debt*, in contrast, the correlation is clear; the question of the debt's origin is answered by historical events. In the chart on *Valuation of Town and City Property*, however, no such correlation between the curve and the text entries is apparent; the reasons for increases to property values do not seem correlated to the items of text. In addition, the terms are not localizable as events within the coordinate system or in relation to the timeline, instead forming part of the structure and the back-

43 The wars in question are those with Spain from 1739–1748, the Seven Years' War from 1755–1762, and the American War of Independence from 1775–1784.

44 For Li, selection and reduction are fundamental operations of narrative—and thus of constructing correlations. See Li, "Visualizing Chinese Immigrants in the U.S. Statistical Atlases," p. 5.

ground. The question is how this change in representational form can be understood.

My suggestion follows on from Olman's approach to propose that the chart breaks the direct correlation of curve to text, challenging the idea of a monocausal relationship and any reductionist explanation of the depicted trend. This is done to illustrate African American lives and realities in Georgia—a complexity that cannot be grasped at a glance or via a chart. Expectations of a correlation between the curve and the accompanying parameters is in keeping with a graphical convention coined by William Playfair in the late eighteenth century, in which complex circumstances are reduced to simplified forms. Playfair's intention was to visually explain the complex problem of national debt and to produce a monocausal correlation. Efforts to see Black resilience in the diagram suffer under our expectations of finding a correlation between the curve and the text labels, as if were precisely *through* the background of violence that the Black population had been strengthened and had gained successes. I wish to propose a different perspective: one that starts by interrupting the correlation, thus allowing us to perceive the background as an independent element. The chart thus opens up a multi-perspectivity that indicates both a positive development—increased property values—and a background of racist violence. This ultimately also means that even in the face of positive developments with regard to property ownership, violence cannot not become invisible and that instead, racist structures are present in the background of any perspectivization or representation of the lives of the African American population. In their subversion and destabilization of convention, the charts highlight expectations of finding causation. If the strategy of the World's Fair photographs is to blur racist stereotypes and, in terms of visual politics, to reject, following Därmann, "slavish servitude," then a deeper refusal of a form of thought

can be observed within the charts. This refusal of form is one that must, in the course of today's decolonializing critiques, be pursued further.

Translation: Matthew James Scown

Lauren Berlant

Unlearning the Common

There can be no change without revisceralization. Throughout this chapter,[1] this summary statement has been indicated in terms of the incitement to break open habits and naturalized norms of association, for example through the use of the commons concept to dispossess the normative analogy of its force. Such change involves all kinds of loss and transitional suspension of our confidence about how things work. It also releases creative energy for worldbuilding.

But it's not simple to move from fight and release to a generative freedom. The transition requires reconditioning what pass as instincts, triggers, gut feelings, true feelings, presumptive ties, the whole default world of emotional and affective expectation. In the affective common, that reconditioning is often what gets in the way of staying with who you're with while also nursing many small and large scars. I flagged this part of the process earlier in the term *unlearning,* which is another way to lose your object. Infrastructuralist perspectives experiment with what can generate ongoing life. So far in this chapter they have used the common to generate tactics for change that are fundamentally concep-

1 Lauren Berlant's text is a revised version of their previously published essay "The Commons: Infrastructures for Troubling Times," *Environment and Planning D: Society and Space* 34, no. 3 (2016), pp. 393–419. Alongside one of its subject matters—Liza Johnson's film *In the Air* (2009)—it served as a basis for discussion during our Resilience vs. Resistance workshop. The revised text is also the concluding part to the second chapter of Berlant's latest and posthumously published book *On the Inconvenience of Other People* (Durham, N.C. and London: Duke University Press, 2022), p. x—"a book about the overcloseness of the world and how we live it [...] about navigating and generating change from within the long broken and fractious middle of life."

tual, experimental in the way they're lived. Such a focus on the transformational infrastructure is central to the anarchist tradition that begins with building from what bodies can do together on the ground, in the weather, through ideas manifest in material practice and living concepts, and not just to get through the ongoing moment but to generate forms of life in resistance to an Oz horizon that doesn't hold up close up. The aesthetics of kinesthetic performance beginning with the body can provide tactics that might grow new proprioceptors. I close with two examples focusing on the sensuality of learning in the middle of the dehiscence of unlearning.

Liza Johnson's film *In the Air* (2009) is about her hometown of Portsmouth, Ohio, although she doesn't name it: it could be many postindustrial US landscapes, except it's predominantly white. The two dominant affects "in the air" are distraction and boredom: the film's central question, posed in different forms every day, is whether the burned-out and "wasted" parents, who spend time drunk and antagonistic in cars and bars, will leave for their children what Patricia Williams describes as the inheritance of a disinheritance.[2] The disinheritance isn't just familial or financial. It's about the exhaustion of language: the heavy silence of what goes without saying sustains this world.

The town in this film has been abandoned not only by its elders but by capital. It seems to have one industry, a junkyard (figure 1). The junkyard's aspiration seems to be to avoid events: a sign announces the string of days without accident. But the feel is as though the world of this town is one punctured membrane away from becoming the scrap it now organizes. The buildings and streets are empty: it seems to be being maintained as a ghost town.

2 Patricia J. Williams, *The Alchemy of Race and Rights* (Cambridge, Mass.: Harvard University Press, 1991), p. 217.

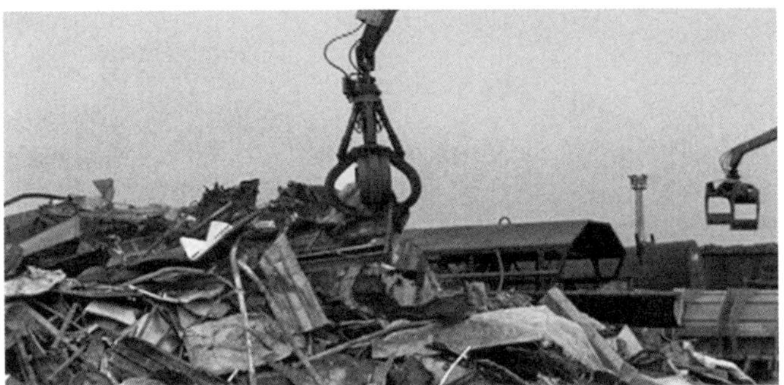

Fig. 1: *In the Air*, directed by Liza Johnson, 2009.

The film is from the perspective of the kids of the town, its current crop of dreamers: they are protagonists in training. The training comes from the only live collective space we see in the town, a circus school that is called, in real life, but not in the film, Cirque d'Art.[3] We see the circus teacher dead serious at the front of the room, getting the group in sync to do tricks. The kids are in many kinds of transition: in late high school about to be sprung and testing the world, still at home living with and against their families, and as student performers veering between kidding around, flirting, and admiring each other's skill and the focus of people in training.

The kids are learning to spin and to fall. They are learning to lean on each other (figure 2). A little light romance might be starting, but autonomy and abs are the focus. You have to be able to hold a whole body in the air while it swings. None of this feels like the pre-enactment of fantasies of stardom or love. It does not feel at all phantasmatic or allegorical: learning to be awkward, to be graceful, to leap, and to fall is a training in attention and also in revisceralizing one's bodily intuition.

3 Cirque d'Art's philosophy of pedagogy and ongoing training apparatus can be found at "Cirque d'Art," Southern Ohio Museum, http://www.somacc.com/cirque-dart/ (accessed June 8, 2020).

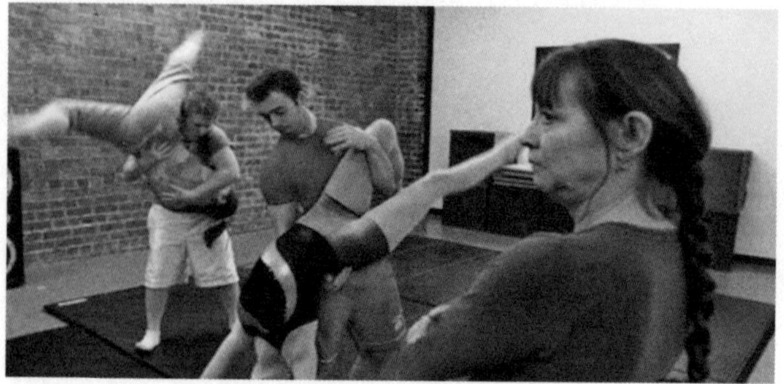

Fig. 2: *In the Air*, directed by Liza Johnson, 2009. Pegi Wilkes teaching Christa Castle Benson, Brian Rushford, Jon Chandler, and Heather White Chandler.

It requires making and breaking habits of response. It involves rethinking gravity. The air is not the common, as in Spahr.[4] Training in collaboration is the thing that collapses breaking forms with making a common life.

This training includes ordinary physical dynamics themselves. Disturbing what threatens and what comforts, the circus schooling shifts what Virno calls the dread and the refuge that shape contemporary ideas of the commons as a relief from life.[5] It does this by foregrounding the difficulty and pleasure of maintaining footing during conversations, in the world, and during performance that requires people to show up for others' bodies.[6]

The high point of the film is difficult to describe because it's so simple, but the point of rebooting relationality through remaking visceral response is that in

4 Berlant is referring to writer Juliana Spahr's 2005 poem *This Connection of Everyone with Lungs*, which is discussed earlier in the chapter (note by Judith Sieber).

5 See Paolo Virno, *A Grammar of the Multitude: For an Analysis of Contemporary Forms of Life*, trans. Isabella Bertoletti, James Cascaito, and Andrea Casson (New York: Semiotext(e), 2004), pp. 29–30.

6 On "footing," see Erving Goffman, *Forms of Talk* (Philadelphia, Penn.: University of Pennsylvania Press, 1981), pp. 124–159.

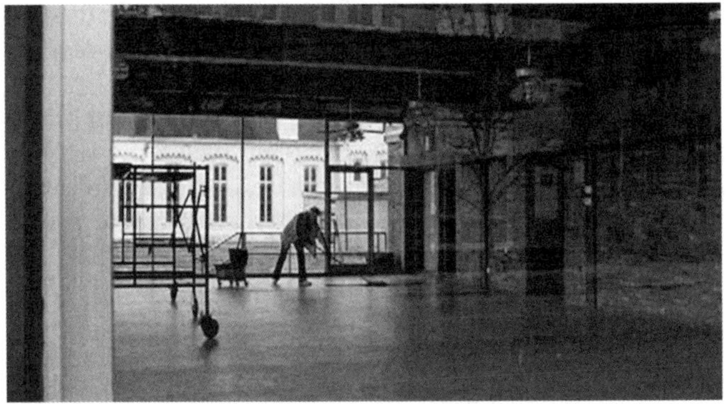

Fig. 3: *In the Air*, directed by Liza Johnson, 2009. Sue Stevenson.

order to reinvent the lifeworld in the present, one must transform what reciprocity can mean.

In the final scene the high school kids want a ride somewhere. The parents have been working, fighting, or drinking, appearing wasted and exhausted, sometimes aggressively deadpan. Finally, they track down a mother while she is doing her job. For a living, she sweeps an empty building by herself (figure 3). She is a maintenance engineer for an abandoned architecture, hired to preserve the hoarded infrastructure of capital just in case it feels like returning for some more exploitation, resource extraction, and real contribution to the atmosphere an abandoned town can only remember as live.

The kids approach her. She barely looks at them, repeating, "What do you want? What do you kids want?" They refuse to speak and assume an expressionlessness interrupted only by the relay of side-eye. These lateral glances shift the film's genre. As though rehearsed, the kids respond to the mother's query by surrounding her and making her flip over them backward, as the music begins. They take their schooling out of the school, but they do not become teachers. No longer tracing the decay of the harsh real, where the remaining fantasy is getting through the day, the magical-realism musical that emerges in this scene derives life from whatever it is that brings people to the situation.

Everyone who has been in the film comes out of an imaginary space of the shot. Collectively, the dispossessed self-possess. Entrained or untrained, they do circus movement. Launching and landing pads mysteriously appear. For the most part the performers are white and working class, but not entirely. For the most part they are strong and skilled, but not entirely. Johnson doesn't stage them as biographical subjects with names and desires, or as stars with untapped auras of magnificence: the elders join the kids as they all learn to use their bodies in sync, which includes counterpoint. Their coordination not only counters the saturation of everyday defeat by work and the absence of work, but also stages a becoming that might lead to belonging. If it works, the revised bodily habit of nonsovereignty creates a collective orientation, a shared subjectivity. It does not erase individuality but creates a mutually transforming affect-sphere where it has no "right" to be. In the hollow spaces of abandoned capital defined by coordinated movement, we are in a different world than the "rights" world.

For the most part their faces are still and composed, so muted as to be inexpressive; they have the stiff bodies of workers entrained by work's rhythms. Johnson isolates only one participant, a young plump woman who makes a victory sign with her arms when she achieves a glorious split, celebrating a victory not over but through her body. Mainly everyone is focused on being in step, but not rigidly: both actors and audience, poised for next phase of movement.

The group embodies, then, not socially necessary labor time or normative intimacy, but something simpler and often inconvenient in ordinary time: socially necessary proximity looking for a way to be. Who would be there to receive a protest? No one: that's how abandoned they are. They turn toward each other without metastatements. The analogy they perform among all persons in a world of people and architectures abandoned by capital becomes the condition of this convergence that isn't a merging; and the propertied space that someone owns becomes a pop-up common defined by skilled, patterned movement that could become a transformational infrastructure. "Space is a practiced place," writes Michel de Certeau.[7] Practice acknowledges the imperfect, the impermanent. As I have argued, the episodic common is not a form of mourning for the loss of the collective ordinary; it's a test to see whether a future can be built through episodes, and what kinds; it's a sensual experiment in breaking down what the body has learned about being in relation. Here, squatting in a space, the people become potential heterotopians.

The soundtrack to this scene is a 1998 song by the group Alice DeeJay called "Better Off Alone." The song's only two lines are, "Do you think you're better off alone?" and "Talk to me," a rhetorical question and an imperative phrase. "Better off Alone" has had a substantial life in clubs and has been remade and remixed a number of times. There's little to it other than the desire to convert the rhetorical into an actual question.[8] Usually it appears in a space where people are alone together, singular and various, intimate and mostly anonymous, looking for a minor release from the solo burden of managing their pseudo-sovereignty. The song delivers the core message of popular culture, that "you are not alone," and challenges its listeners to use their proximity to sense a better lifeworld and build toward

7 Michel de Certeau, *The Practice of Everyday Life*, trans. Steven Rendall (Berkeley and London: University of California Press, 1984), p. 117.

8 Thanks to Luis-Manuel Garcia Mispireta for sending me evidence from the commentary class of this song's credibility as an anthem for solidarity, one that calls not on full subjective or affective convergence but on concerted practical activity that manifests attentiveness, tenderness, respect, and pleasure. See the WhoSampled App, http://www.whosampled.com/sample/view/1427/Wiz%20Khalifa-Say%20Yeah_Alice%20Deejay-Better%20Off%20Alone/.

it together.[9] In this sense the song is air and provides one.

What is "the air" in *In the Air*? As though joining Spahr's inquiry into the common air, the film asks us to wonder about what's the matter with the air, as it recirculates the scrap from the junkyard and the humidity from the lake into lungs and muscles. There's pollution. There's energy for making new genres of convergence. Is there something in the air that might protest the nervous fraying and self-numbing medication of the body politic? How can a discipline of the ordinary body toward pleasure and kindness create an atmosphere for a new economy's good life that does not begin with where the wealth is and judgments of who's deserving?

The film's older figures appear too beaten down to protest the exploitation of supply-chain capitalism, and the abandonment of working populations by the wealth hoarders seems to produce less a politics than rampant and depleting nervous conditions, from irritation to short fuses and numbness (figure 4). The receptive posture of aesthetic attention helps the youths to loosen or unlearn their defenses against taking each other in. They train each other, then the adults, to reoccupy existence in a chilly place. Individuals may be exhausted, but as a whole they've not yet given up on the world.

So in *In the Air*, collaboration clears space for the common, which has no form but offers a point of return through the creative use of proximity, improvised synchronicity, and spiky kinships no less intimate for the ambivalence. In its recessive way the very purposiveness of gymnastics in this final scene makes for a brilliant postwork and antiproductivist performance,[10] with

9 See Lauren Berlant, *The Female Complaint: The Unfinished Business of Sentimentality in American Culture* (Durham, N.C. and London: Duke University Press, 2008), p. 9.

10 The literature on postwork relations to labor begins with the autonomists. For compilations of some of the strongest contemporary arguments, see Doreen Ford, "Abolish Work!," abolishwork.com; Doreen Ford, *Dispatches from the Ruins: Documents & Analyses from University*

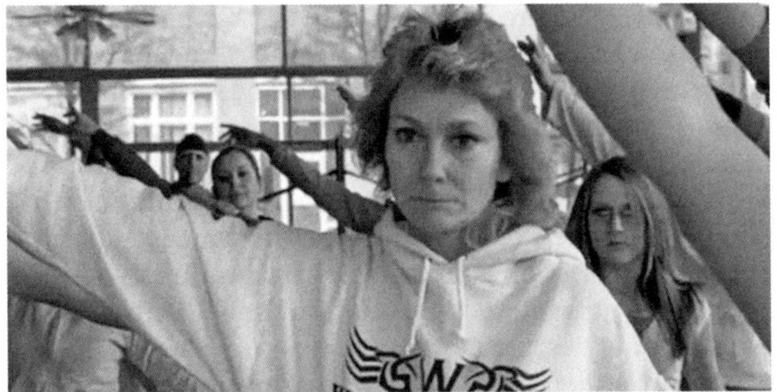

Fig. 4: *In the Air*, directed by Liza Johnson, 2009. Anita Skaggs in front of Misty Windsor Graham and Eugenio Perez.

the musical number serving its traditional function as a placeholder for living otherwise. But the number is in the air while the bodies are quiet and on the ground. Not in the register of the manifesto, the film points to what's there, not proclaiming the reparative solution that is part of the promise that the political holds out. Another use of flatness: to put a wedge in causality. Here the liberal world picture crashes to the floor as the group stands still in the absence of confidence about connection, causality, and building out the world. The first step becomes literally that. No abstraction can provide resources for bearing each other and life's long middle. Unlearning the exhausted gimmicks of normativity, the bodies pause in the space without a satisfying outcome in sight.[11]

Struggles, Experiments in Self-Education, https://1000littlehammers.files.wordpress.com/2010/02/dispatch_ruins_final3.pdf (accessed July 3, 2020) and Kathi Weeks, *The Problem with Work: Feminism, Marxism, Antiwork Politics, and Postwork Imaginaries* (Durham, N.C. and London: Duke University Press, 2011).

11 Sianne Ngai writes, "The gimmick is thus an aesthetic judgment uniquely reflecting on the genre's capacity for absorbing and transcoding nonaesthetic judgments." This description is a good way to talk about the internal dynamics of social form and normativity that organize the conventional world. See Sianne Ngai, *Theory of the Gimmick: Aesthetic Judgment and Capitalist Form* (Cambridge, Mass.: Harvard University Press, 2020), p. 36.

And this is where we are: the "we" who are not one.[12] Those who desire to invent a transformational infrastructure to shape the world that is always in transition often look for something to appear more solid than it can be in order to anchor what's emerging.[13] Charismatic authority is one example of something solid-seeming frequently called on.[14] The commons concept takes up that texture, too, insofar as it stands specifically for cosmopolitan struggles against national-neoliberal privatization strategies such as the massive wealth grab by the 1 percent and "public-private partnerships." These displacements obscure accountability for the offloading of

12 Contemporary thought about being plural often neglects French feminist work on the multiplicity of being both in self- and social relation. I'm referring here to Luce Irigaray's classic, *This Sex Which Is Not One*, trans. Catherine Porter and Carolyn Burke (Ithaca, N.Y.: Cornell University Press, 1985). So, too, does it neglect the non-European traditions that begin with nonsovereign being. My education first came from reading work on ancestral co-existence: Molly McGarry, *Ghosts of Futures Past: Spiritualism and the Cultural Politics of Nineteenth-Century America* (Berkeley and Los Angeles: University of California Press, 2008); Rosalind C. Morris, *In the Place of Origins: Modernity and its Mediums in Northern Thailand* (Durham, N.C. and London: Duke University Press, 2000); and more recently Arnika Fuhrmann, *Ghostly Desires: Queer Sexuality and Vernacular Buddhism in Contemporary Thai Cinema* (Durham, N.C. and London: Duke University Press, 2016).

13 Antonio Negri names the problem of the organization-to-come-after in the face of a deconstituted civil society. See Antonio Negri, "N for Negri: Antonio Negri in Conversation with Carles Guerra," ed. and trans. Jorge Mestre, Ivan Bercedo, Raimon Vilatovà, Glòria Mèlich, Elaine Fradley and Carlos Guerra, *Grey Room* 11 (Spring 2003), pp. 86–109.

14 On charismatic authority, first see Max Weber, *On Charisma and Institution Building* (Chicago: University of Chicago Press, 1968). Much varied use of the concept churns within the literature, especially on narcissistic leadership and contemporary media. See, for example, Nils Gustafsson and Noomi Weinryb, "The Populist Allure of Social Media Activism: Individualized Charismatic Authority," *Organization* 27, no. 3 (2020), pp. 431–440; Walden Flores Bello, "A Dangerous Liaison? Harnessing Weber to Illuminate the Relationship of Democracy and Charisma in the Philippines and India," *International Sociology* (Sept. 2020), https://doi.org/10.1177/0268580920942721 (accessed July 3, 2020); Inderpal Grewal, "Authoritarian Patriarchy and Its Populism," *English Studies in Africa* 63, no. 1 (2020), pp. 179–198, and Stephen Turner, "Charisma Reconsidered," *Journal of Classical Sociology* 3, no. 1 (March 2003), pp. 5–26.

debt, dispossession, and direct violence onto the already structurally vulnerable and violated.

In terms of sloganeering, too, the twenty-first-century translocal cosmopolitan assertion of the commons as the ground of radical democracy became an aspirational performative, acting as a thing that can be collectively asserted, held, achieved and occupied. New analogies were tried out in its name in the United States. The organizing rubric of the commons of Occupy became a way to point to public space reoccupied for constituent power and a trial balloon for the bodily copresence of direct action or "assembly" in the ordinary.[15] It signified something like affective mutuality and feel of what Jonathan Flatley calls a "revolutionary mood."[16] It replaced the uncanny sensation of "the touch of the state" with schooling in respectful social distancing and patience for rhetorical protocols that amplified solidarity and sometimes became intimacy.[17] It proliferated so quickly and intensely through allied cells of Occupy that within a few years it began to irritate some of its early users: "In late July, [Sandy] Nurse pleaded on her Facebook wall, 'Does everything have to be called "Occupy"? Come on, y'all.' A commenter on a similar post a few weeks

15 Regarding reoccupation of public space, in addition to the work of Hardt and Negri, including *Assembly*, it is worth reading slowly and seriously on constituent power in Cesare Casarino and Antonio Negri, *In Praise of the Common: A Conversation on Philosophy and Politics* (Minneapolis: University of Minnesota Press, 2008), especially but not limited to the chapter, "Vicissitudes of Constituent Thought," pp. 134–190. On the copresence of action in the ordinary, see Judith Butler and Athena Athanasiou, *The Performative in the Political: Conversations with Athena Athanasiou* (Malden, Mass.: Polity Press, 2013), and Judith Butler, *Notes Toward a Performative Theory of Assembly* (Cambridge, Mass.: Harvard University Press, 2018).

16 Jonathan Flatley, "Refreshments of Revolutionary Mood," in *Literary/Liberal Entanglements: Toward a Literary History of the 21st-Century*, ed. Corrinne Harol and Mark Simpson (Toronto: University of Toronto Press, 2017), pp. 103–147. On the difficulty of maintaining such a mood, see also Deborah B. Gould, *Moving Politics: Emotion and ACT UP's Fight Against AIDS* (Chicago: University of Chicago Press, 2009).

17 Keith Woodward and Mario Bruzzone, "Touching Like a State," *Antipode* 47, no. 2 (March 2015), pp. 539–556.

earlier put the matter succinctly: 'Burn Occupy on a funeral pyre and move the fuck on.'"[18] Such processes of revision-in-association have tended to link concepts of political voice, atmosphere, proximity and the public sphere to specific sensual qualities of the common as such: the toggle between the affective and political infrastructural imaginary creates space beyond itself. *The commons* still serves as a mere synonym for *public park*. At the same time, it is usually temporally specific and geopolitically local: the resource and spatial common of Occupy Sandy, Occupy the Hood, Occupy London, Occupy Nation. In the meanwhile, occupy/common has changed into a way to describe collaboration and careworlds more generally. Critical work on ecology, states, indigeneity, political movements, knowledge, and research itself blazon Occupy to ally with the desire to transform infrastructures that organize specific resources and concepts necessary for life. It's a kind of dog whistle addressed to a movement dream.

It is hard to avoid making a powerful concept all-absorbent when all you've ever known is how to own, possess, and use action concepts in defense of your existence.

But if the imperative Occupy and ideas of the common have become virtual siblings at this point, their political association during the 2008 economic crash with protests against the reproduction of economic inequality has also been changing. Its legacy endures, for example, in Occupy City Hall, a pop-up common protesting the New York City Police Department's extreme funding privilege and ordinary violence against people of color and the poor.[19] Triggered by the video-recorded

18 Nathan Schneider, "Breaking Up With Occupy," *The Nation*, September 11, 2013, https://www.thenation.com/article/archive/breaking-occupy/ (accessed June 28, 2020).

19 See Juliana Kim, "How the Floyd Protests Turned Into a 24-Hour 'Occupy City Hall' in N.Y.," *The New York Times*, June 28, 2020, https://www.nytimes.com/2020/06/28/nyregion/occupy-city-hall-nyc.html?referringSource=articleShare (accessed June 28, 2020).

police execution of George Floyd in Minneapolis on May 25, 2020, this appropriation of a zoned "public" space as a political common also mobilized the archive of anti-Black murders captured on video with cellphones, already on regular display, to dispersed and local publics. It explicitly created and reanimated knowledges of the genocidal and often barely extrajuridical extermination of Black, Indigenous, and Latinx life in practices such as lynching, as Ken Gonzales-Day has demonstrated across many media.[20] This revision of the Occupy commons also takes energy from the video archive of weaponized joyriding that includes the police and took form in the white supremacist enjoyment-murder of Ahmaud Arbery in Satilla Shore, Georgia, on February 23, 2020.[21]

Writing from the multiple crises of the present in 2020, I resist the desire for performativity for which the commons concept so often stands. Crisis hastily generates multiples of the "we." There have always been bullying, thin, and nostalgic "we's," of course, used for good and ill. Leading to projections of a unity of experience onto a mass, the imperative to posit the atmosphere of belonging works either as assertion or as a hope that if you name it, it will come. During the COVID-19 crisis, before the phase of antiracist protest, corporate and individual pronouncements proliferated with smileys, balloons, and exclamation points. Street corners, posters, shop windows and TV ads proclaimed phrases like "We are in it together!" Who is "we"? What is "it"? Fantasies of democracy as the experience of collectively equal expo-

20 See Ken Gonzales-Day, *Lynching in the West: 1850–1935* (Durham, N.C. and London: Duke University Press, 2006). See also his antiracist photography collection: Ken Gonzales-Day, *Profiled*, ed. Edward Robinson (Los Angeles: Los Angeles Museum of Contemporary Art, 2011).

21 See Richard Fausset, "What We Know About the Shooting Death of Ahmaud Arbery," *The New York Times*, June 24, 2020, https://www.nytimes.com/article/ahmaud-arbery-shooting-georgia.html?referringSource=articleShare (accessed June 28, 2020).

sure to vulnerability tried to establish a ground where there is no ground.

At the current conjuncture, the "we" arises in the contexts of structurally induced suffering-toward-death from anti-Black police torture and murder, food insecurity, medical bankruptcy, drug price inflation, the widening militarization of state tools for control and domination, the racist carceral habit, and so on. These are crises in the ordinary, but not probable and engrained: as Spahr catalogues, as Johnson presumes. Failed state democracies, racist ideologies, life-shattering pandemics, and ordinary fatalism about the suffering of the "essential" worker join the mass refusal to allow the ordinary of racist police violence and specific anti-Blackness to seem like a fate. These conjunctures have multiplied questions about what a life is, what targeted death does, and where and whether any "we" can be said to stretch across communities, bodies politic, epidemiological populations, sets of people with analogous feelings of exposure and vulnerability, consumer addressees, and citizens of the local now defined at all scales: cities, states, neighborhoods, regions and nations.

All of these "we's" are projections from specific visions of a zone of collective experience. The plural is always local but often masked as the name for the general. The same goes for the universal, which always ends up being specific, a failed abstraction. Is "we" ever more than a heuristic coupled with a desire? When is it a way of talking about the effects of a history of defining experience? What does it have to do with liberal and illiberal concepts of "the public"? Is the common effective or a shortcut in generating the plural beyond the moment of the "we" of historical community? None of these questions is rhetorical. No mass politics or any politics exists without some attention to the building out of the "we." This is the power of feeling-with crossed with solidarity in the political sphere.[22] But the very fractures of inequality are also affectively and materially amplified during crisis, in the register of life and death.[23] As the next chapter argues, *life* comes to mean many things. And still there are "die-ins" on the Boston Common, making a bad copy of a literal and pervasive death (figure 5).

Peter Linebaugh proposes that "it might be better to keep the word [*common*] as a verb, an activity, rather than as a noun, a substantive"; he wants us to think about commoning land, life, history, and memory, rather than presuming them, so long as it doesn't serve to further divide the world into local enclaves of value, as it mostly does.[24] Massimo de Angelis argues that the commons is always a doing that is a decoupling from the reproductive energies of a normative life's standards of value, and not a replacement for capitalism.[25] This

22 I would have used the word *sentimentality* rather than *feeling-with* if *sentimentality* wasn't such a trigger, evoking emotional excesses and forced equivalences across difference with which many don't want to identify. I define *sentimentality* as the presumption that shared feeling about something in the domain of desire or threat creates bonds that presume, or hope for, more general likeness across distances of time and lifeworld experience. As an ideologeme, sentimentality links people who don't otherwise share a lifeworld in ways that can fuel world-building and social change from the ground of shared critique, shared outrage, and shared refusal. At the same time though, those very points of convergence can produce infelicitous expectations that the same critique presumes a profound likeness in the world that people want to bring into being. You can't have mass politics without sentimentality, but it does not provide much skill for working through the antagonism or differences among potential comrades. See Berlant, *The Female Complaint*.

23 For a precise summary of this general and contemporary ordinariness of crisis during the pandemic, see Ellen J. Amster, "History's Crystal Ball: What the Past Can Tell Us about COVID-19 and Our Future," *The Conversation*, June, 28 2020, https://theconversation.com/historys-crystal-ball-what-the-past-can-tell-us-about-covid-19-and-our-future-140512?fbclid=IwAR1sJ9TLlGx8hPGGdP2r8B_KJM7-nqAummmHdCFBBqK3AG8ZoNgjpjiIL7c (accessed June 28, 2020).

24 See Peter Linebaugh, *The Magna Carta Manifesto: Liberties and Commons for All* (Berkeley: University of California Press, 2009), p. 279. See also the elaboration of this view in his *Stop, Thief!: The Commons, Enclosures, and Resistance* (Oakland, Calif.: PM Press, 2014).

25 See Massimo de Angelis, *The Beginning of History: Value Struggles and Global Capital* (London: Pluto Press, 2007).

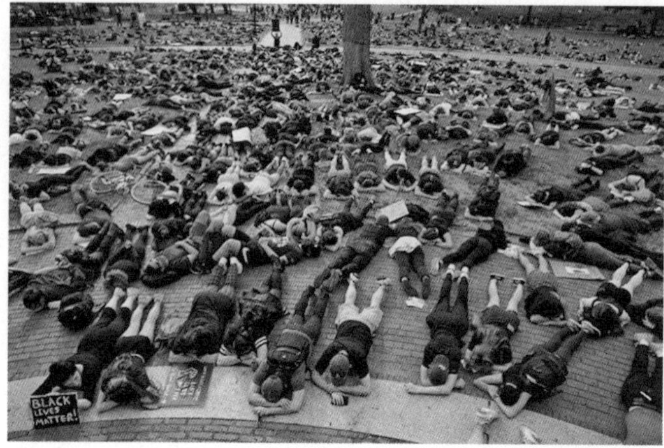

Fig. 5: Die-in at Boston Common, June 3, 2020. Color photograph by Brian Snyder. Copyright: Reuters.

chapter is in sync with these claims. Again, we are talking about the aspirational use of the concept, its destructive function, and not the tradition of lifeworld self-protection in which culture and economic clashing mark a war for a genealogical or an Indigenous community's survival. Linebaugh and de Angelis refer to a rhythm of worlding that resonates with this chapter's project of tracking the growth of an affective infrastructure whose very existence acknowledges the inconvenience of other people in the midst of the struggle to transform life economically and subjectively. Embodied tactics are required for heterotopian praxis. The frictions of counternormative affective infrastructures can bring structural political imaginaries to their knees.

One might respond to my infrastructuralism with the idea that any specific address to transforming the aspiration called the sensus communis is at best a mere episode to hang a wish on. But that's what an episode is: a goad to rethink seriality, continuity, analogy. Every transformative example implicitly disturbs an analogy, decouples coupling. Every broken analogy releases affectively bound energy back into the world. Andrés Green writes that when discourse stops binding "word-presentation, thing-presentation, affect, bodily states, [and] act," the unbound affect might "snap the chain of discourse," inducing a "qualitative mutation."[26] The commons concept requires infrastructures for sustaining the mutations that emerge from the chains that are breaking in the popular resistance to austerity regimes and anti-Black and patriarchal capitalism.

I've argued in this chapter that the inconvenient gesture of breaking analogy, rather than hastily, anxiously, or needfully asserting it, is a prime device for opening up the figural world of what's held to be common. Ian Bogost writes, "Sometimes there is nothing more refreshing than a startlingly bad analogy. It's like a crisp cucumber bursting from the dip of a bad day's sphincter. Like a restorative rain drenching the vomit of last night's bender. Like a cool breeze tousling the blood-matted fur of roadkill."[27] He doesn't mean this in a positive way. I do. The commons produces riffing on the other side of assurance: What isn't mixed? The political and epistemic problem for the politically autopoetic, which is what all world-creating subjects in coordinated struggle are, is that the placeholders for our desire can too easily seem solid and ironed out rather than affective figures for delivering a convergence process we can cling to and with which we draw lines of belonging in the sand, in the air, on the streets, in liveable spaces.

26 André Green, *The Fabric of Affect in the Psychoanalytic Discourse*, trans. Alan Sheridan (London: Routledge, 2005), p. 211. Originally published as *Le Discours vivant* (Paris: Presses Universitaires de France, 1973). This set of linked observations about bound and unbound affects appears throughout Green's work. See, for example, André Green, *Key Ideas for a Contemporary Psychoanalysis: Misrecognition and Recognition of the Unconscious*, trans. Andrew Weller (London and New York: Routledge, 2012), pp. 81, 131.

27 Ian Bogost, "Blogging Stops Unplanned Pregnancy," June 18, 2009, http://bogost.com/writing/blog/blogging_stops_unplanned_pregn/ (accessed June 25, 2020).

What remains for the pedagogy of unlearning that we derive from the aspirational commons, then, is to build affective infrastructures that admit the work of desire and the work of ambivalence as the tactics of commoning. What remains is the potential we have to common infrastructures that can absorb the blows of our aggressive need for the world to accommodate each and all of us and our resistance to adaptation, and, at the same time, to hold out the prospect of a world worth attaching to that's something other than an old hope's bitter echo. A failed episode is not evidence that a project is in error: by definition, forms of common life are always going through a phase, as infrastructures do.

List of Illustrations

Cover Image

Detail from Pallavi Paul, *Bluff check Omitted*, archival print, 11.7 x 16.5 inches, 2015, courtesy of the artist.

Knut Ebeling: War in the Head: Meditating with Bataille

1 Pallavi Paul, *Elsewhere 7*, ink, thread and collage on paper, 9 x 7.5 inches, 2018, courtesy of the artist. **2** Pallavi Paul, *Elsewhere 8*, ink, thread and collage on paper, 9 x 7.5 inches, 2018, courtesy of the artist. **3** Pallavi Paul, *Elsewhere 5*, ink, thread and collage on paper, 9 x 7.5 inches, 2018, courtesy of the artist. **4** Pallavi Paul, *Bluff check Omitted*, archival print, 11.7 x 16.5 inches, 2015, courtesy of the artist.

Akram Zaatari interviewed by Rebecca Hanna John

1 Akram Zaatari, *A Conversation with an Imagined Israeli Filmmaker* (Berlin: Sternberg Press, 2012). Spread courtesy of the artist. **2** Akram Zaatari, *Letter to a Refusing Pilot* (Venice, 2013), no page numbers. Published for the National Pavilion of the Republic of Lebanon at the 55th International Art Exhibition – Biennale Arte, Venice (June 1–November 24, 2013). Spread courtesy of the artist. **3** Akram Zaatari, *Letter to a Refusing Pilot*, 2013, HD video, 34 min, film still. **4** Akram Zaatari, *Letter to a Refusing Pilot*, 2013, HD video and 16 mm installation. Installation view: The National Pavilion of the Republic of Lebanon at the 55th International Art Exhibition – Biennale Arte, Venice. Photo: Marco Milan.

Diana Taylor in conversation with Sebastián Eduardo Dávila and Ulrike Jordan

1 Regina José Galindo, *Earth*, performance, Les Moulins, 2013, courtesy of the artist.

Marivi Véliz: Feeling Presences

1 Regina José Galindo, *Presencia*, performance, Casa Encendida Madrid, 2017, photo: Francisco Magallán, courtesy of the artist.

Pınar Öğrenci: Purple Panic: 43

1 Pınar Öğrenci, *Purple Panic: 43*, performance on Tlatelolco Square, Mexico City, 2015, photo: José Luis Arriaga. **2** Hotel de México: Ely Eduardo G. Rojas, www.monografias.com. **3** Palacio de Lecumberri, Aérea Mexicana, www.rozanamontiel.com. **4** Pınar Öğrenci, *Purple Panic: 43*, performance, Tlatelolco Square, Mexico City, 2015, photo: José Luis Arriaga. **5** The Nonoalco Tlatelolco housing estate in Mexico City, designed by Mario Pani, 1964, copyright: Armando Salas Portugal. **6** Pınar Öğrenci, *Purple Panic: 43*, performance, Tlatelolco Square, Mexico City, 2015, photo: José Luis Arriaga.

Sebastián Eduardo Dávila and Ulrike Jordan: A Psychiatric Clinic, a Monastery, a City and a River

1 Isabel Ruiz, *Matemática Sustractiva*, performance, Antigua Guatemala: Cooperación Española, 2008, photo: Francisco Morales Santos, courtesy of the photographer. **2** Uriel Orlow, *Unmade Film: The Staging*, film still, HD video, silent, 10 min, 2012–2013, courtesy the artist, all rights reserved,

DACS/Artimage 2022. **3** Alex Gerbaulet and Mareike Bernien, *Tiefenschärfe / Depth of Field*, film still, HD video, 15 min, 2016–2017, courtesy of the artists. **4** Gabriel Posada and Yorlady Ruiz, intervention, from the series *Magdalenas por el Cauca*, Cauca River, 2008, photo: Gabriel Posada, courtesy of the artists.

Sofia Bempeza: The Desire of the Exhausted

1 Sofia Bempeza, *Temporäre Adraneia*, 2021, Ausstellungsraum Klingental, Basel, courtesy of the artist. **2** Sofia Bempeza, untitled, courtesy of the artist. **3** Sofia Bempeza, untitled, courtesy of the artist.

Nele Wulff: "Let us be a gear in the machinery and at the same time the obstacle of its operation"

1 House of Tupamaras, *El fracaso es mi estilo. Un manifesto de H.o.T.*, 2021, 12:38 min, film still, courtesy of the artists. **2** House of Tupamaras, *El fracaso es mi estilo. Un manifesto de H.o.T.*., 2021, 12:38 min, film still, courtesy of the artists.

Judith Sieber: Refusal of Form

1 W.E.B. Du Bois, *The Georgia Negro: City and Rural Population. 1890*, ink and watercolor, 710 x 560 mm, ca. 1900. Library of Congress: https://www.loc.gov/. **2** W.E.B. Du Bois, *The Georgia Negro: Illiteracy*, ink and watercolor, 710 x 560 mm, ca. 1900. Library of Congress: https://www.loc.gov/. **3** W.E.B. Du Bois, *The Georgia Negro: Valuation of Town and City Property Owned by Georgia Negroes*, ink and colored ink, 710 x 560 mm, ca. 1900. Library of Congress: https://www.loc.gov/. **4** William Playfair, *Chart of the National Debt of Britain from the Revolution to the End of the War with America*, in: *The Commercial and Political Atlas* (plate 26), 1786. Copyright: Staats- und Universitätsbibliothek Hamburg, C/9050, of which Plate 26 (CC BY-SA 4.0).

Lauren Berlant: Unlearning the Common

1 Liza Johnson, *In the Air*, 2009, film still. **2** Liza Johnson, *In the Air*, 2009, film still showing Pegi Wilkes teaching Christa Castle Benson, Brian Rushford, Jon Chandler, and Heather White Chandler. **3** Liza Johnson, *In the Air*, 2009, film still showing Sue Stevenson. **4** Liza Johnson, *In the Air*, 2009, film still showing Anita Skaggs in front of Misty Windsor Graham and Eugenio Perez. **5** Die-in at Boston Common, June 3, 2020. Color photo by Brian Snyder. Copyright: Reuters.

Contributors

Arnika Ahldag is the Chief Curator at the Museum of Art & Photography in Bangalore. As an art historian her interests cover the representation of labor in Indian contemporary art, institutional critique, exhibition histories and archives. She holds a PhD from the School of Arts and Aesthetics at Jawaharlal Nehru University in New Delhi and an MA from University College London and Albert Ludwigs University in Freiburg. She co-founded the *Feminist Syllabus*, which is part of the workshop series *Pact of Silence—How to break it*, a program for intersectional feminist discourses in the arts. Over the past years she has lectured at the National School of Drama and OP Jindal Global University in New Delhi.

Sofia Bempeza is an art/cultural theorist, artist and author of the book *Geschichte(n) des Kunststreiks* (2019). She writes on dissent and polyphonic aesthetics, queer-feminist art and knowledge practices, forms of collectivity, and on the aesthetics of the (new) right. She is the founder and co-curator of the art festival Aphrodite* and member of the poetry gang *She-Dandies* in Athens. https://sofiabempeza.org

Lauren Berlant (1957–2021) was George M. Pullman Distinguished Service Professor of English at the University of Chicago and the author and coauthor of many books, including *The Queen of America Goes to Washington City* (1997); *The Female Complaint* (2008); *Cruel Optimism* (2011); *Sex, or the Unbearable* (2013); and *The Hundreds* (2019), all published by Duke University Press.

Kathrin Busch is a Professor of Philosophy at the University of the Arts, Berlin. Her research focuses on French philosophy, art theory, and aesthetics. She publishes on topics such as knowledge in the arts and the aesthetics of passivity, incapacity and sensibility. She launched the Berlin funding program for artistic research (kuenstlerischeforschung.berlin) and has collaborated on various art projects, most recently curating the exhibition *Radical Passivity: Politics of the Flesh* at nGbK Berlin.

Helen Cammock is a multimedia artist based between Brighton and London. She works across film, photography, performance and print and her practice is characterized by its fragmented, non-linear nature; questioning mainstream historical narratives around Blackness, gender, wealth, power, poverty and vulnerability. Mining her own biography in addition to the histories of oppression and resistance with multiple and layered narratives, Cammock reveals the cyclical nature of histories. Her work makes leaps between different places, times and contexts, asking us to acknowledge complex global relations and the inextricable connection between the individual and society. Cammock was the recipient of the 7th Max Mara Art Prize for Women and joint recipient of The Turner Prize 2019.

Knut Ebeling is Professor of Media Theory and Aesthetics at Weissensee Academy of Art, Berlin. He has published numerous works on contemporary theory, art and aesthetics, most recently: *Archivologie. Theorien des Archivs in Philosophie, Medien und Künsten* (2009, ed. with Stephan Günzel), *Wilde Archäologien 1. Theorien materieller Kultur von Kant bis Kittler* (2012), *Wilde Archäologien 2. Begriffe der Materialität der Zeit von Archiv bis Zerstörung* (2016), *There is No Now. An Archaeology of Contemporaneity* (2017), and *Sorge. Autotheorie der Trauer* (2021).

Sebastián Eduardo Dávila's PhD project deals with materiality in art practices from postwar Guatemala. He forms part of the DFG graduate program "Cultures of Critique" at Leuphana University Lüneburg. His articles and reviews have been published in journals such as *Miradas*, *Re:Visions*, *Revista Poiésis* and *insurgencias.net*, in the anthology *Museums, Transculturality and the Nation State* (ed. Susanne Leeb and Nina Samuel, 2022), and in the context of art exhibitions. He has spoken at conferences like "Worldviews: Latin American Art and the Decolonial Turn" (London/online, 2021) and "Seeing more Queerly in the 21st Century" (Miami, 2020), and is part of the collective *VOCES de Guatemala en Berlín*.

Mutlu Ergün-Hamaz is an author, and currently lives as a parent, consultant, performer, trainer and social researcher in Berlin. Since 2001, Ergün-Hamaz has been a member of the antiracist NGO Phoenix e.V. and works as a White Awareness and Empowerment trainer. His research focuses on racialization and empowerment in Germany. Ergün-Hamaz received his PhD from the Sociology Department of the London School of Economics in 2021. Since spring 2022 he also works part-time at the University of Arts Berlin as Diversity & Anti-Discrimination Officer.

Stefanie Graefe is a private lecturer and sociologist at the Friedrich Schiller University of Jena. She researches and teaches on the relationship between politics, economics, and subjectivity in late neoliberal contemporary society. In 2019, she published the book *Resilienz im Krisenkapitalismus. Wider das Lob der Anpassungsfähigkeit*.

Rebecca Hanna John is an art historian and author invested in transnational perspectives on art. She studied art history, literature and media studies at the University of Konstanz, Paris University Diderot, Humboldt University of Berlin, as well as at the School of Arts and Aesthetics of Jawaharlal Nehru University in New Delhi. In 2019, she joined the DFG graduate program "Cultures of Critique" at Leuphana University Lüneburg, with a PhD project on archival critique and transnational narratives in contemporary art practices.

Ulrike Jordan is an art historian and cultural producer. Prior to joining the DFG graduate program "Cultures of Critique" at Leuphana University Lüneburg in 2019, she was working in various cultural institutions in Berlin like Haus der Kulturen der Welt, Kunstraum Kreuzberg/Bethanien and Maxim Gorki Theater. She is an active member of neue Gesellschaft für bildende Kunst (nGbK), where she collaboratively realized the projects *Im Dissens* (2019) and *50 Jahre neue Gesellschaft* (2019). Together with Naomi Hennig she curated the exhibition *Context is Half the Work. A Partial History of the Artist Placement Group* (Kunstraum Kreuzberg/Bethanien, 2015 / Summerhall Edinburgh, 2016).

Pınar Öğrenci is an artist and filmmaker from Turkey living in Berlin. She has a background in architecture, which informs her poetic and experiential video-based works and installations that accumulate traces of "material culture" related to forced displacement across geographies. Her works are decolonial and feminist readings from the intersections of social, political and anthropological research, everyday practices, and human stories that follow agents of migration. Öğrenci's works have been exhibited internationally, including documenta fifteen (2022). She has been nominated for the Kunstpreis der Böttcherstraße in Bremen (2022) and her first documentary film *Gurbet is a home now* won the Special Jury Award of the Documentarist Istanbul Film Festival (2021).

Pallavi Paul's artistic practice, founded on her academic research, encompasses film, installation, text, photography and performance. She holds a doctorate in cinema studies from Jawaharlal Nehru University and a postgraduate degree in media from Jamia Millia Islamia University. Both these universities in New Delhi have been repeatedly targeted by the right wing for promoting critical thinking and progressive politics. This experience has left its mark on her work. Her work has been shown, for example, at Savvy Contemporary (2022), the International Film Festival in Rotterdam (2021), Haus der Kulturen der Welt (2020), The Rubin Museum (2019), Beirut Art Centre (2018), AV Festival (2018, 2016), Contour Biennale (2017) and Tate Modern (2013).

Thorsten Schneider is an author and art historian with a transdisciplinary background, who also teaches at several universities. Since 2019 he is part of the DFG graduate program "Cultures of Critique" at Leuphana University Lüneburg, where he is researching on ideology in the context of German art history since 1968 and its potential for a contemporary art critique. In 2018 he was curator in residence of the German state North Rhine Westphalia at Schloss Ringenberg. In 2019 he was honored by the Austrian artmagazine for his art critique. He is a member of the German section of AICA (Association Internationale des Critiques d'Art).

Judith Sieber lives and works in Berlin. She was a member of the DFG graduate program "Cultures of Critique" at Leuphana University Lüneburg, from 2017 until 2022. Her dissertation, titled *Kritik linearer Zeit,* formulates a critique of the universalistic concept of the directed and linear timeline established via diagrams in eighteenth century England. Together with Marius Hanft and Lotte Warnholdt she edited the volume *Weiterschreiben. Anschlüsse an Rebecca Ardners "Affirmation und Negation als Figuren der Kritik"* (2020). Her texts and exhibition reviews have been published in, among others, *AQNB, Arts of the Working Class* and *Rundbrief Fotografie*. From 2015 to 2016 she was a Global Humanities Junior Fellow at the Johns Hopkins University in Baltimore.

Diana Taylor is University Professor and Professor of Performance Studies and Spanish at New York University. Her books include: *Theatre of Crisis* (1991), *Disappearing Acts* (1997), *The Archive and the Repertoire* (2003), *Performance* (2016), and *¡Presente! The Politics of Presence* (2020). She co-edited *Holy Terrors* (2003), *Stages of Conflict* (2008) and *Lecturas avanzadas de Performance* (2011), among others. In 1998 she founded the Hemispheric Institute of Performance and Politics, which she directed until 2020. She received a Guggenheim Fellowship and other major awards. Taylor was President of the Modern Language Association (2017) and was inducted into the American Academy of Arts and Science (2018).

Deniz Utlu is a novelist and essayist living in Berlin, where he also curates the literary series *Prosa der Verhältnisse* (present conditional prose—a reading series) for the Maxim Gorki Theater and conducts research on human rights. His first novel, *Die Ungehaltenen*, was published by Graf Verlag in 2014 and his second novel, *Gegen Morgen*, in 2019 by Suhrkamp Verlag. Most recently, he received the Alfred Döblin Prize 2021 for the manuscript of his forthcoming third novel *Vaters Meer*. www.denizutlu.de

Marivi Véliz holds a PhD in Literary, Cultural and Linguistics Studies (University of Miami, 2021) and a BA in Art History

(Havana University, 1999), with experience in Cultural Anthropology (2000–2002). In 2003, she moved to Guatemala to work as a contemporary Latin American art lecturer, curator, journalist, and independent researcher in the Central American region. Currently, she is a Visiting Professor at Wichita State University and is working on her book project *Healing, Deceleration, and the Digital*, which focuses on the connections between the Americas through performance and media studies.

Nele Wulff is an arts scholar and cultural producer and is pursuing her PhD in the DFG graduate program "Cultures of Critique" at Leuphana University Lüneburg. Her work focuses on artistic institutional critiques as well as queer-feminist critique. She has worked for various art projects and institutions, including dOCUMENTA (13), the Venice Biennale, and the Hamburg-based exhibition project *Krankheit als Metapher*. She has published articles in the journal *feministische studien* and the magazine *Kultur und Gespenster*.

Akram Zaatari lives and works in Beirut. He has produced numerous films and videos, books, and installations of photographic material, all sharing an interest in writing histories, excavation, political resistance, and the play of tenses inherent to various letters that have been lost, found, buried, discovered, or otherwise delayed in reaching their destinations. Zaatari was a co-founder of the Arab Image Foundation, an artist-driven organization devoted to the research and study of photography in the Arab world. Zaatari's work has been featured at dOCUMENTA (13). He represented Lebanon at the Venice Bienniale in 2013. His films include three features: *The Landing* (2019), *Twenty-Eight Nights and A Poem* (2015) and *This Day* (2003).